GUIDELINES

FOR THE

ECONOMIC ANALYSIS

OF PROJECTS

Economics and Development Resource Center
February 1997

FOREWORD

A Bank Task Force on Project Quality established in 1993 considered several means of enhancing the effectiveness of Bank operations, in conjunction with borrowing member countries. A number of steps were identified to improve the quality of projects at the preparation stage as well as at the implementation stage. To this end, an Interdepartmental Working Group was established to reconsider the nature and role of the economic analysis of projects, and in particular to review the existing guidelines for project economic analysis, as a means of enhancing project quality "at entry". This review has led to these new Guidelines for the Economic Analysis of Projects.

Bank staff and consultants are required to undertake economic analysis of Bank loan projects in a relatively uniform way. Guidelines for this purpose were issued last in 1987. Several factors have come together to make it necessary to produce this new general guidelines.

First, the Asian Development Bank has reconsidered its own priorities. A new set of objectives for classifying Bank projects has been established, resulting in a greater emphasis on projects producing nontraded outputs that meet people's needs directly. Second, the source of finance for many types of project is changing with a greater role for the private sector. Greater emphasis therefore needs to be placed on the appropriate roles of the public and private sectors in the provision of goods and services before specific project proposals are brought forward for analysis. Third, Bank staff and consultants now have to deal with a broader range of issues than before. This can be summarized under the title of sustainability, the realization that the economic benefits of projects will not fully materialize unless attention is also paid to cost recovery and financial sustainability, to environmental effects and to the distributional effects of projects. Finally, the subject matter of project economic analysis has itself undergone some change. Greater attention is now paid to the broader aspects of economic analysis, the way project alternatives are identified and assessed, the treatment of uncertainty, and the policy context in which projects are undertaken.

These new guidelines have been prepared by the Project Economic Evaluation Division of the Economics and Development Resource Center, in consultation with the Interdepartmental Working Group and after comments from staff in the Bank's Projects Departments. They outline the principles upon which the economic analysis of projects should be based. The appendices provide illustrations of their application. The guidelines provide the basis for quantifying and valuing project costs and benefits where all relevant data are available. However, it may not always be possible to quantify and value all the costs and benefits of a particular project. The guidelines provide for the ideal situation to which Bank practice should aspire.

Whilst continuing to focus on economic viability, or on economic cost effectiveness of alternatives where benefits cannot be valued, as the key criterion for assessing Bank loans, these guidelines now provide a more integrated approach to the economic analysis of projects. Not every form of analysis contained in these guidelines will be equally applicable to every project. Projects Departments will need to take a decision early in project processing about the forms of economic analysis appropriate to a particular project.

These guidelines are issued to assist Bank staff and consultants to answer the basic economic questions that need to be asked about any of its project loans. It is hoped that through their application the underlying purpose of enhancing project quality will be better served.

VISHVANATH V. DESAI
Director and Chief Economist
Economics and Development Resource Center
January 1997

ACKNOWLEDGMENTS

These guidelines were produced as a joint effort by several persons. The overall structure and content of the guidelines were subject to external review at different stages by William Ward and J. Price Gittinger. However, the text of the guidelines was written by members of staff of the Project Economic Evaluation Division of the Bank's Economic and Development Resource Center. Stephen Curry and George Whitlam drafted the main text and the majority of the appendixes, while selected appendixes were provided by Anneli Lagman, Bo Lin, Rita Nangia, and Arlene Tadle. The document benefited several times from the comments of Jungsoo Lee, Assistant Chief Economist, Project Economic Evaluation Division, and its preparation was undertaken with the encouragement of Vishvanath Desai, Director and Chief Economist.

Drafts of the guidelines were subject to several internal reviews, first by an interdepartmental working group chaired by Jungsoo Lee, and subsequently by the Directors and staff of operational departments. Reviews of earlier drafts were provided by Piyasena Abeygunawardena, Ifzal Ali, Nihal Amerasinghe, Peter Darjes, David Edwards, Preminda Fernando, Morimitsu Inaba, Thomas Jones III, Bindu Lohani, Bruce Murray, Lester Neumann, Gene Owens, Frank Polman, Narhari Rao, William Staub, Phiphit Suphaphiphat, Etienne Van De Walle, Jean-Pierre Verbiest, and Chi-Nang Wong of the interdepartmental working group. Subsequent comments from operational departments were received particularly from Elisabetta Capannelli, Bruce Carrad, Brian Fawcett, Kazi Jalal, Toshio Kondo, Loh Ai Tee, Takashi Matsuo, Mark Mitchell, Patricia Moser, Eustace Nonis, and Frederick Roche.

The preparation of the manuscript was undertaken through many drafts and revisions by Digna Real. It was edited by Judith Banning and processed through the several stages of production by Virginita Capulong, Marcelia Garcia and Regina Sibal. Assistance with printing was provided by Victor Angeles and Raveendranath Rajan.

This version of the guidelines, produced particularly for distribution outside the Bank, is intended as a means of creating a better understanding of the purposes and content of the economic analysis of projects by several groups of users. It is hoped that a consistent application of principles will develop between Government officials from borrowing countries, consultants employed by the Bank in project preparation, and Bank staff. Prior acknowledgment, therefore, is given to the users of these guidelines who have the joint task of improving the quality of Bank-assisted projects.

ABBREVIATIONS

AIEC	-	average incremental economic cost
AIFC	-	average incremental financial cost
BCR	-	benefit-cost ratio
BOOT	-	build-own-operate-transfer
BPEV	-	border price equivalent value
CEA	-	cost effectiveness analysis
CF	-	conversion factor
CIF	-	cost insurance freight
CS	-	consumer surplus
DMC	-	developing member county
DMP	-	domestic market price
DP	-	demand price
DRC	-	domestic resource cost
EAC	-	effective assistance coefficient
EAR	-	effective assistance ratio
EC	-	economic cost
EDR	-	equalizing discount rate
EIA	-	environmental impact assessment
EIRR	-	economic internal rate of return
ENPV	-	economic net present value
EOCK	-	economic opportunity cost of capital
EP	-	economic price
EQDR	-	equalizing discount rate
FIRR	-	financial internal rate of return
FNPV	-	financial net present value
FOB	-	free on board
FP	-	financial price
GEB	-	gross economic benefit
HDTP	-	handling, distribution, transport, processing
HLD	-	healthy life day
IRR	-	internal rate of return
LIBOR	-	London interbank offer rate
NEB	-	net economic benefit
NFB	-	net financial benefit
NGO	-	nongovermental organization
NOER	-	nominal official exchange rate
NPV	-	net present value
O&M	-	operation & maintenance

OCR	-	ordinary capital resources
OER	-	official exchange rate
PAR	-	project assistance ratio
PAC	-	project assistance coefficient
PIR	-	poverty impact ratio
PV	-	present value
PVC	-	present value of cost
ROER	-	real official exchange rate
SCF	-	standard or average conversion factor
SER	-	shadow exchange rate
SERF	-	shadow exchange rate factor
SI	-	sensitivity indicator
SP	-	supply price
SV	-	switching value
SWR	-	shadow wage rate
SWRF	-	shadow wage rate factor
UFW	-	unaccounted for water
WMP	-	world market price
WTA	-	willingness to accept
WTP	-	willingness to pay

CONTENTS

FIGURE/TABLES

APPENDIXES

GUIDELINES FOR THE ECONOMIC ANALYSIS OF PROJECTS

I. INTRODUCTION

1.   These guidelines provide a general approach for the economic analysis of projects for application by the Asian Development Bank.[1] While the guidelines focus on the objective of maximizing net output or income, which is often referred to as the "economic" or "efficiency" objective, they do so in a broad manner to ensure consistency with the Bank's focus on

- the social sectors and the environment, and
- greater project and program support to develop institutions and organizations that facilitate economically efficient market activity in the Bank's developing member countries.

2.   The economic analysis of projects includes an assessment of the sustainability of project effects to ensure that

- the project provides sufficient incentives for producers,
- sufficient funds are available to maintain project operations,
- the least cost means of providing the project benefits is used,
- the distribution of project benefits and costs is consistent with project objectives, and
- environmental effects are included in the analysis (see Appendix 1).

II. BACKGROUND

3.   Several factors have combined in recent years to change the context within which Bank lending operations occur. The Report of the Task Force on Improving Project Quality (1994) recommended that the Bank's guidelines and procedures for the economic analysis of projects be reviewed with the aim of strengthening project quality. At the same time, the Medium-Term Strategic Framework adopted by the Bank requires greater emphasis to be placed on social and environmental concerns. This has resulted in the need to widen the scope of economic analysis to account more fully for nonmarket benefits and costs.

4.   Other factors include evolving changes in the theory and practice of development, and the role of the public sector; the related shift toward stronger support for environmental sustainability; and greater emphasis on organizational and institutional change and provision of social, legal, and institutional infrastructure to facilitate private economic activity.

---

[1]   These guidelines are a revision of the previous edition published in 1987. The revision draws on research undertaken by the Bank and other multilateral lending institutions.

5.   The application of economic logic to the identification of appropriate investment operations and to the economic analysis of such projects derives from the prevailing views and theories on economic development, and on the most effective role for government in the economy. During the 1980s and 1990s, both of these bodies of theory experienced major and continuing change. Development is now seen less as a process of transferring physical capital, and more as assisting in human capital and institutional development. In economic management, government is seen as playing more of a facilitative, rather than a command and control, role. In particular, direct investment in government activities in industry, finance, and agriculture takes a decreasing share of the Bank's loan portfolio. Instead, Bank investment in the form of loans and credits to these sectors is increasingly directed at facilitating private sector development.

6.   The view that has emerged is that the facilitative role of government includes four primary sets of activities:

- providing the institutional framework within which market-based transactions can expand and appropriate government investments can be rationally made, such as, political stability, commercial codes, legal systems, budgeting and control systems, consumer protection, and respect for property;
- provision of an economic environment in which private investment can expand efficiently and equitably, for example, price and exchange rate stability, neutrality between sectors, access to global financial and capital markets, and access to export and import markets;
- development and maintenance of human capital and technological capability, for instance, an educated and healthy workforce, access to technology, and ability to adopt and adapt; and
- provision and maintenance of economic and social infrastructure, such as transport, communications, and health and welfare systems.

7.   At the same time, project planning and project economics are now affected by environmental issues; various aspects of sustainability, including those of a financial, environmental, economic, social, and political nature; equitability; participation; and governance, including the role of women and nongovernment organizations in development. Economic analysis must facilitate the analysis of these additional issues whilst maintaining the basic focus on economic viability.

III.   THE ECONOMIC RATIONALE OF A PROJECT

8.   The application of economic logic should occur early in the project cycle, rather than simply at the appraisal stage. It should lead the analyst to ask whether the investment operation being analyzed represents an appropriate role for government or whether a policy change or institutional change might be broader reaching and more sustainable than a

proposed physical investment. The analysis of investment operations and the analysis of policy-based alternatives can flow from the application of the same forms of economic logic.

9.   The inadequacy of markets to produce what society wants provides the main rationale for Bank operations. Where financial returns are less than cost recovery, or revenues are nominal or nonexistent, there is a case for financing public projects. Because external benefits and costs are not a part of financial production decisions, too little output will tend to be produced where externalities are net benefits, and too much where they are net costs (see Appendix 2).

10.   Many goods and services are still produced in relatively monopolized markets, both by the public sector and by the private sector. Bank assistance should be combined with development of a legal and regulatory framework that limits the effects of monopoly structures. The extent to which competitive market structures can be created or simulated depends on transactions costs. Transactions costs include the costs of negotiating and enforcing contracts, and the costs of collecting charges for goods and services provided. The Bank can assist with the introduction of new technologies and institutional arrangements which reduce transactions costs and increase accountability. In some sectors, the Bank will therefore achieve a longer term aim of ensuring sustainable private production of both private goods and public goods.

11.   The Bank seeks to provide finance primarily for public and near-public goods, and for those elements, such as roads, irrigation systems or enterprise restructuring, which help to create the conditions under which a larger number of goods can be produced as private goods. The two common criteria used to distinguish between public and private goods are

- subtractability—how much the consumption of a good or service by one person subtracts from the ability of others to use the good or service; and
- excludability—the extent to which a potential user can be excluded if the user does not meet conditions set by the supplier.

The Bank is also involved in reducing public bads such as environmental costs or poverty, and in funding some private sector developments where they can play a catalytic or demonstration role.

12.   Bank operations must also cope with the consequences of nonmarket failure. Many projects, both private and public, underperform because they are not implemented and operated effectively and because the project benefits are captured by some groups, especially the nonpoor, and not by others. Nonmarket failure helps to explain why projects often yield higher costs and lower benefits than those forecast at appraisal. Bank projects and operations can reduce nonmarket failure through capacity building for strengthening organizational capacity, and for restructuring institutional roles in a sector.

IV.   MACROECONOMIC AND SECTORAL CONTEXT

13.   Project proposals should be derived from, and placed in the context of, broader development objectives. These objectives may be explicitly stated in a government plan document, or implicitly given through a public investment program. They will form the basis of the Country Operational Strategy Study. A statement should be given of the main development objectives of a country to which a proposed project will contribute. This statement is separate from the classification of projects according to the Bank's own system of priorities, and includes the time period in which specific objectives are to be achieved or programs of investment are to be implemented.

14.   There will be constraints to the achievement of development objectives and implementation of sector programs. At the sector level

- forecasts should be provided of future demands or needs for the type of output to be produced;
- existing sources of supply, the costs of supply, and intended investments should be outlined;
- a statement should be provided of the contribution of the proposed project to meeting sector demands or needs, and any cost reduction or technology innovation it may contribute; and
- a statement should be provided of the extent of direct government involvement as a supplier and the extent of government subsidy to the sector.

15.   Many investments will work well only if there are complementary investments in related sectors or activities. For example, for an irrigation project to raise agricultural output, the appraisal report must elaborate the necessary extra requirements for transport and processing. Projects to improve urban services should consider the capacity of the existing systems to deliver additional power and water. Potential constraints in supplies, whether they can be overcome, and the necessary timing of complementary investments, must be considered.

16.   Because a project takes place within a given macroeconomic and sector context, an investment project can be seen as an incremental change to an existing structure. In fact, the context may be more important than the project itself. Moreover, a project that is financially sound within one sector and macroeconomic context may be financially unsound in another. Thus policy changes may be as important as the physical investment to the achievement of development objectives.

17.   The macroeconomic and sector context will result in differences between financial and economic prices. The policy context that affects financial and economic prices can be analyzed on a country basis by determining

- how levels for the key macroeconomic parameters—exchange rate, interest rates, and wages—are determined;
- the impact of microeconomic policies, such as import quotas, rationing schemes, and special financial incentives, on a particular investment;
- which border policies, such as import duties and export subsidies, will affect project outputs and inputs and how; and
- what are the existing market structures, such as the degree of monopoly supply and pricing for public utilities and other inputs, and the degree of competition for project outputs.

18.   Brief statements on each of these four factors will focus attention on the macroeconomic and sector framework. Where any of the factors are deemed very significant, then the efficiency of project investments is likely to be reduced as consumers and suppliers respond to distorted prices. In addition, substantial differences between financial and economic prices as a result of any of these four factors can be a prelude to policy changes that increase the risk of project investments. Therefore, the statement of the macroeconomic and sector context should be accompanied by a statement on whether the intended investment project and associated policy dialogue are likely to facilitate adjustments in the framework or are likely to bolster resistance to change.

V.   AN INTEGRATED APPROACH TO ECONOMIC ANALYSIS

A.   Scope of Economic Analysis

19.   The purpose of the economic analysis of projects is to bring about a better allocation of resources, leading to enhanced incomes for investment or consumption. For a directly productive project, where the output is sold in a relatively competitive environment, choices are made within the economy to ensure that projects selected for investment meet a minimum standard for resource generation and to weed out those projects that do not. For an indirectly productive project, where the output is not sold in a competitive environment, choices are made within the project between different means of achieving the same objectives. Economic analysis is used to choose the means using the least resources for a given output. All resource inputs and outputs have an opportunity cost through which the extent and value of project items are estimated. Projects should be chosen where the resources will be used most effectively.

20.   Economic viability depends upon the sustainability of project effects. Projects are sustainable if their net benefits or positive effects endure as expected throughout the life of the project. Sustainability is enhanced if environmental effects are internalized, and if financial returns provide an adequate incentive for project-related producers and consumers. Sustainable development is concerned also with distributional issues. When looking at the distribution of project effects and judging project social acceptability, it is important to determine who

benefits and who pays the costs. An assessment of the capacity of the project to cope with an uncertain future is another measure. Sensitivity analysis is applied when testing projects for both productive and allocative efficiency.

21.   The scope of economic analysis contained in these guidelines seeks to address several issues in the economic analysis of Bank project loans (see Figure 1). Previous practice focused on forecasting demand, choosing least-cost options, and, where possible, calculating the economic internal rate of return. The demand forecasts themselves depend upon project charges and affordability, which also affect financial incentives for different participants. At the same time, environmental effects can now be incorporated into the analysis, and policy dialogue requires a statement of the distribution of project effects. This broadening of the scope of economic analysis must be tailored to the particular project and the issues it generates.

22.   In some cases, project preparation does not end with the decision to accept a project. In process projects, design and appraisal are continual and go along with project implementation. This allows for greater participation by project beneficiaries in the design and testing of different options. Economic analysis can be applied at the outset of such projects to test the underlying rationale. The principles of economic analysis contained in these guidelines can be applied at key decision points in the process.

23.   The procedure for undertaking economic analysis follows a sequence of interrelated steps:

- defining project objectives and economic rationale;
- forecasting effective demand for project outputs;
- choosing the least-cost design for meeting demand or the most cost-effective way of attaining the project objectives;
- determining whether economic benefits exceed economic costs;
- assessing whether the project's net benefits will be sustainable throughout the life of the project;
- testing for risks associated with the project;
- identifying the distributional effects of the project, particularly on the poor; and
- enumerating the nonquantifiable effects of the project that may influence project design and the investment decision.

For indirectly productive projects, economic analysis would comprise all of the above steps, except determining whether economic benefits exceed costs.

Figure 1: Scope of Economic Analysis

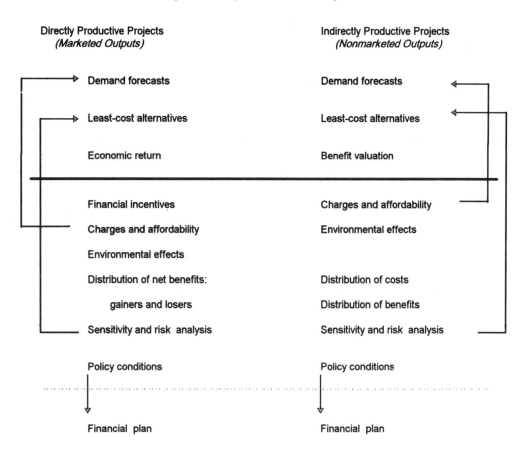

Directly Productive Projects *(Marketed Outputs)*	Indirectly Productive Projects *(Nonmarketed Outputs)*
Demand forecasts	Demand forecasts
Least-cost alternatives	Least-cost alternatives
Economic return	Benefit valuation
Financial incentives	Charges and affordability
Charges and affordability	Environmental effects
Environmental effects	
Distribution of net benefits:	Distribution of costs
gainers and losers	Distribution of benefits
Sensitivity and risk analysis	Sensitivity and risk analysis
Policy conditions	Policy conditions
Financial plan	Financial plan

B.   The Project Framework

24.   The Project Framework provides a conceptual framework for analyzing both directly productive projects, for which a direct market demand exists for valuing project outputs, and indirectly productive projects, for which demand is derived from nonmarket goals. Such an integrated approach to project appraisal helps to prevent the misallocation of resources. It is particularly appropriate for projects where benefits are difficult to quantify and value. It provides a framework for identifying and comparing alternative means of achieving objectives.

25.   In the Project Framework, a project is seen as being made up of a series of means-ends relationships, beginning with input-output linkages, then output-purpose linkages and, finally, purpose-goal linkages. For each foreseeable year of project implementation and operation, explicit verifiable targets are set at each level for each objective. The Project Framework is thus both an appraisal tool and a means by which the project can be monitored for

- implementation efficiency—testing the input-output linkage;
- operational effectiveness—testing the input-output-purpose linkage; and
- impact significance—input-output-purpose-goal linkage.

26.   The Project Framework provides for the identification, quantification, and valuation of project objectives or targets for inputs, outputs, project effects, and sector impacts. The approach adopted for economic analysis depends on the extent to which project inputs, outputs, effects, and impacts can be identified, quantified, and valued. For directly productive projects operating in a relatively competitive market environment, the economic effects of purpose level achievements can be measured mainly in terms of incremental income. On the other hand, in the case of indirectly productive projects, the best that can be expected is to be able to value project effects indirectly in terms of the project's impact on the market value of the product for which the project produces an intermediate input or of the cost of an alternative, in terms of cost savings.

27.   The application of the Project Framework approach to project design provides an analytical framework for both the economic and social analysis of directly and indirectly productive projects. By enabling the application of the same criteria, the integrated framework ensures transparency and accountability, and promotes efficient resource use (see Appendix 3).

C.   Financial and Economic Analysis

28.   The economic analysis of projects is similar in form to financial analysis: both appraise the profit of an investment. The concept of financial profit is not the same as economic profit. The financial analysis of a project estimates the profit accruing to the project-operating entity or to the project participants, whereas economic analysis measures the effect of the project on the national economy. For a project to be economically viable, it must be financially sustainable, as well as economically efficient. If a project is not financially sustainable, economic benefits will not be realized. Financial analysis and economic analysis are therefore two sides of the same coin and complementary.

29.   Both types of analysis are conducted in monetary terms, the major difference lying in the definition of costs and benefits. In financial analysis all expenditures incurred under the project and revenues resulting from it are taken into account. This form of analysis is necessary to

- assess the degree to which a project will generate revenues sufficient to meet its financial obligations,
- assess the incentives for producers, and
- ensure demand or output forecasts on which the economic analysis is based are consistent with financial charges or available budget resources.

30.   Economic analysis attempts to assess the overall impact of a project on improving the economic welfare of the citizens of the country concerned. It assesses a project in the context of the national economy, rather than for the project participants or the project entity that implements the project. Economic analysis differs from financial analysis in terms of both (i) the breadth of the identification and evaluation of inputs and outputs, and (ii) the measure of benefits and costs. Economic analysis includes all members of society, and measures the project's positive and negative impacts in terms of willingness to pay for units of increased consumption, and to accept compensation for foregone units of consumption. Willingness to pay and willingness to accept compensation are used rather than prices actually paid or received because

- many of the project impacts that are to be included in the economic analysis either will be nonmarketed, for example, biodiversity preservation, or incompletely marketed, such as, water supply and sanitation benefits. Thus, some form of nonmarket value must be estimated.
- many project impacts that are marketed will be bought and sold in markets where prices are distorted by various government interventions, by macroeconomic policies, or by imperfect competition.

Shadow prices may be used in estimating the willingness to pay and willingness to accept compensation values in the face of these market absences and market imperfections.

31.   The benefits from a project constitute the extent to which the project contributes to increasing the value of the consumption available to society. Consumption can be defined broadly. Societal consumption may apply equally well to a society's willingness to pay for preservation of plant or animal species, as to society's willingness to pay for the consumption of agricultural produce or clean drinking water.

32.   Costs reflect the degree to which consumption elsewhere in society is sacrificed by diverting the resources required by the project from other uses. The total net changes in consumption available to the society represent the net impact of the project. When the units of consumption are valued in terms of marginal willingness to pay for the units of increased consumption and marginal willingness to accept compensation for foregone units of consumption, the resulting economic net benefits from the project will reflect the summation of the changes in the net income of the society as a whole, resulting from the situation with the project compared with that without the project.

33.   Shadow prices are used to take into account the major impacts of a project where economic values differ from financial values. In many developing member countries, many prices paid and received in the project accounts may come from relatively complete markets where the major impacts are captured in the transaction between buyer and seller, and are reflected by the prices paid and received. As structural adjustment and sectoral adjustment measures proceed, and as projects involving institutional and organizational approaches to

market development are successfully implemented, the differences between financial values and economic values may lessen. The overall objective of the structural and sectoral adjustment programs, and of the projects financed by the Bank, is to attempt to create just such an economic environment in the Bank's developing member countries.

VI.   IDENTIFICATION AND QUANTIFICATION OF COSTS AND BENEFITS

A.   General

34.   There are four basic steps to analyzing the economic viability of a project:

- identify the economic costs and benefits;
- quantify the costs and benefits, as much as possible;
- value the costs and benefits; and
- compare the benefits with the costs.

The first two steps can generally be undertaken together. However, there will be some types of benefits, and sometimes costs, that cannot be quantified and valued for inclusion in the cost-benefit comparison. They will simply be stated alongside the results of the economic analysis.

35.   To identify project costs and benefits, the situation without the project should be compared with the situation with the project. The without-project situation is not the same as the before-project situation. The without-project situation can sometimes be represented by the present levels of productivity of the relevant resources. However, present levels of productivity would frequently change without the project, and this should be taken into account in defining the without-project situation.

36.   The comparison of without-project and with-project situations is at the heart of the estimation of net benefits for any project. While, in practice, appraisal reports provide a clear specification of the with-project situation, they frequently provide little analysis of the without-project situation. The without-project situation is often inaccurately described. The without-project situation is that which would prevail without the project. It is not the implementation of the next best project alternative, unless there is clear evidence to suggest that this is most likely to be the case. Similarly, the without-project situation is not the delayed implementation of the same project. In most cases, it is a modification of the existing circumstances. In comparing project alternatives, the without-project situation follows the same scenario, and provides the basis for comparing with-project net benefit flows for each project alternative.

37.   Most projects or subprojects are regarded as marginal in the sense that they will not have any effect upon the prices of project inputs and outputs, and will not have a substantial impact on the government budget or the exchange rate. Additional factors will have to be

taken into account in the case of large projects that have a considerable impact on the regional, national, or international economy.

38.   An important distinction in identifying project benefits and costs is that between nonincremental and incremental output, and between incremental and nonincremental inputs. The distinction is important because nonincremental and incremental effects are valued in different ways. It should therefore be used in the identification and quantification of project effects. Nonincremental outputs are project outputs that substitute for existing production. For example, a new hydropower plant may in part substitute for existing coal-fired generation. Incremental outputs are project outputs that expand supply to meet new demands, for example, the growing demand for electricity as generation and transmission costs decline. Incremental inputs are project demands that are met by an increase in total supply of the input, for example, where an increase in demand for water is met by an overall expansion of the water supply system. Nonincremental inputs are project demands that are met not by an expansion of overall supply but from existing supplies, that is, by competing supplies away from existing producers. Each project will exhibit different degrees of nonincremental and incremental effects for both outputs and inputs. Part of the process of forecasting involves analyzing these effects for the main project outputs and inputs.

B.   Identification and Quantification of Benefits

39.   For directly productive projects, the main benefits will be in the form of production that is sold. It is important to determine whether a project's output is incremental to existing supplies. If the project is small relative to the size of the market, it is likely that the project output will be fully incremental. This is the case for most outputs that are traded internationally. In the case of an output that is nontradable, project supply can cause price effects where nonincremental output displaces sales from higher-cost producers.

40.   The need for services from indirectly productive projects will depend on underlying factors, such as the rate of economic growth for freight transport or the rate of population growth for water and health services. A key feature of a sector or project analysis will be the phasing of investments to match the demand for services. For most indirectly productive projects, the type and extent of expected benefits can be quantified through such factors as time and cost savings, increased access, improved health, and so on, most of which have a productive effect, as well as a direct effect on welfare.

41.   Some benefits of indirectly productive projects will not be quantifiable. For example, a newly sited bridge may not only reduce travel time for haulage trucks, but may also encourage greater social and political interaction by those on both sides of the river. A dam project may create a reservoir that not only can be used for fishing or recreational purposes, but also can have a scenic value for existing inhabitants. Such benefits should be stated along with an estimate of the number of beneficiaries.

42.   Project benefits also include the extent of any consumer surplus. A project may lower the price of the output for all consumers. The savings to existing consumers, because of the difference between what they are willing to pay and what they will now have to pay, is not reflected in the financial effects. Consumer surplus can also arise when the output price is fixed by government below the demand price. The difference between the actual price and what consumers are willing to pay can be estimated through a price elasticity of demand, if available. If no direct estimate of the elasticity is available or can be estimated, then the likely magnitude of this form of benefit should be discussed (see Appendix 4).

C.   Identification and Quantification of Costs

43.   While several types of cost need to be included in the economic analysis of a project, some types of financial cost must be excluded. The underlying principle is that project costs comprise the difference in costs between the without and with project situation, that is, the extra use of resources necessary to achieve the corresponding benefits.

System Costs

44.   If a project is part of a larger system, then the expected benefits may not accrue unless some matching investments are made. For example, power generation benefits rely on investments in transmission and distribution. A highway section may need investment in preceding sections or interchanges for the expected traffic flow and cost savings to occur. The project boundary must include the total system investment required to achieve the benefits and, correspondingly, the total system benefits. If the total system of investments is viable, then the project can also be considered viable.

Sunk Costs

45.   A project may require the use of facilities already in existence. The costs of such facilities are sunk costs and should not be included in the project cost, provided their use in the project involves no opportunity cost. Put another way, sunk costs are those costs that would exist both without and with the project, and thus are not additional costs for achieving project benefits.

46.   Many projects will be implemented through existing enterprises or agencies. The project analysis must separate the additional agency costs from the whole cost structure of the enterprise. At the same time, the project may succeed only if the enterprise itself is stable. The analysis of the whole enterprise, including sunk costs together with the project, is necessary to determine financial sustainability (see *Guidelines for Preparation and Presentation of Financial Analysis, 1989*).

Contingencies

47.   Contingency allowances, which are determined by engineering and financial considerations, also have implications for economic appraisal. When estimating project costs for financial planning purposes, both physical and price contingencies are included. Since economic returns are measured in constant prices, general price contingencies should be excluded from the economic cost of the project. Physical contingencies represent the monetary value of additional real resources that may be required beyond the base cost to complete the project, and should be treated as part of the economic cost of a project.

Working Capital

48.   Working capital is commonly defined in financial analysis as net current assets, consisting of inventories, including goods in process; net receivables; marketable securities; bank balances; and cash in hand. A certain amount of working capital is normally required to run project facilities created by investment in fixed assets. For purposes of economic analysis, only inventories that constitute real claims on the nation's resources should be included in the project economic costs. Other items of working capital reflect loan receipts and repayment flows, and are not included in the economic cost (see Appendix 5).

Transfer Payments

49.   Some of the items included in the financial costs of a project are not economic costs, as they do not increase or decrease the availability of real resources to the rest of the economy. These items will, however, affect the distribution of financial costs and benefits between the project entity and other entities, and among project beneficiaries. They are thus referred to as transfer payments, as they transfer command over resources from one party to another without reducing or increasing the amount of resources available as a whole. Taxes, duties, and subsidies are examples of items that, in some circumstances, may be considered to be transfer payments. They can affect the income of the government, and that of the payer and the recipient simultaneously and in opposite and identical amounts, thus canceling out in an economic analysis summation. However, there are circumstances when tax and subsidy elements should be included in the price of an input or output. The economic cost of an input should include the tax (subsidy) element, if the demand is nonincremental. If the government is correcting for an externality by applying a tax or a subsidy to reduce or to increase production, for example, where a tax is levied on project output that is equivalent to the costs of waste processing undertaken by a government agency, the economic cost of the input should also include the tax element. Finally, the economic value of incremental outputs will include any tax element imposed on the output which is included in the market price at which it sells.

Depreciation

50.   The financial accounts of agencies implementing a project will include provision for depreciation and amortization on the basis of prevailing accounting practice. However, for project economic analysis, the stream of real investment required to realize and maintain project benefits is included in the resource flow, together with a residual value for these assets at the time they are released from project use at the end of the project's life. The stream of investment assets includes initial investment and replacements during the project's life. This stream of expenditures generally will not coincide exactly with the time profile of depreciation and amortization in the financial accounts.

Depletion Premium

51.   Many projects involve the exploitation of a nonrenewable natural resource, such as oil, natural gas, or mineral deposits. The economic cost of using these natural resources must be included in the economic analysis. Because they cannot be replenished, and when depleted must be replaced by imports or domestic substitutes, the opportunity cost of the resource includes the cost of the substitutes when the resource is exhausted. The depletion premium or allowance depends on this economic price and the proportion of the total reserves exploited during each year. It is added to the economic cost of exploitation to arrive at the full economic cost of using the nonrenewable resource. If the resource will not be exploited to exhaustion, the salvage value of the land at the end of the project must include the economic value of any remaining undepleted reserves (see Appendix 6).

External Costs

52.   In many projects, effects will go beyond the financial analysis from the point of view of the implementing agency. These external effects may include significant costs that must be accounted for in an economic analysis from the national perspective. For example, increased air and water pollution from an industrial plant may be measured and its effects on surrounding entities estimated. In some cases, it may be helpful to internalize these external costs by including all relevant effects and investments in the project statement, including, in this case, pollution control equipment costs and effects.

VII.   VALUATION OF ECONOMIC COSTS AND BENEFITS

A.   General Considerations

53.   Once the costs and benefits of a project have been identified and quantified, they should be valued according to a common criteria. This allows them to be aggregated and compared. Decisions by producers and users of project output will be based on financial prices. However, to evaluate the consequences of their decisions for the national economy,

costs and benefits need to be valued at economic prices that represent their value from the national economic perspective.

54.   Costs and benefits should be valued in constant prices, that is, in terms of the price level prevailing in the year in which the project is appraised. Any expected change in the general price level can be ignored. However, if it is expected that there will be significant changes in relative prices over the life of the project, for example that the output of a food production project will decline in value relative to prices in general, then this relative price change must be incorporated in the valuation of the cost or benefit item (see Appendixes 7 and 8).

55.   In an economic analysis, market prices are adjusted to account for the effects of government intervention and market structure. The result is shadow prices. For project outputs, the shadow price is based on the supply price, the demand price, or a weighted average of the two. Where project output is nonincremental, that is, where it substitutes for alternative forms of supply, then the shadow price is based on the supply price of these alternative forms of supply—on the market price, less any production taxes, plus any subsidies on the alternative supplies. This supply price in turn must be adjusted for the effects of government intervention and market structure on the inputs going into the alternative production. Where project output is incremental, that is, where the project provides additional output compared to the without project case, then the shadow price is based on the demand price for that output-on the market price inclusive of any consumption tax and exclusive of any subsidy falling on the buyer. This demand price also must be adjusted for the average difference between economic and market prices, as explained further below. In many cases, a project will produce a combination of nonincremental and incremental output. In such instances, the shadow price of the output is based on a weighted average of the supply and demand prices (see Appendix 9).

56.   For small projects producing an import substitute good, the whole output will be nonincremental. It can be valued through its supply price, that is, through its import price. For small projects producing an export good, the whole output will be incremental. It can be valued through its demand, or export, price. For a project producing a combination of import substitute and export goods, the output can be valued through a weighted average of the import and export prices. This valuation process becomes more complicated when the project that produces traded goods is large and will have an impact on international prices. The impact must be considered when applying supply and demand prices.

57.   The same principles of valuation apply to projects producing outputs that are nontraded. Generally, some of the nontraded output will be nonincremental. The shadow price is based on the supply price of the alternative supply being displaced. Also, some of the nontraded output will be incremental. The shadow price is based on the demand price or willingness to pay of the new users. The shadow price of total nontraded output will be based on a weighted average of the supply and demand prices.

58.   In practice, it may be difficult to identify and separate the nonincremental from the incremental output of a project. This is particularly so for projects producing nontraded outputs that are quite large and may have an impact on demand and supply prices. The proportion of nonincremental to incremental output will depend on the elasticities of demand and supply. The data available, and interview structure needed to estimate the willingness to pay of new users, may not provide sufficient information to provide reliable estimates of relevant elasticities and, therefore, output proportions. In such circumstances, an estimate of the supply price for alternative supplies, that is, the cost of supply without the project, may be applied to the whole of the nontraded output, both nonincremental and incremental.

59.   The shadow price of project inputs is also valued through a weighted average of their supply and demand prices. However, in the case of inputs, the valuation of nonincremental and incremental inputs is the reverse of the case for outputs. For nonincremental inputs, that is, for input supplies that are competed away from other uses, the shadow price is based on the adjusted demand price or willingness to pay for the input. For incremental inputs, that is, for nontraded inputs where production is expanded, or for traded inputs where additional supplies are imported or substitute for exports, the shadow price is based on the adjusted supply price of the input, that is, on the supply price of additional domestic production for a nontraded input, and on the import or export price for traded inputs. In the case of a nontraded input in fixed supply, or in the exceptional case of a very large increase in demand for a traded input that affects its price, the shadow price is based on with-project supply prices that may require relevant elasticity estimates to predict.

60.   The basis for valuing incremental and nonincremental outputs and inputs is summarized in Table 1. The relevant supply or demand prices have to be adjusted for the effect of trade controls and market structures that create a difference between financial and economic values. Therefore, the shadow price of an output or input is the weighted average of its supply and demand prices adjusted for these additional factors.

Table 1: Basis of Economic Valuation of Project Outputs and Inputs

	Incremental	Nonincremental
Outputs	Adjusted demand price or willingness to pay	Adjusted supply price or opportunity cost
Inputs	Adjusted supply price or opportunity cost	Adjusted demand price or willingness to pay

B.   Role of World Prices

61.   One approach to estimating the value of outputs and inputs from the national point of view uses world market prices. The extra outputs and demand for inputs created by a project will have a direct or indirect effect on international trade. World market prices are also subject to national and international policy effects and, in some cases, to monopolized market structures. However, trade represents an alternative to domestic production for most goods

and services. Hence, world prices can be used to measure the value of project inputs and outputs from the national perspective.

62.   The valuation of outputs and inputs through world prices requires that the trade effect of each project item be identified. Incremental outputs that are exported can be valued at the export demand price and outputs that substitute for imports can be valued at the import supply price. Where a project's output involves both substituting for imports and an expansion of exports, it should be valued at the weighted average of import supply and export demand price. Incremental inputs that are imported can be valued at the import supply price, while inputs that reduce the level of exports can be valued at the export demand price. Where extra inputs involve both a reduction in exports and an increase in imports, they should be valued at the weighted average of the export demand and import supply price. World prices will differ from the domestic prices used in the financial analysis of the project because of

- the effects of trade controls and net taxes on traded goods;
- the monopoly pricing of some traded goods; and
- subsidy levels, especially for utility prices.

Adjusting prices to world prices in effect excludes all tax and subsidy elements from project input costs and ensures that outputs are valued at their worth to the national economy. Any excess operating surplus, over and above production or supply costs including a capital charge, resulting from monopoly supplies of nontradable outputs or inputs, should also be excluded.

63.   Applying world prices to measure the marginal value of project outputs and inputs can be directly applied to traded project items. They can also be applied indirectly to the incremental production costs of project inputs that are nontraded. However, they cannot be applied directly or indirectly to outputs that have no trade effect (see Table 2).

Table 2: Valuation of Main Project Outputs and Inputs

	Category	Project Impact	Basis of Economic Price	Basis of Valuation
Output	Tradable	Incremental	Demand price	WMP (=FOB)
		Nonincremental	Supply price	WMP (=CIF)
	Nontradable	Incremental	Demand price	DMP + CT
		Nonincremental	Supply price	DMP - PT - OS
Input	Tradable	Incremental	Supply price	WMP (=CIF)
		Nonincremental	Demand price	WMP (=FOB)
	Nontradable	Incremental	Supply price	DMP - PT - OS
		Nonincremental	Demand price	DMP + CT

CIF	-	Cost insurance freight	OS - Operating surplus
CT	-	Net consumption tax	PT - Net production tax
DMP	-	Domestic market price	WMP - World market price
FOB	-	Free on board	

64.   All project items should be valued using the same reference point. There are different levels of prices: producer prices, wholesale prices, and retail prices. The economic prices of all outputs and inputs should be valued at the project level. Generally, this means at the point of production for the project or subproject. World prices and other forms of valuation should be adjusted to the level of the project for purposes of comparing the economic value of project costs and benefits.

C.   Economic Prices of Traded Goods and Services

65.   Project effects estimated in terms of traded goods and services can be measured directly through their border price equivalent value–the world price for the traded product for the country concerned, adjusted to the project location. The steps involved are summarized at the end of Appendix 10. The world price for the country is the border price, the price in foreign exchange paid for imports inclusive of insurance and freight at the port or, for landlocked countries, at the railhead or trucking point; or the world price received for exports at the port, railhead, or trucking point. Border prices for exported outputs can be adjusted to the project location by subtracting the cost of transport, distribution, handling, and processing for export measured at economic prices. Border prices for imported inputs have to be adjusted by adding such costs to the project site. Outputs that substitute for imports should be adjusted by the difference in transport, distribution, and handling costs between the existing point of sale and the project site. Project inputs that reduce exports should be adjusted by the difference in costs between the point of production and the project location. In each case, the traded good or service is estimated through its border price equivalent value (BPEV), adjusting for the economic cost of local costs (see Table 3 and Appendix 10).

Table 3: Border Price Equivalent Value Adjustments

Outputs Exported Import substitutes	FOB price CIF price	less PTDH from project plus TDH to market less TDH market to project
Inputs Imported Export substitutes	CIF price FOB price	plus TDH to project less PTDH production to port plus PTDH production to project

CIF   -   Cost insurance freight
FOB   -   Free on board
PTDH   -   Processing, transport, distribution, handling in economic prices
TDH   -   Transport, distribution, handling in economic prices

66.   World prices are not stable. They fluctuate from year to year. The world price from which border price equivalent values are derived should be expressed as an annual average price over successive fluctuations. Also, it should be adjusted for any quality differences between the world price reference product and project outputs and inputs. World prices are also subject to long-term relative price changes. Where it is forecast that the real price of a

traded product, the forecast nominal price deflated by an index of world prices, such as the unit manufacturing value added index, will increase or decline over time, then the forecast real price for future years should be used in the project economic statement. This applies to major outputs and major inputs that are traded internationally. Bank analysis uses the forecast real prices of commodities published quarterly by the World Bank.

67.   In most cases, world prices will not be affected by a single new project. However, where a country produces a high proportion of world output, for example production of timber, the effects of extra output on the world price itself should be taken into account. The marginal export revenue allowing for the effects on price of greater supply should be estimated. Similarly, where a project creates additional demand for an input that is large relative to world supplies, such as for lucretia extract, the input should be valued at its marginal border price equivalent value allowing for the effect on world prices of the additional demand. In these cases, elasticity estimates are required at present world price levels to estimate the marginal export or import effect (see Appendix 10).

68.   Differences between domestic market prices and border prices of traded goods occur because of net tax and trade controls, the project location, and the monopolization of domestic markets. Valuing traded goods at their border price equivalent values and adjusting for the effects of net taxes and controls, the economic costs of local costs, and monopoly rents, removes the differences between domestic and world market prices. Initially, border price equivalent values will be estimated by converting all foreign exchange values into domestic currency at the official exchange rate. However, the exchange rate, through which traded goods and nontraded goods valued at domestic market prices are made comparable, may itself be a cause of difference between domestic and border price equivalent values. The use of a shadow exchange rate or its converse, the standard conversion factor, is discussed later.

D.   Economic Prices of Nontraded Goods and Services

69.   The Bank is increasing its lending in areas where the project outputs are nontraded. The steps involved in estimating the economic value of nontraded output and inputs are summarized at the end of Appendix 11. While public utility, social sector, and environmental projects produce effects that are nontraded, many directly productive projects also have nontraded effects. Some will be marketed, such as port services or urban water and sanitation supplies.

70.   Goods and services may be nontraded for different reasons. By their nature, some goods and services, such as domestic transport and construction, are products that must be produced and sold within the domestic economy. Sometimes goods and services are nontraded because of government policy decisions that they should not be exported or imported. Finally, some goods and services may be nontraded because their cost and quality are such that, although they can be sold in the domestic market, there is no international market. In some cases, nontraded inputs and outputs have close substitutes that are traded. For example,

domestic firewood can be converted into the calorific equivalent of kerosene or gas. In these cases, the equivalent in traded products can be used to provide an economic price for the nontraded products. However, in most cases of nontraded products there will be no close substitute that is traded.

71.   Nontraded goods and services used as project inputs, where additional project demands result in increased supply, can be valued in terms of their supply price, the marginal economic costs of extra supply. The marginal cost will differ between situations where spare capacity already exists and only variable operating costs will increase, and situations where there is no existing spare capacity, and the marginal cost will include a capital element as well. In either case, the traded component of the marginal cost structure can be valued at border prices, and the economic value of any remaining nontraded element in the marginal cost structure can be approximated by use of a group or standard conversion factor (see Section H below). Use of the marginal cost of supply converted to its economic value will fully account for the differences between domestic market and world prices.

72.   It is not relevant to estimate a marginal cost of production for nontraded inputs in fixed supply. The demand price must be applied. Here the valuation of the input must rely on the willingness to pay principle: an estimate should be made of the price that different users are willing to pay for receiving or retaining input supplies. This will provide a value for the nontraded input in fixed supply.

73.   Extra demand by a project for nontraded inputs, such as transport, construction, water, and power, may have both an incremental effect, where additional supplies are provided, and a nonincremental effect, where supplies are competed away from existing users. The economic price of the nontraded input will be the weighted average of the marginal supply cost and the demand price.

74.   Most nontraded outputs will be incremental; they will provide additional supplies of a nontraded good. Incremental nontraded outputs should be valued at their demand price, that is at the average of their value to the new consumers with and without the project. The value to consumers is inclusive of any indirect tax on the output and net of any subsidy. Nonincremental nontraded output should be valued at its supply price, that is, taking into account the cost of supply of the alternative output being displaced.

75.   Because nontraded outputs and nontraded inputs are, by definition, produced and used in the domestic economy, the effects on the domestic markets of extra output and extra demand may be significant. In each case, the effect on the price of the nontraded good and the responsiveness of demand to price changes need to be considered.

76.   Where an increase in transport services, or a road improvement scheme, brings about a reduction in transport charges, in addition to the value of the output with the project, there will be a benefit to existing users of transport services given by the without-project demand

times the price reduction. Most of this benefit will be offset by a decline in producer surplus. The net effect is equal to the nonincremental output valued through the average supply price. There will also be additional benefits to new users. The value is generally approximated by the average of the price with and without the project, times the change in demand. However, to estimate both effects, an estimate is required of the effects of the project on total supplies, and on the price of the nontraded good. Reaching an estimate of the without- and with-project quantities and the price is the key step in evaluating project effects. The corresponding financial prices need to be converted to their equivalent economic values for economic analysis.

77.   In many instances, the supply of nontraded output will be monopolized in public or private hands. An increase in supply may not be associated with a decrease in price. In this case, benefits will accrue to new, but not to existing, users. Similar modifications can be made for valuing nontraded inputs and outputs in differing circumstances (see Appendix 11).

78.   Many Bank projects produce nontraded outputs that are also nonmarketed; these are generally public goods. Public goods can be defined in terms of excludability and subtractability, as in paragraph 11 above. Public goods, such as uncongested roads, have low subtractability and low excludability. The marginal cost of using them is generally close to zero. However, public goods usually provide considerable economic benefits.

79.   Nonmarketed outputs can be valued through direct willingness to pay measures, such as contingent valuation, travel cost, or other surrogate market techniques. More frequently, public goods are valued in terms of the changes they cause in the value of closely related private goods, or in the productivity of private sector activities. The public good is treated as an intermediate good in the production of a final private good. The value of the "intermediate" public good is then derived from the value of the private good it ultimately produces. This is particularly relevant when valuing infrastructure services, such as roads and bridges, and social services, such as education and health, which can have a measurable effect on private sector productivity.

E.   The Economic Price of Labor

80.   Labor is an important component of any project. The demands for labor for the project should be broken into two basic categories: types of labor that are scarce and types that are in surplus supply. Scarce labor consists of those workers who would be able to find alternative employment in a short time, that is, where supply is more or less in fixed supply in the short term. This generally includes vocational and technical occupations; it also generally includes managerial and professional occupations, although in some countries there is a surplus of labor with educational rather than vocational qualifications.

81.   For most labor that is scarce, the cost of labor inclusive of benefits can be taken as its demand price. This provides an estimate of its opportunity or economic cost—the output

foregone elsewhere in the economy when labor moves to the new project. In some cases, where as a matter of policy wages have been held down in the public sector, or in transitional economies where substantial pay differentials have been discouraged, the value of production foregone may be greater than the demand price of scarce labor, and an upward adjustment to the cost of labor may be made. For foreign labor drawn into an economy, the economic cost to the economy will include the cost of its local consumption at economic prices, plus any remittances from the country of employment, plus the cost of any additional benefits or facilities such as health or education provision that has to be made.

82.   Surplus labor consists of categories for which there would, in general, be a long search time between jobs. For these types of labor, the project wage is usually at or above the supply price. Analysis of the impact of additional project employment generally involves interlinked labor markets. The ultimate effect may be far from the project itself, and this effect will differ from project to project. The cost to the economy of surplus labor in a new project is its supply price, which approximates the opportunity cost of net output lost elsewhere; plus additional economic costs of social infrastructure provision not borne by the project itself.

83.   Often the effect of a project may be to draw surplus labor from rural areas or from agricultural production. An estimate can be made of the lost production that would result from labor migration. This estimate can be expressed in terms of a traded good that has a border price equivalent value. Some lost production will include nontraded agricultural output where, in the case of well-developed local markets, the demand price can be used as an estimate of the opportunity cost.

84.   Identifying the lost rural production associated with one additional project job can be time consuming. It may include nonagricultural, as well as agricultural, products. It may include an imputed value for lost production that is produced by family labor but not marketed. An indirect alternative is to use rural wage estimates as a proxy for opportunity costs. Rural casual wage rates in competitive markets represent the value placed on surplus labor in the region from which it is drawn, and hence its supply price. Casual wage rates can be reexpressed in annual terms and used as a measure of opportunity cost.

85.   With increasing city size and growing numbers of urban poor, many projects draw labor from urban rather than rural areas. Surplus labor in the urban context supports itself through many informal activities. The outputs of these informal activities are generally nontraded products sold only in the domestic market. Estimates of annual incomes in the urban informal sector can be used as a measure of opportunity cost for labor drawn into projects from urban areas. The estimate of income can be associated with a range of urban goods and services for purposes of estimating an economic value.

86.   Some projects, especially in the industry sector, use predominantly young female labor. Such labor may play a different role in the rural or urban economy from which it is drawn, depending on local customs and family structure. Generally, there are further costs

associated with female rather than male labor. These relate to the provision of goods and services in the household. The migration of female labor to new jobs, especially where it involves geographic migration as well, may lead to a decline not just in marketable production, but also in household production that is not marketed. Estimates of this additional element of opportunity cost can be made through the purchase cost of equivalent services and should be included in the economic cost of labor for projects using predominantly female labor.

87.   The economic price of different categories of labor can be expressed in relation to the full wage of the same category of labor to form the shadow wage rate factor (SWRF). The SWRF for surplus rural labor is the ratio of the opportunity cost of rural labor plus the economic costs of migration to the project wage for surplus labor. Similarly, the SWRF for scarce labor is the ratio of its economic and financial price. In each case, the supply price of surplus labor and the demand price of scarce labor have to be adjusted for the general level of distortions in the economy (see Paragraph 104 and Appendix 12).

F.   The Economic Price of Land

88.   All projects involve some use of land. Even where land has no financial cost, its economic value should be estimated and included in the calculation of economic viability. The demand price for land does not always give an accurate reflection of the economic value of land because supply cannot be expanded and land can be held for speculative, as well as productive, purposes or to meet immediate needs. The value of land is best determined through its opportunity cost—what it would have been used to produce without the project. In a relatively competitive land rental market, land rent is generally a good estimate of the opportunity cost. Where relevant, the economic costs of resettlement should be included in the cost of land, if such costs are not included already in the project costs.

89.   For rehabilitation and improvement projects, the same area of land may be included as in the original project. Here the economic price of land will be included in the without-project net output estimates. However, for new and expansion projects, the economic price of land needs to also include the opportunity cost of land undergoing a change of use. The alternative net output from the land undergoing a change of use, at economic prices, will differ from project to project.

90.   For new projects in rural areas, the opportunity cost of the land will be the net agricultural output foregone, measured at economic prices. This opportunity cost should be estimated on an annual basis. Over the life of the project there may be an increasing or decreasing trend in agricultural productivity, which should be incorporated into the opportunity cost estimate. A similar approach can be used for city-edge land, where agricultural uses are displaced by infrastructure, industrial, or housing projects. In this context, owing to greater access to urban markets and facilities, the future opportunity cost is likely to considerably exceed the present productivity of the land.

91.   The same principle can be applied, but with greater complexity, in the city center context; for example, when road construction displaces housing, offices, commercial and industrial activities, and recreational uses. The extent of land use change for each type of activity can be calculated and valued accordingly, considering the lost production at economic prices for directly productive industrial and commercial activities; the cost savings through relocation of indirectly productive activities; and the willingness to pay for recreational and other public amenities. The economic cost of land also includes the opportunity cost of land used for the resiting of the displaced activities, which may be at other city-edge locations.

92.   Many countries are implementing a series of special export or development zones. Here the opportunity cost of the land may change dramatically over a short period of time. Previously, relatively unused, poor agricultural land could be transformed through infrastructure investment into highly valued land for industrial, financial, or commercial purposes. Where land markets develop or where rents are set on a competitive basis, the market price of the land can be used to estimate its productive value in this context. In addition to the opportunity cost of land use, the costs of land development should also be included as an economic cost of the project (see Appendix 13).

93.   Many natural resources, such as land, are depletable. When a natural resource is depletable, its economic cost will comprise both its opportunity cost in terms of benefits foregone from its best alternative use and its scarcity rent. While the consequences of land degradation represent an increasing threat to agricultural production, other natural resources, such as groundwater, are closer to exhaustion. In the case of groundwater, the finite capacity of aquifers means that when withdrawal rates exceed the rate of recharge, an alternative water source must eventually be found. The higher future cost of obtaining water implies a scarcity rent or depletion premium (see Appendix 6). Even in the case of surface water, scarcity rent is relevant when pricing raw water. When a water utility approaches its legal entitlement from a river source, it has to find an additional source if it is to meet growing demand. Typically, only higher cost sources are left, and this in itself implies a scarcity rent. If, on the other hand, a water utility is able to purchase new water rights on the open market, the scarcity rent becomes an explicit part of the price paid for raw water, and the market price of raw water is equal to its economic price. Similar considerations apply in valuing other depletable national resources, such as mineral deposits or national fish stocks.

94.   Many Bank-funded projects involve resettlement of people and economic activities. Sometimes resettlement may be a major component of project planning and costs; other times it may affect only a small number of people and activities. Generally resettlement cannot expect to recreate exactly the living conditions or income opportunities that are displaced. Resettlement itself should be seen as a development subproject, requiring its own institutional structure and financial resources. There will be economic costs, both direct and in terms of lost output, as well as potential benefits that can be identified by analyzing the situation with and without resettlement (see Appendix 14).

G.   Bringing Economic Prices to a Common Base

95.   If the above principles are followed in estimating economic benefits and costs, then most project effects will be valued at their border price equivalent value. This will apply for traded goods and services, for the opportunity cost of surplus labor, for the opportunity cost of land, and indirectly for nontraded inputs with increasing supply. However, other items, such as the opportunity cost of scarce labor, nontraded products in fixed supply, and especially nontraded outputs, will be valued initially in domestic market price values. These two forms of valuation need to be brought to a common base so that they can be aggregated and compared.

96.   The aggregation of costs and benefits requires a unit of account to be established in terms of the currency and the price level in which the analysis is to be conducted. Economic analysis can be undertaken in the currency of the borrowing country or a foreign currency, and at the domestic or the world price level. Bank economic analysis generally will be undertaken in the currency of the borrowing country. For reasons given below, there is also a preference for using the domestic price level to conduct economic analysis. However, there may be circumstances when the world price level is preferred.

97.   Domestic market price values differ from border price equivalent values. Generally, domestic prices are higher than world prices. This means that purchasers in the domestic market, in general, place a higher value on imported and exported goods and services than is indicated by the border price equivalent value of those items. The difference between the domestic market price and the world market price equivalent represents the extent to which purchasers are willing to pay above the direct foreign exchange cost or value of the goods and services. The economic price of foreign currency—the shadow exchange rate—rather than the actual price of foreign currency—the official exchange rate—should be used in the economic valuation of goods and services. The shadow exchange rate is the weighted average of imports and exports in domestic prices to the border price equivalent value of the same goods.

98.   The shadow exchange rate is greater than the official exchange rate to the extent that domestic market prices for goods and services exceed their border price equivalent value. Even where the official exchange rate is market-determined, it will differ from the shadow exchange rate. The former is affected by income and capital flows; the latter refers only to goods and services. Where foreign exchange markets themselves have been liberalized, there will remain a difference between the domestic market price and world market price values for traded products, because of trade controls and taxes, and monopolized markets.

99.   The shadow exchange rate is estimated by comparing the demand for, and supply of, foreign exchange for trade purposes. Where demand and supply are elastic with respect to price, the shadow exchange rate can be estimated by directly comparing the domestic market price value of all traded products with their world market price value. The shadow exchange rate factor (SERF) is calculated as the ratio of the shadow exchange rate to the official exchange rate. This factor will generally be greater than 1. The SERF is applied to all outputs

and inputs, including labor and land, that have been valued at border price equivalent values. Project effects measured at domestic market price values are left unadjusted. In this way, all project effects are brought to a common basis of measurement in the currency of the borrowing country at the domestic price level.

100.   This method of adjusting border price equivalent values to the equivalent domestic price level is called using the domestic price numeraire. Project effects, as far as possible, are still measured at border price equivalent values. These values are reexpressed to correspond to the level at which the remaining project items are measured. This use of the domestic price to express all economic costs and benefits has the distinct advantage of corresponding to the price level at which the constant price financial analysis is undertaken. The distribution of net economic benefits among project participants can therefore be traced more easily in assessing financial and fiscal sustainability, as well as affordability and acceptability (see Section XII).

101.   An alternative approach can be used to adjust all project items to a common basis of comparison. Domestic market price values are in general higher than border price equivalent values. Instead of adjusting border price equivalent values upward, using the SERF, the domestic market price values of project items, measured through willingness to pay or other nontraded measures, can be adjusted downward. This can be done using the standard conversion factor (SCF), which is simply the inverse of the SERF. It represents the extent to which border price equivalent values, in general, are lower than domestic market price values. It is applied to all project items valued at their domestic market price to convert them to a border price equivalent value. If this is done, they can be aggregated together and compared with all other project items valued at their border price equivalent values, in the currency of the borrowing country at the world price level.

102.   Use of the standard conversion factor in this way is called using the world price numeraire. Most project effects are still measured at border price equivalent values. All project effects are brought to this level of valuation. The use of the world price numeraire may be preferred in small open economies, where it is simple to think in foreign exchange terms. It may also be preferred in transitional economies, where there remain numerous administered prices or subsidized enterprises and products. In the latter case, the unit of account may also be changed. Instead of expressing all effects in domestic currency, project effects may be expressed in foreign exchange units directly, but still using the standard conversion factor as well as the official rate of exchange to convert nontraded values to border price equivalent values. However, use of the world price numeraire in domestic or foreign currency units when assessing economic viability means that to make further comparisons with the distribution of net financial benefits in sustainability analysis, project effects would all have to be converted back to domestic market price values.

103.   Estimation of the shadow exchange rate factor or the standard conversion factor can be done from time to time on a country basis. Which is applied, that is, which numeraire is chosen for the analysis affects the absolute value of economic costs and benefits, but not the

economic internal rate of return (EIRR) of the project. All values using the domestic price numeraire—both costs and benefits—will be greater than the corresponding values using the world price numeraire by a fixed amount given by the SERF. Conversely, all values using the world price numeraire—both costs and benefits—will be less than their domestic price equivalent by a fixed amount given by the SCF. Of course, it is important not to confuse the two methods by using both the SERF and the standard conversion factor together. However, if the shadow exchange rate factor and standard conversion factor have been consistently estimated, that is, if one has been estimated from the other, then there will be a fixed proportion between all costs and benefits using the two methods, and, correspondingly, the EIRR will be the same. The choice of which numeraire to use will depend on how easily the analysis of economic viability fits together with the analysis of financial and fiscal sustainability.

104.   The SWRF can also be expressed in both numeraires. The ratio between the economic and financial cost of labor for different categories forms the basis of the SWRF. Where the economic costs are measured in domestic market price values, the SWRF can be used directly in a domestic market price analysis. Where economic viability is being measured in world market price values, the SWRF also has to be expressed in world market price values, using a specific or the standard conversion factor. Hence, the SWRF for domestic market price analysis is multiplied by the specific or standard conversion factor to give the equivalent SWRF for world market price analysis (see Appendix 15).

H.   Conversion Factors

105.   Conversion factors can be calculated and used when testing the economic viability of a project. A conversion factor is the ratio between the economic price value and the financial value for a project output or input. This ratio can be applied to the constant price financial values in project analysis to derive the corresponding economic values. Conversion factors can be calculated for

- specific project items, for example, the main outputs and inputs;
- groups of typical items, such as, petrochemicals or grains; and
- the economy as a whole, as in the SERF or standard conversion factor.

Specific conversion factors can be calculated to convert financial values into economic values using the domestic market price numeraire or the world market price numeraire.

106.   Where the domestic price numeraire is being used, no adjustment for economic values is necessary for the outputs of indirectly productive projects, where an economic value has been attributed based on the willingness to pay or the willingness to accept compensation; or for nontraded inputs valued in the same way. For economic analysis using the world market price numeraire, the willingness to pay or willingness to accept values should be adjusted by

the standard conversion factor to bring them in line with other items in the economic resource flow.

107.   Conversion factors for groups of products, as well as the SERF and the standard conversion factor, are often estimated using only an adjustment for net trade taxes. This approach generally underestimates the difference between the domestic market and border price equivalent values. The corresponding group conversion factors are minimum estimates, together with the SERF, using the domestic price numeraire, or maximum estimates, along with the standard conversion factor, using the world price numeraire. Results of economic viability analysis can be tested through higher (domestic price numeraire) or lower (world price numeraire) values of the SERF and the standard conversion factor, respectively, and conversion factors for groups of products.

108.   Several nontraded inputs occur in nearly all projects: construction, transport, water, power, distribution, and financial services are the most obvious. It may be desirable to calculate specific conversion factors for these commonly occurring inputs on a country basis so that consistent values are used across different projects in a country. Where the supply of these nontraded inputs is being expanded, specific conversion factors can be calculated through a cost breakdown at financial prices. The cost breakdown should include the proportion of the financial value spent on surplus labor, scarce labor, net taxes to government, traded items, and domestic resources. Such a cost structure can be used to estimate a conversion factor for the item if there also exists an estimate of the SERF and SWRFs for the different categories of labor, or a standard conversion factor and adjusted SWRFs for the labor categories (see Table 4).

109.   Table 4 illustrates the importance of two national parameters, the SERF (or standard conversion factor) and the SWRF. The SERF and standard conversion factor are estimated at the national level. There are different approaches to estimating a SERF/standard conversion factor, including the use of semi-input-output methods, or an estimate of the sustainable trade balance (see Appendix 16). The SWRF may differ from project to project for different types of labor and should be estimated on a project basis. Moreover the opportunity cost of surplus or scarce labor in physical terms may differ between projects—in one region it may be represented by paddy, in another it may be represented by livestock products. Specific conversion factors for different labor categories can also be used in the above procedure if they can be estimated.

Table 4: Specific Conversion Factors from Cost Breakdowns

		Adjustment	
Item	Proportion (%)	Using Domestic Price Level Numeraire	Using World Price Level Numeraire
Traded goods	60	SERF	1.0
Surplus labor	10	OCSL	OCSL * SCF
Scarce labor	10	OCSCL	OCSCL * SCF
Net taxes	10	0.0	0.0
Domestic resources	10	1.0	SCF
Total	100	DMP adjusted	WMP adjusted
Conversion Factors		DMP CF	WMP CF

CF   - Conversion factor
DMP   - Domestic market price
OCSCL   - Opportunity cost of scarce labor
OCSL   - Opportunity cost of surplus labor
SCF   - Standard conversion factor
SERF   - Shadow exchange rate factor
WMP   - World market price

I.   Economic Viability: A Procedure

110.   In a project context, the methods outlined above need to be applied in a cost-effective manner. The focus must be placed on those economic prices that are important for testing the economic viability of the specific project. Economic price calculations can be carried out in more or less detail. The following iterative procedure can be used to determine what level of detail to pursue:

First Iteration
    (i)   Choose the numeraire and unit of account for the analysis.
    (ii)   Obtain the SERF or the standard conversion factor.
    (iii) Revalue the main outputs and inputs having a trade effect at border price equivalent values. Use a simple SERF or the standard conversion factor estimate to bring traded/nontraded items to a common basis.
    (iv)   Obtain willingness to pay or other valuations for incremental nontraded outputs.
    (v)   Identify any nontraded inputs that are crucial to the project and for which financial prices incorporate a significant tax or, more likely, subsidy element. There is likely to be only one or none for any project. Calculate a specific conversion factor for such an item.
    (vi)   Estimate a SWRF for project labor.
    (vii) Estimate the economic value of land using the SERF or the standard conversion factor.

    (viii)   Calculate the project net present value (NPV) and internal rate of return (IRR) using:
- border price equivalent values for the main traded outputs and inputs;
- a willingness to pay or other estimate for incremental nontraded outputs;
- a specific conversion factor for any major, subsidized nontraded input;
- a SWRF for project labor adjusted by the standard conversion factor, if necessary; and
- a SERF estimate for other trade items, or a standard conversion factor estimate for other nontraded items.

    (ix)   Test the sensitivity of the results to the SERF or the standard conversion factor value used, and the SWRFs used.

    (x)   If the project or subproject is not marginal, and if the result is not sensitive to the national parameter estimates used, present the results of the economic viability tests.

111.   If the project or subproject is marginal, or if the results are sensitive to the national parameter estimates used, proceed to the second iteration:

Second Iteration

    (i)   Estimate specific conversion factors for other nontraded inputs, labor, and land. Sometimes these can be taken from studies of national parameters carried out at the national level.

    (ii)   Reestimate the NPV and IRR of the project or subproject.

    (iii)   Present the results of the tests of economic viability (see Appendix 17).

VIII.   LARGE PROJECTS, LINKAGES, AND NATIONAL AFFORDABILITY

112.   Most projects can be treated as marginal projects in the sense that they do not have any substantial influence on other sectors or projects. However, some large projects may have considerable repercussions within the local and the national economy. A large project can be seen as one that affects production levels and prices in the sector of output and in supplying sectors. For such projects, there should be a discussion of linkage effects. A project can also be seen as large in a national context, where it may have a substantial impact upon foreign exchange revenues, expenditures, or budget resources, particular for Bank-financed projects in borrowing countries with smaller population and economies. For such projects, there should be a discussion of national affordability.

113.   The linkage effects of large projects will be considerable. Where possible, a quantitative estimate should be made of the main linkage effects. This could include

- effects on capacity utilization of supplying sectors,
- employment generation—direct and indirect,
- effects on prices of output and inputs, and
- direct and indirect income generation and its distribution.

114.   The issue of national affordability needs to be discussed in the context of investment possibilities for the country as a whole, and projected macroeconomic forecasts. Where a significant proportion of investment funds or foreign exchange resources will be committed, a statement should be provided of

- other large projects that may compete for resources simultaneously,
- the net foreign currency flows over the project life,
- the net flows to the government over the project life,
- the effect on the national debt measured by increases in debt and debt servicing ratios, and
- possible effects on the exchange rate of substantial capital inflows at the beginning of the project.

In the case of both foreign currency and government budget flows, it can be expected that positive net flows will be delayed until late in the project, especially where incentives are given in the form of tax holidays.

115.   The assessment of large projects will be more extensive than for smaller projects. This is generally justified in terms of the funds being committed within a particular country. A range of indicators can be used, incorporating wider considerations of economic impact and national affordability. The results of these wider assessments can be summarized alongside the basic project worth criteria (see Appendix 18).

IX.   LEAST-COST AND COST-EFFECTIVENESS ANALYSIS

116.   After determining the scope of the project on the basis of demand and other factors, and having identified, quantified, and valued the costs and benefits of the project alternatives, the next step is to identify the least-cost or most cost-effective alternative to achieve the purpose of the project. A comparative analysis of the scale, location, technology, and timing of alternative project options or designs is often required. Such an analysis will take into account both market and nonmarket costs in testing for least-cost or productive efficiency. In cases in which alternatives can be defined that deliver the same benefits, it is possible to estimate the equalizing discount rate between each pair of mutually exclusive options for comparison. Alternatively, if the effect or outcome of a project can be quantified but not valued, the average incremental economic cost can be estimated, with the aim of establishing the project alternative with the lowest per unit cost.

117.   Least-cost analysis aims at identifying the least-cost project option for supplying output to meet forecast demand. Least-cost analysis involves comparing the costs of the various mutually exclusive, technically feasible project options and selecting the one with the lowest costs. For example, it may be that the cheapest way of increasing water supply is through more efficient management of the existing supply system rather than through augmenting capacity.

118.   Mutually exclusive project options must be alternative ways of producing the same output of a specified service quality. If differences in output or service quality exist, a normalization procedure that takes the foregone incremental benefits of one option relative to another as a cost to the deficient option must be followed to ensure equivalence.

119.   Procedures for the calculation and interpretation of the equalizing discount rate should be made explicit, with the least-cost project being identified by comparing the capital and operating costs of the project alternatives and calculating the equalizing discount rate for the difference in cost streams. The project with the highest equalizing discount rate for all comparisons is the least-cost alternative. Using a more straightforward approach, the alternative with the lowest present value of costs, is the least-cost alternative.

120.   Alternatively, the average incremental economic cost for each alternative can be estimated, with the aim of identifying the alternative with the lowest per unit costs. The average incremental economic cost is the present value of incremental investment and operation costs, with and without the project alternative, divided by the present value of incremental output, with and without the project alternative.

$$\text{Average incremental cost} = \sum_{t=o}^{n}(C_t / (1+d)^t) / \sum_{t=o}^{n}(O_t / (1+d)^t)$$

where C_t is incremental investment and operation cost in year t
        O_t is incremental output in year t
        n is the project life in years
and d is the discount rate.

121.   Because of the uncertainty involved in forecasting future demand and the complex interrelationships between the cost of output and the price charged, least-cost analysis should also take into account the value of flexibility. For example, in the case of uncertain demand in a water supply project, it may be more costly but preferable to consider staging construction. Adding capacity in small amounts gives the water enterprise flexibility, but is also more costly. Hence, it is important to be able to value this flexibility. One way to do this is to find out how much lower the capital cost of the smaller plant would have to be to make it the preferred choice. The economies of scale associated with the larger cheaper-cost option would have to be

equal to, or greater than, that amount to make giving up the flexibility of the smaller project economical (see Appendix 19).

122.   Least-cost analysis applies to projects where the benefits can be valued or to projects where the benefits take the form of a single commodity, such as treated water or power. Cost-effectiveness analysis also deals with alternative means of achieving given ends. However, the ends may be estimated only indirectly. For example, different means of organizing activities to raise reading abilities in primary schools may be under discussion. The costs associated with each alternative can be calculated on a without project / with project basis. The effectiveness of each alternative may be measured through setting reading tests for groups of students subject to the different methods.

123.   Cost-effectiveness analysis requires the increase in reading test scores to be divided by the costs for each method. The most cost-effective method is the one that raises reading test scores by a given amount for the least cost. If this method is chosen and applied to all similar students, the same increase in reading test scores can be obtained for the lowest cost, in other words, there would be the largest overall improvement in reading test scores per unit of cost expended. However, it should also be noted that the most cost effective method is not necessarily the most effective method of raising reading test scores. Another method may be the most effective, but also cost a lot more, so it is not the most cost effective. The cost effectiveness ratios - the cost per unit increase in reading test scores for each method - can be compared to see how much more it would cost to implement the most effective method. Which method is chosen for implementation then depends jointly on

- the desired target increase in reading test scores, and
- the extra cost involved in implementing the most effective method.

124.   There will be circumstances where project alternatives have more than one outcome. For example, there are different dimensions of literacy - comprehension, writing, speed. Different interventions to improve literacy may have different impacts on each dimension. In order to assess the cost effectiveness of the different interventions it is necessary to devise a testing system where the results for the different dimensions can be added together. It is also necessary to decide on some weights for adding the different dimensions together, reflecting their importance in relation to the objectives of the project. Such a use of cost-effectiveness analysis is called weighted cost-effectiveness analysis. It introduces a subjective element, the weights, into the comparison of project alternatives, both to find the most cost-effective alternative and to identify the extra cost of implementing the most effective alternative.

X.   INVESTMENT CRITERIA: ECONOMIC VIABILITY

A.   Project Decisions

125.   The preceding sections outlined the principles for identification, quantification, and valuation of project costs and benefits. The resulting streams of costs and benefits are used to make project choices. Essentially, there are three types of project decisions for which criteria are needed:

- choice of the least-cost option for achieving the same benefits,
- choice of the best among project alternatives, and
- testing the economic viability of the best option.

126.   The first type of decision occurs when benefits cannot be valued for comparison with project costs. Such situations are discussed in Chapter IX. The purpose is to achieve the same benefit effect at the lowest cost. The second type of decision occurs at the early stages in all projects, when choices are being made about project location, scale, size, and other features of project design. Costs and, to some extent, benefits may differ between mutually exclusive alternatives. The purpose is to choose the best alternative from the point of view of the national economy. The third type of decision is the basis for agreeing to fund a project or not. The best project alternative may not be economically viable. A test is needed of the economic viability of the best alternative for a project, in short, whether a proposed project is acceptable for investment or not.

127.   To make these decisions, all cost and benefit streams are discounted to present value. Present costs and benefits are accorded a larger weight than those in the future. Moreover, the weights on future costs and benefits are treated as decreasing at a constant rate each year. To determine the least-cost option or to compare project alternatives, the same discount rate should be applied to the various cost and benefit streams. For this purpose, the Bank uses a discount rate between 10 and 12 percent. The same discount rate should be used to determine if a project is economically viable. In choosing the best alternative or testing economic viability, where costs and benefits are measured in economic prices, this discount rate for decision-making purposes should be regarded as the economic discount rate relevant for economic prices (see Section XI).

B.   Choosing Between Alternatives When Benefits Are Not Valued

128.   Where the benefits of a project cannot be valued, they cannot be aggregated with the costs of the project. In these circumstances, a decision can be made only about which option has the lowest present value of costs for providing a given level of output. If the full costs of each alternative are laid out over the full life of the project, including any residual value at the end of the project life, then for each alternative the present value of costs can be calculated

using the chosen discount rate between 10 and 12 percent. The best alternative is the option with the lowest present value of economic costs.

>   Criterion: Choose option with lowest present value of economic costs at chosen
>   discount rate (between 10 and 12 percent)

129.   The choice between cost alternatives can also be approached another way. The discount rate that equalizes the costs of different options compared in pairs—the equalizing discount rate—can be calculated. Comparison of the equalizing discount rate with the Bank's discount rate for decision-making purposes will identify the least-cost option between successive pairs of options.

130.   Where the cost alternatives do not provide exactly the same level of output, or where different cost alternatives have multiple and differing outcomes, it is difficult to identify the option with lowest present value of costs without placing weights on the outcomes from the different alternatives. In these cases, the approach has to be adjusted to consider both the target level of attainment of different outcomes that is desired, and the extra costs of the different alternatives of achieving higher levels for the outcomes.

C.   Choosing Between Alternatives When Benefits Are Valued

131.   Where the benefits of a project and project alternatives can be valued, they can be aggregated and compared with the costs of the project or project alternatives. Three criteria are commonly used to aggregate and compare costs and benefits. However, they cannot all be used in the same way to choose from project alternatives.

132.   The benefit-cost ratio compares the present value of the cost streams with the present value of the benefit streams, each discounted at the same rate. The comparison is made by forming the ratio of the present value of benefits to the present value of costs. However, the benefit-cost ratio should not be used for choosing from alternatives as the ratio is sensitive to the way in which benefits and costs are grouped, for example, whether residual values are subtracted from the cost streams or added to the benefit streams.

133.   The net present value (NPV) also compares the present value of the cost streams with the present value of the benefit streams. However, it does so not as a ratio but by taking the cost stream away from the benefit stream to obtain the net benefit stream, which can then be discounted. In choosing between project alternatives, the alternatives can be ranked according to their NPVs, which at economic prices represent the present value of net output that will be generated in the economy over the life of the project. The economic net present value (ENPV) is calculated for each project alternative using the Bank discount rate of 10 to 12 percent.

134.   The third criterion for summarizing the benefit and cost effects of a project alternative is the internal rate of return (IRR). The IRR represents the rate of return in economic prices that would be achieved on all expenditures of the project. The EIRR is

calculated using the net benefit stream obtained by subtracting year by year all costs from all benefits. The EIRR is the rate of discount for which the present value of the net benefit stream becomes zero. Put another way, it is the rate of discount at which the present value of the cost stream is equal to the present value of the benefit stream.

135.   The ranking of project alternatives according to these three criteria may differ. The overriding purpose of the economic analysis of projects is to increase the net output measured at economic prices in the national economy. The ENPV criterion measures this directly. The choice between project alternatives should be made using the ENPV criterion at the chosen rate of discount, between 10 and 12 percent.

> Criterion: Choose project alternative with the highest ENPV at the chosen discount rate (between 10 and 12 percent)

D.   Testing the Economic Viability of the Best Alternative

136.   The best project alternative may not be economically viable. A test of viability needs to be applied to the chosen alternative, and to any subprojects within it. The basic test for economic viability is whether or not there are other projects in the national economy that, when estimated in the same way, would yield a greater increase in net output. In practice, not all investment opportunities are collected together and compared. The way this comparison is done is to specify a rate of discount representing the next best alternative project in the economy, and to ensure that the project being analyzed creates net benefits in present value at a rate that exceeds those of the next best alternative. This can be done using any of the three criteria discussed above.

137.   The chosen rate of discount for decision making is between 10 and 12 percent. At a discount rate within this range, the two main criteria can be used as follows:

- *Net Present Value*: the discounted value of economic net benefits should be positive.
  Criterion: Accept all independent projects and subprojects for which the ENPV is greater than 0.

- *Economic Internal Rate of Return*: The economic internal rate of return on resources should exceed that on the next best alternative project.
  Criterion: Accept all independent projects and subprojects for which the EIRR is greater than the chosen discount rate.

138.   These two criteria are equivalent. They will lead to the same acceptance and rejection of independent projects and subprojects.

E.   The Chosen Discount Rate

139.   It has been standard practice for the Bank to use the EIRR criterion. The project is considered economically viable if its EIRR exceeds the economic opportunity cost of capital in the country concerned. Because it is difficult, in practice, to estimate precisely what this value should be for each country, 10 to 12 percent is used for all member countries as the minimum rate of return for projects for which an EIRR can be calculated, and the rate at which to choose least-cost options.

140.   Most directly productive projects have some element of benefits or costs that cannot be quantified or valued. The minimum rate of return within the range of 10-12 percent could be interpreted to take account of these factors. The Bank would expect to

- accept all independent projects and subprojects with an EIRR of at least 12 percent;
- accept independent projects and subprojects with an EIRR between 10 and 12 percent for which additional unvalued benefits can be demonstrated, and where they are expected to exceed unvalued costs;
- reject independent projects and subprojects with an EIRR between 10 and 12 percent for which no additional unvalued benefits can be demonstrated, or where unvalued costs are expected to be significant; and
- reject independent projects and subprojects with an EIRR below 10 percent.

F.   Project Investments and the Budget

141.   The Bank operates with an indicative program of lending for each country. These programs are, in part, determined by an assessment of absorptive capacity within the country, and what other external funds are being used. Some countries will operate under an investment budget constraint at the national or sector level. In addition, investments tend to be lumpy and not to fit easily within any constraint. Foreign borrowing relaxes such constraints on investment. When a country is faced with a budget constraint, implying more investment opportunities than it can implement, because of a shortage of investment funds or budget resources for counterpart funds, or a lack of appropriate personnel, then the appropriate response is to raise the discount rate for project and subproject selection above the 10-12 percent band usually adopted. When funds and resources are in short supply, it is even more important to look for viable projects with high rates of return.

XI. DISCOUNT RATE

142.   Bank practice is to use a rate of 10 or 12 percent to calculate the net present value of a project, or to compare with the internal rate of return, for economic analysis. However, economic rates of return differ considerably between sectors and countries, and different

countries vary in their capacity to repay foreign borrowing. From time to time, an appropriate discount rate for economic analysis should be calculated for each country to compare with the existing practice. The concern here is with a discount rate for economic analysis with benefits and costs estimated in economic prices.

143.   A discount rate for economic analysis can be estimated in different ways. Four of these approaches to estimation focus on

- the economic rate of return on alternative marginal projects or the economic opportunity cost of capital, so that investments can be selected that show a minimum rate of return that is not exceeded by other possible investments;
- the real cost of foreign borrowing, which ensures that investment funds are committed to projects that will be able to meet the country's debt obligations, especially where investment is highly dependent on inflows of foreign capital;
- the real rate of return in the capital market, which will indicate the return a project must earn before investors will forego more liquid types of investment to invest in physical assets; and
- the overall demand and supply of investment funds, to provide an overall estimate of the economic price of capital.

144.   Various sources of information can be used to obtain an estimate of the rate of return on investments in the economy. At one level, national income accounting data converted to economic prices can be used to calculate a national level profit estimate. This should then be compared with a national capital stock estimate, which may not be available. At a second level, sector or corporate data is used to estimate a weighted average return in financial prices. This return then needs to be converted to economic prices using national parameter estimates. At a third level, studies of recently accepted and rejected projects are used to identify a minimum economic rate of return that appears acceptable to the government. These approaches generally give a range of estimates for the economic opportunity cost of capital, on the basis of aggregate data at the national and sectoral level, and data incorporating appraisal optimism at the project level.

145.   The real costs of foreign borrowing may be easier to estimate where it is appropriate. The cost of foreign borrowing varies between different sources. The relevant cost is the marginal or highest cost of borrowing on current or projected loans, where the cost of borrowing includes the interest rate and other costs, such as front-end and commitment fees, and risk premiums. This cost needs to be converted into real terms. The marginal cost of foreign borrowing can be deflated by an export or import price index depending on whether the major source of repayments in foreign currency will come from expanded exports or imports foregone. In the absence of specific data on foreign loans, a world rate, such as the London interbank offer rate (LIBOR) adjusted for administration fees and a risk premium, can be used. In the absence of data on export and import prices, a world price index, such as the manufacturing value-added index, can be used for deflating purposes. The resulting real cost of

foreign borrowing provides the minimum rate of return a project or subproject should achieve at economic prices.

146.   There are different sources of capital funds in the domestic economy: insurance or pension funds, investment and commercial banks, venture capital operations, and bond and stock markets. Rates of interest or return on these different sources of capital can be deflated to real terms and converted to economic prices. Moreover, the return must be acceptable to those using the funds. The real cost of domestic borrowing will be the rate that balances the supply of funds from savers with the demand for funds from investors. Projects should provide a return greater than the sources of funds that finance them. However, capital markets and, especially, interest rates, are frequently regulated, controlled, or small, and may not provide an appropriate measure of economic return on financial investment.

147.   More generally, the economic price of capital can be estimated as a weighted average of the demand and supply price. The marginal productivity of capital provides an estimate of the demand price for investment funds. The supply price of savings will be given by a social rate of time preference, a rate beyond which savers are willing to give up present for future consumption. The supply of savings from different groups of lenders can be compared with the demand for investment funds from different groups of borrowers. Elasticity estimates of the responsiveness of supply and demand to changes in real interest rates are used to arrive at the weighted average of the demand and supply price of capital (see Appendix 20).

XII.   UNCERTAINTY: SENSITIVITY AND RISK ANALYSIS

148.   The EIRR or ENPV for Bank projects is calculated using the most likely values of the variables incorporated in the cost and benefit streams. Future values are difficult to predict and there will always be some uncertainty about the project results. The effects of different values should be investigated. For directly productive projects, this means assessing the effect of possible changes on the ENPV or EIRR and, hence, on the project decision. For indirectly productive projects, this means assessing the effects of possible changes on a basic project parameter, such as the unit cost of service provision.

149.   Sensitivity analysis is a simple technique to assess the effects of adverse changes on a project. It involves changing the value of one or more selected variables and calculating the resulting change in the NPV or IRR. The extent of change in the selected variable to test can be derived from postevaluation and other studies of similar projects. Changes in variables can be assessed one at a time to identify the key variables. Possible combinations can also be assessed. Sensitivity analysis should be applied to project items that are numerically large or for which there is considerable uncertainty. To facilitate mitigating action, variation should be applied separately to underlying variables, such as areas and yields in agricultural projects, and not just to aggregate values. The effects of variation in the basic parameters for shadow price analysis, the SERF or standard conversion factor, and the SWRF, should also be assessed.

150.   The results of the sensitivity analysis should be summarized, where possible, in a sensitivity indicator and in a switching value. A sensitivity indicator compares the percentage change in a variable with the percentage change in a measure of project worth. The preferred measure is the ENPV. A switching value identifies the percentage change in a variable for the ENPV to become zero, the EIRR to fall to the cut-off rate, and the project decision to change. Where percentage changes in the variable cannot be measured, for example, for delays, simply the percentage change in the ENPV can be presented.

151.   Where the project is shown to be sensitive to the value of a variable that is uncertain, mitigating actions should be considered. This can include project level actions, such as long-term supply contracts or pilot phases; sector level actions, such as price changes or technical assistance programs; or national level actions, such as changes in tax and incentive policies. Where there is exceptional uncertainty, the project may have to be redesigned or implemented first on a pilot basis.

152.   Quantitative risk analysis associates a probability of occurring with different values of key variables. When such variables are varied simultaneously through a random selection of outcomes, a frequency distribution for the ENPV or EIRR can be produced showing the probability that the project is not acceptable. Decision makers will compare the scale of net benefits from different projects with their riskiness in selecting an individual project or a portfolio of projects. Quantitative risk analysis can be carried out for large and marginal projects, or projects where there is considerable uncertainty about a key variable, such as the world price for the project output.

153.   Sensitivity and risk analysis can be used to assess the effects of changes in project variables that are quantified. The results can be presented together with recommendations on what actions to take or which variables to monitor during implementation and operation. However, many projects involve institutional and social risks that cannot be readily quantified. A statement of such risks and any mitigating actions should be included alongside the conclusions from the sensitivity and risk analysis (see Appendix 21).

XIII.   SUSTAINABILITY OF PROJECT EFFECTS

154.   Economic viability depends upon the sustainability of project effects. The economic analysis of projects should include an analysis of the financial sustainability of project agencies, and the environmental sustainability of outputs and inputs. The ENPV and EIRR measure the value of a project over its estimated full life. However, the transience in practice of some project effects has drawn attention to the way in which financial and environmental effects impinge on benefit sustainability. Postevaluation experience also shows that, unless such factors are taken into account, economic benefits will not be sustained at the level necessary to generate an acceptable EIRR.

A.   Financial Sustainability

155.   There are three aspects of financial sustainability:

- the availability of adequate funds to finance project expenditures, especially funds drawn from the government budget,
- the recovery of some of the project costs from the project beneficiaries, and
- the financial incentive necessary to ensure participation in the project.

Project Funding and Fiscal Impact

156.   A financial plan at constant financial prices is necessary to ensure there will be adequate funds to finance project expenditures. This applies to the implementation period to ensure capital funds are available to cover investment and working capital requirements, and to the operating period to ensure sufficient funds to cover operating expenditures. Where the project will generate revenue, this revenue will be the main source of funds during the operating period.

157.   For indirectly productive projects that do not generate sufficient funds to cover operating expenditures, the full fiscal impact of the project for each year of its life should be calculated. The financial requirement becomes a fiscal requirement, and steps should be taken to ensure that the government commits adequate funds for operational purposes. Directly productive projects will also impact on the government budget, through tax revenues and concessions, and the net budget effect also can be calculated. The fiscal impact calculations should be linked to policy discussions over the extent and scale of user charges, operators fees, and tax revenues.

158.   For many public sector projects the government budget will be the principal source of funds to meet investment and operating expenditures. These funds could come from different sources. One possible source is a reallocation from other public expenditure programs. Another source is efficiency improvements in other public expenditures. In either case, the additional project expenditure should be considered in the context of public expenditure policy as a whole. Where the funds are not met from reallocations or efficiency improvements, they will be met from extra taxation or from borrowing. The economic effects of extra taxes, in particular what are the likely sources and what disincentives might they create, can be assessed at the national level. The economic effects of extra domestic borrowing by government can also be assessed at the national level. In either case, it is important to consider particularly the effects of extra taxation or borrowing on the groups who are the principal project beneficiaries, especially when these are the poor.

Cost Recovery

159.   The introduction or adjustment of user charges to finance project expenditures from project beneficiaries involves four important issues:

- the economic effect of the charges,
- the degree of revenue generation or cost recovery,
- the scope of charges between existing and new users, and
- the affordability of charges by different users.

The basic principle behind user charges is that users should pay the economic cost of the good or service being provided. In practice, this does not happen in many cases for government services or utilities. The appropriate cost for users to pay is the marginal cost of providing the good or service in question. However, over the life of a project the marginal cost must include the additional investment costs of expanding supply. The average incremental unit economic costs of investment and operation, on the basis of the least-cost method of supplying a good or service, should be taken as the appropriate target for charging users. This long-run marginal cost should be calculated at future, rather than historic, costs of supply.

160.   Three measures should be calculated and compared for each project or subproject producing an output for which charges can be levied, for example, port or water charges. These measures are:

- the average incremental financial cost of supply,
- the average incremental economic cost, and
- the average tariff to be charged.

The average incremental financial cost and the average incremental economic cost of supply should both be calculated using the economic discount rate of 10-12 percent. Where a project or project component stands alone, the tariff charged to the users should be related to the average incremental cost of supply for the service provided. Where a project extends an existing network, the tariff charged should be related to the average incremental cost of supply, but spread over existing, as well as new, users. In most cases, either situation will require an increase in charges from present levels.

161.   The government may decide to regulate or set charges so that the full costs of supply are not met by users. For example, the government may decide that only the operation and maintenance costs of government services need to be met from user charges, but not the capital costs of the project or project component. If so, the grounds upon which this implicit subsidy is given, should be stated. The extent of the effective subsidy should also be calculated. The effective subsidy is the difference between user charges and the average incremental cost of supply. Any subsidy implicit in the level of user charges will have to be met from funds or resources elsewhere in the economy through the budget system.

162.   Bank policy is to seek the elimination of subsidies over time where they are not justified or where they can be replaced by more effective measures, for example, income transfers. Subsidies may be justified on efficiency grounds in selected contexts such as for decreasing cost activities, or activities with substantial external benefits, or even to compensate some producers or consumers for the effects of other government policies. Targeted subsidies may also be justified, where necessary, to ensure access to a limited number of basic goods, that is, basic food, a basic quantity of water, basic education, and primary health care; or to provide a social safety net during a period of general economic transition. In all cases, the economic effects of financing a subsidy must also be assessed. The raising of user charges to cost recovery levels to eliminate unjustified subsidies must be pursued at the sector as well as the project level.

163.   Where a project provides a range of services on the basis of joint costs, it may not be possible to identify the marginal costs for providing each service. In this case, an overall financial internal rate of return can be calculated for the activities as a whole, for comparison with the chosen discount rate between 10 and 12 percent. Where the financial internal rate of return at constant prices falls below the chosen discount rate, the extent of the financial subsidy can be stated by calculating the extent to which tariff levels would have to be increased to provide a financial internal rate of return at least equal to the discount rate.

164.   A key issue in deciding on the extent of cost recovery is the structure of the tariff charged. Increases in charges will be more affordable for some users than for others. Maintaining a single average tariff, where costs are not fully recovered, in effect subsidizes those who are better off to the same extent as those who are worse off. Tariff structures can be designed to ensure that those who use the service more pay more, and, in general, that those who are better off pay more.

165.   The introduction or increase of user charges may affect the scale of the investment to be undertaken and its organization. Charges provide a form of demand management where users react by adjusting their use to the level of charges. These effects can sometimes be estimated through the use of price elasticities of demand. It is uneconomic to provide capacity at a level that would exceed demand at future charge levels. Typically, charge increases would reduce the need for investment somewhat and may, in turn, influence the average incremental economic and average incremental financial cost of supply. Demand management of this sort is particularly important where governments lack investment and operating resources. User charges are therefore a means not just of recovering costs but of determining the overall scale of investment, and should be considered at the early stages of project design (see Appendix 22).

Financial Incentives

166.   For a project to be sustained, each of the main participants should benefit from it. However, each also will have a certain standard against which to measure the expected benefits of project participation. A project statement of costs and benefits at financial prices can be

constructed for the directly productive elements of a project, for example, the commercial farm, the port authority, the build-own-operate-transfer sponsor, or the tomato paste factory. This project statement also includes the effects of taxation and of loan funds. The basic test of financial sustainability is whether the financial internal rate of return for the project participant exceeds the opportunity cost of capital for that participant. This may also include a risk element where revenues are in the form of charges or fees negotiated with, or regulated by, the government. The economic analysis of the project should include a statement based on realistic assumptions about taxation and the real costs of borrowing on the financial returns to investors (see Appendix 23).

167.   For some project participants, a full financial internal rate of return analysis cannot be undertaken. This will include the government, which may benefit from tax revenues unrelated to its proportion of costs. A statement of the effect of the project on the government budget should be included. It will also include small-scale participants whose investment is small or provided in kind, for example small landholders or tenants. Here a statement should be provided of the expected increase in annual income after allowing for any taxes, charges, and the real cost of borrowing.

168.   In many cases, the sustainability of project effects will depend upon specific investors or public corporations. A statement should also be included of how the project fits into the overall corporate structure, and whether any restructuring is required. These issues should be followed up in more detail in the financial analysis of the project.

Financial and Economic Analysis

169.   Project financial analysis should be undertaken in conjunction with project economic analysis. Financial prices influence the decisions of project participants; economic prices record the consequences of those decisions for the national economy. Financial prices help determine the level of demand for project outputs and the level of supply of project inputs. Prices or user charges, demand, and the scale of investment all need to be considered simultaneously. Financial prices provide the incentive for investment. For example, the extent to which traffic will divert to a new expressway, and the return to the expressway investor, will vary with the projected level of toll. The consequences of these responses for the economy as a whole are calculated in economic prices. The extent of traffic diversion will affect the level of traffic cost savings, and hence, also the EIRR of the project.

B.   Environmental Sustainability

170.   Sustainable development is development that lasts. A specific concern is that those who enjoy the fruits of economic development today may be making future generations worse off by excessively degrading the earth's resources and polluting the earth's environment. A general principle of sustainable development, that current generations should meet their needs

without compromising the ability of future generations to do the same, has become widely accepted.

171.   The value of environmental effects can be included in the economic analysis of projects. Although it is not possible to put monetary values on all types of environmental effects, such costs and benefits should be as explicit as possible so as to inform policymakers and citizens. For some projects, beneficial environmental effects will be the main objective of the project and should be valued. For other projects, environmental benefits or environmental costs should be valued as far as possible, and incorporated into the economic analysis, together with related mitigation or monitoring costs.

172.   Four broad approaches can be used to value environmental costs and benefits: market prices, costs of replacement, surrogate markets, and surveys. Transference modeling, that is, inferring input-output relationships and values from studies and experiences elsewhere, can be used to take account of environmental effects. In all cases, environmental costs and benefits based on financial values are in turn converted to economic values. These economic values need to be expressed using the same numeraire as other project items.

173.   Market prices are used in valuation when environmental damage leads to losses in productivity. Common applications include valuation of damage due to soil erosion, deforestation, and air and water pollution. In applying this approach, the physical or ecological relationship between environmental damage and its impact on output or health is estimated and combined with prices to derive monetary values. For environmentally related health risks, income foregone because of illness or premature death can be used to measure welfare losses. However, such estimates are only partial because they rely solely on income losses.

174.   People and firms can respond to environmental degradation by making expenditures to avert damage or compensate for possible consequences. Although some effects of degradation are not accounted for, these expenditures can provide an estimate of environmental damage. For example, when water supplies are polluted, factories can invest in private tubewells, and households can buy water from vendors. Losses of soil fertility caused by erosion can be approximated by the cost of using purchased fertilizers to replace nutrients.

175.   Environmental degradation can sometimes be valued through its effect on other markets, especially on property values and wages. For example, clean air is implicitly valued in property markets, since buyers will consider environmental attributes as characteristics of property. Similarly, environmental risks associated with different jobs are traded in labor markets, and wage levels for higher risk jobs will include larger risk premiums. This technique is difficult to apply when property owners or workers are unaware of environmental problems or are constrained in responding to them.

176.   Direct questioning can be used to find what value people place on environmental change or natural resources. This approach is particularly relevant where markets are nonexistent or where people value environmental resources that they do not use. Such surveys can be employed to determine the amenity value of species or landmarks and to determine willingness to pay for better access to clean water and improved sanitation.

177.   Governments may seek to internalize environmental costs and benefits into financial prices. The main advantages of market-based instruments is that they directly alter incentives through the price mechanism. They also tend to have positive fiscal effects because they involve a reduction in environmentally damaging subsidies and increase environmentally improving taxation (see Appendix 24).

XIV. DISTRIBUTION OF PROJECT EFFECTS

178.   Project sustainability is strongly affected by who benefits, and by how much, relative to who pays. In lending to the private sector for provision of public goods and services, for example, the distribution of project benefits among government, consumers, and private investors is a key input in negotiating build-own-operate-transfer agreements, in pricing services, and in the economic return to the national economy. One form of distributive analysis considers the distribution among operators, customers, and government, and how it is affected by different charge levels. This is pertinent to water supply, airport, and port projects, for example.

179.   The identity of the groups that gain or lose, and the size of the gains and losses, can be documented during the project design and appraisal process. The analysis of distribution effects begins with analyzing financial benefits and costs. This first step disaggregates the financial impact of the project on the main beneficiary groups. Six groups can be considered:

- the owners of project operating entity,
- those working in the project,
- the government,
- the consumers of project outputs, and
- those providing material inputs to the project, and
- lenders to the project.

180.   The second step is to account for the distribution of the economic benefits and costs, over and above financial benefits and costs. The differences between financial and economic costs and benefits should be allocated to owners, labor, government, consumers, suppliers, and lenders, or to different categories of producers in agricultural projects. The adoption of the domestic price numeraire enables financial benefits and costs to be compared directly with economic benefits and costs to identify the effects of government policies, externalities, and user charges.

181.   Distribution analysis can show the extent to which public pricing policy can affect the share of the private and public sectors in the net benefits of a service project. It can also be used to test the extent to which the project design directs benefits to particular income groups. Distribution effects can be important in the economic analysis of private sector projects in which the Bank takes an equity position (see Appendix 25).

182.   A second form of distribution analysis considers the distribution of net benefits among beneficiary groups according to their income level. A particular focus on net benefits going to the poor is pertinent to many agricultural, social sector, urban development and public utility projects that often focus on or at least include the least well-off. A statement can be provided of the incremental financial benefits to different project participants. For agricultural projects, for example, the benefits to producers can be broken down among farmers with different income levels. For road sector projects, the benefits to different final users can be broken down among users with different income levels. Such statements, showing the distribution of financial benefits, can be the basis of assessing the division of benefits between the poor and nonpoor (see Appendix 26). For several projects, financial benefits cannot be calculated. It is still desirable to obtain information on the income level of different beneficiaries. Where possible, the proportion of benefits, in physical terms, going to the poor and the nonpoor should be stated.

183.   In general, the analysis of the impact of projects on the poor should be based on specific information about direct project beneficiaries, and not merely about the district or province in which a project is located. Poverty reduction will be assisted where projects are targeted in ways that will assist groups of poor people directly. Obtaining information about likely beneficiaries is part of the process of project identification and design, and not just appraisal.

184.   Project costs and benefits may impact differently on men and women. Where a project generates substantial net benefits, and extra incomes for project participants, this will be at the cost of additional work. The burden of additional work rarely falls equally on all members of a household. At the same time, those who benefit or who control the additional financial resources may not be those who contribute most of the extra effort. For some types of project, for example, health, education or agricultural development projects, a distribution analysis can be undertaken on a gender basis, to identify the additional costs and benefits to women in particular.

185.   A third form of distribution analysis considers the effects of using foreign resources in production and funding. The economic analysis of foreign investment projects should be undertaken from both the project and host country perspective. The use of foreign financing, either equity or loans, results in an initial inflow of capital into the host country, but an outflow in later years to service foreign debt and interest payments and the repatriation of foreign equity, capital gains, and earnings. From these two flows, the net foreign capital flow to the host economy can be calculated.

186.   More generally, the division of benefits between the host country and the foreign investor typically will depend upon government policies. For example, taxes are a source of revenue to the host country and a cost to the foreign investor, reducing the level of repatriated profits. Subsidies are a cost to the host economy and a benefit to the foreign investor. To encourage foreign investment, protection might be provided to the foreign investor. Tariffs on project outputs will increase the profits of the foreign investor and, therefore, potentially increase the outflow of benefits from the economy. Tariffs on project inputs will increase the benefits to the economy. Fees paid by the government for privately provided services represent a benefit to the investor, but a cost to the national economy.

187.   Economic prices should be used to estimate net economic benefits of the foreign investment project from the efficiency viewpoint. However, financial prices determine the share of overall benefits that accrue to the foreign investor and to the host country. Changes in financial prices affect the distribution of benefits between the host country and the foreign investor without necessarily affecting the total economic benefits of the project. Both the underlying economic return and the net benefits to the foreign investor and country should be calculated for such investments, particularly when the Bank both extends a loan and takes an equity position in the project company.

XV.   Projects and Policies

188.   Investment projects take place in an economic environment shaped by government policy. Increasingly, governments are using market mechanisms in conjunction with investment projects to achieve their objectives. There are important relationships between policies, sector programs, markets, and projects.

189.   Most investments funded or supported by government play an enabling role in the wider economic framework. The provision of physical infrastructure and an appropriate institutional framework allow producers of goods or services to adjust their activities to achieve higher levels of real income and other more direct benefits. These adjustments rely on additional activities, the supply of inputs, or the selling or distribution of outputs, also adjusting themselves to the new opportunities. In some cases, these adjustments will be easier to achieve than others.

190.   Governments also act where market mechanisms produce ambiguous results. Relying on private investment and commercial credit to build up the productive sectors may be successful, but at the same time it may involve a displacement of labor from other sectors and an increase in income disparities. The government may want both to facilitate this process, through reallocation of water, health, and other government services, and to compensate for some of its effects, for example by promoting projects in outlying regions and activities where people remain poor. Investment projects are one means of both promoting the growth of incomes and services in the country and ameliorating some of the effects of this process.

Project analysis can help in shaping sector and national policies, as well as providing the means of implementing them.

A.   Comparing Financial and Economic Prices

191.   Comparison of project rates of return at financial and economic prices, or the financial and economic costs of indirectly productive projects, can reveal the effect of current policies on investments within the sector. Ideally, projects will provide an adequate economic rate of return and a sufficient financial return to the main participants. However, cases will arise in which a project appears favorable to producers, but does not appear to be economically viable; and cases in which an economically viable project does not provide sufficient incentive to project participants. For each project, the basic question should be asked: Why do the financial and economic prices differ?

192.   Generally, there are some factors that account for a small part of the differences. This can be the level of wages in the project, which may be above the opportunity cost of labor. However, for most projects this would not provide the main difference between financial and economic values. It could also be the effect of monopoly pricing of certain inputs, in transport, distribution, and construction, for example, which increases project costs. Where pricing of utilities and other services is a major cause for financial and economic prices to differ, then an appropriate system of regulation should be considered, in the case of autonomous suppliers, and a reduction in subsidy levels, where prices are low.

193.   In most cases, it is the level of domestic taxes and subsidies, and trade taxes and controls, that cause financial and economic prices to differ. Differences in costs at economic and financial prices occur because of subsidies and taxes on input supplies. Differences in the value of traded outputs occur because of the levels of trade taxes and controls. There may be significant differences between the financial and economic price of foreign exchange because of government management of the foreign exchange market. Identifying these differences is part of the process of analyzing the distribution of project benefits. It is the first step in linking project investments and policy changes (see Appendix 27).

194.   Where significant differences do exist between financial and economic prices, the question should be asked whether the underlying policies are likely to change during the life of the project. This is particularly the case for private sector projects, or projects that basically stimulate private sector activities: commercial returns that rely on significant differences between financial and economic prices indicate an additional risk of possible policy changes. If the government is planning for a reduction or standardization of tariff levels on imports, this should be built into the project estimates. If the government has already adopted a policy of reducing subsidies in utilities provision, the effects of this on the financial returns to project participants should be considered. A key question relates to exchange rate management and future levels of the real exchange rate (see Section XV.C below).

195.   Conversely, analyzing the differences between financial and economic values for a project may suggest desirable changes in government policy, such as:

- actions that are specific to the project; or
- general changes in sector or national policy.

Project-specific actions include additional access to concessional credit to promote worthwhile projects, foreign exchange retention or access to foreign exchange at a favorable exchange rate, or meeting the costs of staff training. General changes in sector policy might include raising the target for cost recovery, applying competition policy in the sector, reducing the level of net protection through taxes and subsidies, and changing the administered or regulated prices. The main difficulty with these broader policy changes is that they will impinge on all existing producers and consumers in the sector, not just on those involved in the project.

B.   Effective Protection or Effective Assistance

196.   Analysis of the level of financial and economic prices in a sector, the reasons why they differ, and the effects of possible changes in policy should be part of the Bank's sector work in each country. Such an analysis should be focused on showing where the structure of incentives leads and what the effects of policy reform on incentives might be. A starting point is the measurement of protection using financial and economic price estimates.

197.   Protection coefficients for sectors use the comparison of financial and economic prices. Such comparisons indicate the extent to which domestic policy and market structures protect producers from foreign supplies and, in the process, affect incentives for domestic production and consumption. The nominal protection coefficient compares the financial and economic price of a marketed output. The effective assistance ratio considers the total return to the activity, considering the protective effect of net taxes on outputs and net subsidies on inputs. It can also be calculated at the project level.

198.   The effective assistance ratio for a sector can be compared with those of other sectors to identify which receive the most protection. Where the effective assistance ratio shows a high value relative to other sectors, it can be claimed that the sector or project is particularly favored by the structure of taxes and subsidies. In these cases, caution should be exercised in projecting the current policy framework into the future. If adjustments are to be made to policy in the direction of reduced protection, then those sectors that have high protection indicators will be particularly affected. It is preferable to support investment in sectors and projects that are economically viable anyway and would therefore survive substantial changes in policy (see Appendix 28).

C.   The Real Exchange Rate

199.   In assessing the economic viability of a project, an estimate must be made of the SERF or the standard conversion factor. The SERF expresses the difference between the economic cost of traded goods at the official exchange rate and at the domestic market prices actually paid for them. The SERF can be affected by changes in the structure of taxes and subsidies, and trade controls. It can also be affected by long-term changes in the real exchange rate.

200.   Nominal exchange rate changes can quickly be overtaken by changes in relative prices. Where the exchange rate change itself sets off changes in domestic prices, the initial effect of the exchange rate change may be short-lived. However, where there is a sustained difference in the rates of inflation for domestic goods and for foreign goods, and where this is unlikely to be compensated by improvements in productivity or by inflows of capital or income, then a permanent effect on the exchange rate may occur. If there is a change in the real exchange rate, this will alter the incentive between producing traded goods and services and producing nontraded goods and services. If it is expected that the real exchange rate will change—that it will depreciate, encouraging exporters, or that it will appreciate, encouraging producers of nontraded goods—then this expectation should be built into the project cost and benefit streams. However, this should be done for all investment projects in the country in question, so that economic viability is tested on a consistent basis.

201.   A change in the real exchange rate will also affect the returns to investors and borrowers in a project. Loan payments especially will differ depending on the currency in which the loans are denominated and the rate of real appreciation or depreciation relative to the domestic currency. This effect should be taken into account in the financial analysis from the borrower's point of view, and in the distribution analysis of project effects (see Appendix 29).

APPENDIX 1
KEY QUESTIONS FOR THE ECONOMIC ANALYSIS OF PROJECTS

1.   These guidelines are for use by

- consultants producing project feasibility studies in project preparation,
- consultants updating and reviewing government feasibility studies, and
- Bank staff working directly on feasibility studies and project loan documents.

2.   The scope of economic analysis of projects should be broadly understood to answer a series of questions relating to project design, and to bring together the information required to make a decision whether to proceed with the project or not. Table 1 below summarizes the main issues that should be addressed in making an economic analysis of a project. They follow the structure of the guidelines.

3.   In each case there is a limit on the resources available for economic analysis of projects. Early in project processing, as early as writing the terms of reference for project preparation consultants or agencies, an explicit decision should be made on a project by project basis about the emphasis to be placed on the series of issues to which the questions relate. For example, not all projects will place the same emphasis on distributional issues. Environmental sustainability will be much more important for some projects than for others. A view should be taken on the balance of time to be devoted to the basic assessment of economic viability or cost-effectiveness, including sensitivity analysis, to financial incentives and fiscal impact, and to environmental and distributional issues.

Key Questions in Economic Analysis of Projects

1. Project rationale	What is the rationale of the project: what market or government failure does it address? What is the rationale for public sector involvement / private sector operations? What is the main alternative to the project? Have changes in policy been considered as an alternative to investments? Have efficiency improvements been compared with capacity expansions?
2. Macroeconomic and sectoral context	How does the project relate to the overall development strategy? What particular development problem does it address? What is the policy environment for the project: taxes & subsidies, trade controls, exchange rate & interest rate policy? How does the project relate to sectoral strategy? What is the sectoral policy context in terms of market structure and regulation? Is the project a priority public investment?

3. Project alternatives	Have project alternatives been considered in terms of location, scale, timing? How has the best alternative been chosen? Have the subprojects been ranked in an appropriate way? Has the least cost alternative been identified for the project or major subprojects? Has cost-effectiveness analysis been used when benefits cannot be quantified or valued? Has the most cost-effective means been identified? Is it also the most effective means? What is the additional cost of the most effective means? Does the project have several outcomes: how have they been weighted to assess cost-effectiveness?
4. Demand Analysis	What is the basis for projecting the demand for project output? How will demand be affected by income growth? What other sources of supply are there for meeting the demand? How will demand be affected by an increase in price or user charge?
5. Identification of costs and benefits	Have the without and with project situations both been described? Have all project costs, comparing the with and without project situations, been identified? Have all project benefits, comparing the with and without project situations, been identified? Which benefits have been quantified and valued, and which have not?
6. Use of shadow prices	Has an economic rate of return been calculated? Which numeraire has been used in the application of shadow prices? Has it been used consistently? Have project outputs been identified as nonincremental and incremental? Have they been valued appropriately? Was all the data available for valuing project outputs and inputs? Has a cost-effectiveness analysis been conducted where benefits cannot be measured? Have the major project costs been identified as incremental or nonincremental, and valued appropriately? Have benefits and especially costs been broken down into traded and nontraded items? What value of the SERF/SCF has been used: has it been correctly applied? Have more specific conversion factors been used for some items: how were they derived? What discount rate has been used: to choose between alternatives, and to assess economic viability?
7. Sensitivity analysis	What type of sensitivity analysis has been applied? Does it relate to underlying benefit and cost variables? Have the key variables been identified? Have switching values been calculated? What measures are proposed to monitor the key variables?

8. Risk analysis	Is there a quantitative risk analysis? Have probabilities been attached to any of the key sensitivity variables? Have institutional risks been assessed? Are there sufficient incentives for government participants in the project? What measures have been proposed for reducing project risks?
9. Financial and fiscal sustainability	Has the FIRR for the project been calculated? Have the financial returns to different project participants been calculated? Are they adequate to attract investment/ensure active involvement? What is the level of charges for goods and services? Is the economic analysis related to the charge level? What is the difference between the FIRR and EIRR, and what accounts for the difference? Have the average incremental financial and economic costs been calculated? What is the level of cost recovery? Is there any explicit or implicit subsidy to the project? What is the justification for the subsidy? Has the fiscal impact on the capital and recurrent budget been calculated? What will be the source of funds to meet net fiscal requirements: extra taxation, extra borrowing, or a reallocation of expenditure?
10. Environmental sustainability	Have the environmental effects of the project been identified: costs and benefits? How have they been quantified and valued? Are they expressed in the same numeraire as the basic economic analysis? Have they been integrated into the economic analysis: for choosing between project alternatives; for assessing economic viability? Have required mitigatory and monitoring expenditures been identified?
11. Distribution analysis	Has a distribution analysis been undertaken for the project? Have levels of income been projected both without the project and with the project? Has the effect of different levels of charges for goods and services been assessed for operators, customers and government? Has the distribution of costs, especially on the poor, been identified? Has the distribution of benefits, especially to the poor, been identified? What proportion of net benefits will go to poor people? Is the distribution of costs and benefits analyzed by gender? Is there a substantial foreign involvement in investment and operation? Has the proportion of incomes and revenues going to foreign investors, lenders and workers been identified?

12. Benefit monitoring and valuation	What are the key variables necessary to identify project impact during implementation and operation? Does this include key performance variables, physical or financial, for the implementing agency? Is a system in place to collect data on all the key variables?
13. Overall assessment	Have the major conclusions of the economic analysis been clearly spelt out? Does the project incorporate the best alternative? Is the project economically viable? Are any policy changes necessary to complement project implementation? Are any capacity building measures necessary: to provide incentives or training to the executing agency and other participants?

SERF - Shadow exchange rate factor
SCF - Standard conversion factor
FIRR - Financial internal rate of return
EIRR - Economic internal rate of return

APPENDIX 2

PROJECT ECONOMIC RATIONALE: MARKET AND NONMARKET FAILURES

I.   ESTABLISHING THE ECONOMIC RATIONALE OF A PROJECT

1.   The main rationale for Bank operations lies in the inadequacies of markets to produce what society wants. However, this rationale provides only a necessary, not a sufficient justification for project investments. Sufficiency requires that specifically identified market failures be compared with potential nonmarket failures associated with project implementation and operation. Such an assessment is needed to arrive at a balanced appraisal of whether and what kind of Bank operation will come closer to a socially preferred outcome.

II.   MARKET FAILURE

2.   In a relatively undistorted environment, the economic internal rate of return (EIRR) and financial internal rate of return (FIRR) of a project tend to converge. The exception is projects producing pure public goods, such as rural roads and primary education. Public goods create positive external benefits that do not enter into financial production decisions. Markets therefore underproduce goods and services whose provision entails positive externalities, and overproduce goods and services whose provision entails negative externalities. Projects should aim at producing public goods or at reducing negative public goods, such as negative environmental impacts and poverty, while assisting the production of some private goods through private production and regulation.

3.   Eligibility for Bank assistance will vary by project or subsector, depending on how much the output of each subsector approximates a public good. Criteria for distinguishing between public and private goods are excludability and subtractability:

- *Excludability* is the degree to which a potential user of a good or service can be excluded if the user does not meet conditions set by the supplier. Users cannot be excluded from using public goods.

- *Subtractability* refers to how much one user's consumption of a service subtracts from the ability of others to consume without raising production costs. Subtractability is a matter of degree: virtually all public goods experience crowding out at sufficiently high levels of use, thus increasing marginal costs of supply.

4.   These two characteristics enable a fourfold classification of the publicness of projects:

- *public goods*, for example, urban and rural roads, wastewater treatment, and unpiped water, have low subtractability and low excludability.

- *private goods,* such as rail, urban, and road transport services, have high subtractability and high excludability.

- *toll goods,* such as highways, telecommunications, piped water, and power transmission and distribution, have low subtractability and high excludability.

- *common property goods,* for example, power generation, and irrigation systems, have high subtractability and low excludability.

Public goods should be produced by the public sector and private goods by the private sector. The practical issue is how far toll and common property goods can, through technological and institutional development, approach the conditions of private goods and be operated under competition.

5.   Publicness varies with government policy. For a project producing toll goods or services in a relatively undistorted economic environment, public provision should be compared with the alternative of private provision. The economic and financial rates of return may not differ very much. On the other hand, if the policy environment was not conducive to private sector investment, the acceptability of the project's EIRR and unacceptability of the project's FIRR provides a case for policy reform rather than for Bank-assisted investment. However, policy reform takes time. The large size and long maturity of many projects bring high risks. In such cases, the Bank could make greater use of guarantees, taking on those political risks that participants in private markets are unwilling to shoulder.

6.   Publicness also varies with affordability. In a distorted environment, if a project producing private goods yields an acceptable EIRR but unacceptable FIRR solely because the project benefits the poor, there is a case for Bank assistance. If the project yields an unacceptable FIRR as a result of both the inability of the poor to pay and nonmarket distortions, then policy reform would be a necessary precondition for the project to be viable, even with concessional credit.

III.   NONMARKET FAILURE

7.   Nonmarket failure helps to explain why projects often yield higher costs and lower benefits, as well as different consequences, from those forecast at appraisal. Nonmarket failure results in projects underperforming for four main reasons:

- the private goals of nonmarket organizations are not congruent with the public objectives set for them,
- implementation and operation is inefficient,
- externalities are derived, and
- there is distributional inequity.

These reasons can apply just as well to the private as well as to the public sector, but the extent to which they do is limited by competition.

8.   The sources of nonmarket failures generally lie in the monopolistic structure of supply. Government interventions to correct market failure can generate unanticipated side effects, often as a result of premature action or inefficient regulation. Unless located in areas in which poor people live, projects typically benefit the nonpoor more than the poor. Bank projects and operations can reduce nonmarket failure by strengthening organizational capacity and improving institutional efficiency. With both being related, "Getting the institutions right" is as important as "getting the prices right". Fostering competition between state enterprises, and promoting financial autonomy and accountability, reforms both prices and institutions.

APPENDIX 3
THE PROJECT FRAMEWORK

1.   The first step in economic analysis of projects is to define the economic rationale of a project and, in doing so, to establish its objectives. For some projects, especially those that may have multiple outcomes which cannot be adequately valued, these are best defined in a logical framework setting out the objectives of the project at the input, output, purpose, and sector goal levels. In this way, the project can be more precisely defined and the important relationships on which the success of the project depends, both internally and externally, better understood.

2.   Projects are conceptualized as hierarchical causal structures. They are seen as being made up of a series of means-ends relationships, beginning with input-output linkages, continuing with output-purpose linkages, and ending with purpose-goal linkages. If specified inputs are provided on time, then outputs are produced. If there is demand for project outputs, then the project purpose is achieved. If the project purpose is achieved, it will contribute to the achievement of sector goals. The external conditions on which these linkages are based can be stated as assumptions. The internal project linkages and the external conditions are the basis on which project risks can be enumerated.

3.   The Project Framework integrates the evaluation of the economic and social effects of projects and provides a common framework to evaluate directly and indirectly productive projects. The Project Framework encourages clarification of the economic logic underpinning project design: whether the project represents an appropriate role for the government or whether a policy change or institutional change might be broader reaching and more sustainable than a proposed project investment.

4.   The feasibility of applying economic analysis can be shown in terms of the Project Framework. The following table shows the extent to which project inputs, outputs, effects, and impact can be identified, quantified, and valued by project type: directly productive or indirectly productive.

**Table 1. Feasibility of Economic Analysis Procedures for
Directly Productive and Indirectly Productive Projects**

	Identification	Quantification	Valuation
Goal/Impacts	DP&IDP		
Purpose/Effects	DP&IDP	DP&IDP	DP
Output	DP&IDP	DP&IDP	DP&IDP
Input	DP&IDP	DP&IDP	DP&IDP

DP - directly productive; IDP - indirectly productive.

5.   The main difference between directly productive and indirectly productive projects for economic analysis is in the valuation of project outputs and effects. For directly productive projects operating in a relatively competitive market environment, the economic effects of purpose level achievements can be measured in terms of incremental income. In the case of indirectly productive projects, on the other hand, the best that can be expected is to be able to value project effects indirectly, in terms of the project's impact on the market value of the product for which the project produces an intermediate input or on the cost of an alternative in terms of cost savings.[1] Contingent valuation and benefit transfer techniques are also useful in quantifying and valuing the outputs and effects of indirectly productive projects.

6.   The approach to and reliability of economic analysis therefore vary, depending on whether the project is directly productive or not. There are related sectoral similarities and differences in applying economic analysis. Directly productive projects, typically in agriculture and industry, lie at one end of a continuum for the direct application of project analysis. Indirectly productive projects in education, population, health, and human nutrition lie at the other, along with projects aimed at environmental quality management, institutional change, and public sector organizational development and improvement. Infrastructure projects lie somewhere in the middle, depending on their specific production and consumption characteristics.

7.   The reach of economic analysis widens with the project producing a private good type service and operating in a competitive market environment. Infrastructure services, for example, differ substantially in their economic characteristics, across sectors, within sectors, and between technologies. Infrastructure projects producing private services, such as telecommunications, urban transport, and rail transport, are subject to financial analysis on which economic analysis can be based and with which it can be compared. However, those infrastructure services producing public good type services or common property type services, such as urban sewerage, wastewater treatment, rural roads, and rural water supplies, are more difficult to analyze from both the economic and the financial point of view. Although the public sector has dominated the production of infrastructure services, the potential for competitive markets for these services is higher now than previously. Technological innovation has reduced economies of scale, resulting in the break-up of natural monopolies. Competition can also be enhanced through contestability arrangements and competition for the market. Regulatory innovation enables unbundling of services to enhance competition. These changes influence the approach to be used in the economic analysis of public, private, and hybrid projects.

8.   In the case of public utility projects producing private good type services, project outputs are sold on noncompetitive markets and financial analysis can be undertaken and, for purposes of economic analysis, supplemented by cost savings on displaced alternative sources

---

[1]   There can be difficulties in quantifying the effects of alternative ways of achieving project effects. In the case of health projects, for example, to quantify the full loss of healthy life, the index DALY (disability adjusted life years) was estimated to compare the relative cost of health care investments.

of supply and consumer surplus with and without the project. Markets, whether competitive or not, do not often exist through which to directly value purpose level achievement for indirectly productive projects.

9.   The application of the Project Framework approach to project design provides a conceptual framework for both the economic and social analysis of directly and indirectly productive projects. An integrated framework ensures transparency and accountability, and promotes the efficient use of resources.

APPENDIX 4
IDENTIFICATION AND MEASUREMENT OF CONSUMER SURPLUS

1.   Market competition is rarely perfect and large projects affect prices. The extent to which a project affects its output price depends on the price elasticity of demand for project output. If demand is less than fully elastic, the project faces a downward sloping demand curve, and buyers paying the market price for project output are paying less than what they and others would be willing to pay. The difference between the market price and what they and others would be willing to pay for project output is called consumer surplus. An increase in consumer surplus represents an increase in economic welfare.

2.   The gross benefits of a large project, therefore, are made up of sales revenue and consumer surplus. Sales revenue equals the quantity of project output sold, multiplied by the actual price paid. Consumer surplus equals the sum across all consumers of the differences between the price actually paid for the project output and what buyers would be willing to pay for it. It is only when demand is perfectly elastic, such as for most internationally traded outputs, that no consumer surplus is created by an increase in project supply. In that case, the market price for project output does not fall and no consumer surplus is created. A project sometimes may create consumer surplus without reducing the price of its output. If supply is rationed at a price below what buyers would be willing to pay, an increase in supply capacity at the same price produces incremental consumer surplus.

3.   Estimating consumer surplus requires knowledge of the demand curve for project output; but demand curves are difficult to estimate. Demand is often suppressed by nonprice factors, such as supply constraints. Econometric analysis using historical data is not always reliable, and the results are often controversial because estimates of the quantity demanded without the price change are counterfactual. The use of before and after price change data, instead of with and without price change data, may fail to account for shifts in the demand curve over time, and therefore mixes price consumption points on different demand curves.

4.   Segments of demand curves are often built for the purpose of estimating consumer surplus. This approach is applicable where prices charged for an output are full cost recovery prices, that is, they are not depressed by subsidies to the supplier or by regulation. A segment can be drawn from two price consumption points. Alternatively, what is required is one price consumption point and an estimate of price elasticity of demand at that point.

5.   The first step in measuring consumer surplus is to forecast the quantity demanded without the project (Q_{WO}). Over time, the demand for project output will be affected by population and income growth, as well as prices. If the price elasticity of demand, quantity demanded without the project, and the output price with and without the project (P_W and P_{WO}) are known, then the quantity demanded with the project (Q_W) can be estimated as part of the formula for an arc elasticity:

$$e = \left[(Q_W - Q_{WO}) / ((Q_W + Q_{WO}) / 2) \right] * \left[((P_{WO} + P_W) / 2) / (P_W - P_{WO}) \right]$$

where e is an arc estimate of the price elasticity of demand.

6.   The project will have an incremental and a nonincremental effect. Incremental project output is equal to $(Q_W - Q_{WO})$. At the same time, the lower price of output with the project means that existing production is displaced. The total project output, Q_P, consists of the incremental output $(Q_W - Q_{WO})$ plus the nonincremental output (Q_N) that displaces existing producers. Nonincremental output, Q_N, is, by definition, equal to $(Q_P - (Q_W - Q_{WO}))$.

7.   By assuming a linear demand segment, consumer surplus (CS) from incremental output can be estimated as half the product of the difference between the price of project output without and with the project, and the quantity of incremental output (area d in Figure 1).[1] Consumer surplus from nonincremental output is estimated by multiplying the difference between the price of project output with the project and the price of project output without the project by the quantity of nonincremental project output (area a in Figure 1). Together, this gives total consumer surplus from:

$$CS = \tfrac{1}{2} (P_{WO} - P_W)(Q_W - Q_{WO}) + (P_{WO} - P_W)(Q_P - (Q_W - Q_{WO}))$$

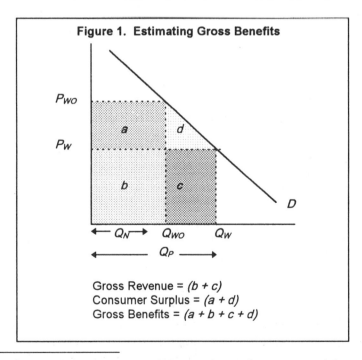

Figure 1. Estimating Gross Benefits

Gross Revenue = (b + c)
Consumer Surplus = (a + d)
Gross Benefits = (a + b + c + d)

---

1   In principle, the demand curve segment should be treated as nonlinear. However, it is frequently convenient to treat the demand curve segment as linear, as in the text, especially where the CS from incremental outputs is much smaller than the CS from nonincremental output. A value of less than ½ can also be used in the text calculation to approximate the result for a nonlinear demand curve.

8.   The following example shows the estimation of gross benefits, consisting of sales revenue and consumer surplus, for a rural electrification project that supplies electricity to households. In year 10, for example, the quantity of illumination demanded without the project Q_{WO} is forecast at 14,331 kWh. Without the project, households would continue using kerosene lanterns for illumination. The price of illumination (equivalent to that supplied by a 10 watt bulb) without the project (P_{WO}) is Rp189.6/kWh, depending on (i) the rate of kerosene consumption by a kerosene lantern (0.0076 l/hr); (ii) the price of kerosene (Rp235/l); (iii) the illumination produced by a kerosene lantern (0.01 kWh); and (iv) the cost of kerosene lantern operation other than for kerosene (Rp11/kWh). The price of electricity with the project (P_W) will be Rp140/kWh.

9.   Market research in the project area shows that the price elasticity of demand for illumination is -0.8. Using the arc elasticity formula above, Q_W is calculated as 18,254 kWh. Consumer surplus on incremental output is Rp97,290 and consumer surplus on nonincremental output is Rp710,818. Adding total consumer surplus to sales revenue of Rp2,555,560, gives a total gross benefit in year 10 of Rp3,363,668.

10.   Gross benefits, made up of consumer surplus and sales revenue, are estimated at the domestic price level. Project costs may be denominated at either the world price or the domestic price levels. To be able to compare gross benefits with project costs, tradable components valued at the border price level must be converted to the domestic price level using the shadow exchange rate factor. Alternatively, nontraded components of costs and the gross benefits must be converted to the border price level using the standard conversion factor (see Appendix 16).

11.   In many projects in which consumer surplus is an important benefit source, the price of project output is set by the government, not the market. If project output is not rationed by price and demand exceeds supply, the price of project output would not reflect marginal willingness to pay. If project supply remains constant, as demand shifts over time and the quantity demanded without the project approaches the quantity demanded with the project, the magnitude of consumer surplus increases to reach a maximum, equal to the difference between the price of project output with the project and the price of project output without the project multiplied by project output (see Figure 2). Thus, in the case of many public utility projects, with markets exhibiting high levels of suppressed demand, this approach to measuring consumer surplus would be warranted.

12.   In some cases, projects supply services to new markets and empirical price-quantity data are not yet available. Market surveys have been used to provide willingness to pay data in such circumstances. Surveys often take the form of a contingent valuation when a respondent is asked what he or she would do in a hypothetical situation.[1] For example, a consumer may be asked whether she would be willing to pay $x per cubic meter for a 24-hour piped water

---

[1]   Refer Water and Sanitation for Health Project, USAID, *Guidelines for Conducting Willingness-to-Pay Studies For Improved Water Services in Developing Counties*, Field Report No. 306, 1988.

service. Each consumer would be asked this question for a range of tariffs. It is on the basis of a sample of households' willingness to pay bids that statistical demand curves can be estimated.[1]

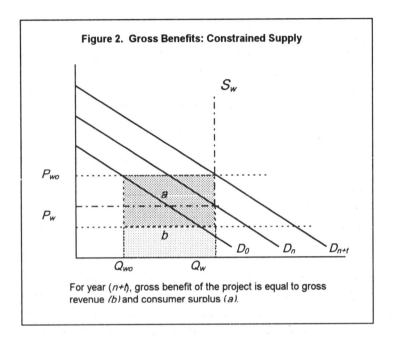

Figure 2. Gross Benefits: Constrained Supply

For year ($n+t$), gross benefit of the project is equal to gross revenue (b) and consumer surplus (a).

13.   Unlike private goods and services, public goods, such as rural roads, and social services, such as primary education, are not sold. With the output of projects producing such goods and services being supplied free of charge, consumer surplus accounts for all of project benefits and can be estimated using a willingness to pay approach.

---

[1]   The problem of uncovering the true preferences of community members cannot be underestimated. Surveys have shown many households felt that the government had a responsibility to provide them with clean water, and that understating its value would reduce the price they would be charged for it. However, most practitioners now generally agree that the greatest problem for contingent valuation arises not from strategic behavior, but from "hypothetical bias". Simply put, hypothetical bias occurs because people have little practical experience evaluating hypothetical offers and so are more likely to make mistakes when they respond to hypothetical offers than when they respond to cash offers. This does not suggest that the opinions of beneficiaries should not be solicited, but rather that care must be taken to design mechanisms that minimize potential sources of bias.

APPENDIX 5
TREATMENT OF WORKING CAPITAL

1.   Stocks of materials and spares need to be available to facilitate the smooth functioning of a project's operations. Stocks of final goods may be held before their sale and distribution. Other materials and inputs will be tied up in partially completed production outputs. For some projects, particularly in agroprocessing or industry, such working capital stocks need to be allowed for in the estimates of initial project investments and included in the project statement at financial and economic prices. They are separate from the annual project costs on operations and maintenance.

2.   Several types of projects involve negligible working capital. For example, irrigation and road projects require considerable resources for regular operation and maintenance, including labor. However, they require very small amounts of resources tied up and available as materials and spares. Other projects may require stocks of materials but not outputs, for example, power generation from coal that requires coal stocks at power plants but where the product is not storable.

3.   In the economic analysis of projects, the value of working capital is calculated at constant prices. If the level of stocks varies over the year, as for many agriculture-based activities, annual average stock levels are used in the calculations. The project statement for economic analysis should contain a cost row showing annual increases in working capital in early project years. The total stocks held as working capital are released at the end of the project and should be shown as a residual value.

4.   For agroprocessing and manufacturing investments, and some other projects, working capital may be an important cost for project assessment and financing. Here a full treatment of working capital is required (see paras. 5, 6, 7, and 8 for an example).

5.   The components of working capital are

- initial stocks of materials equivalent to two months requirement for the following year's production level, valued at shadow prices;
- final stocks of outputs equivalent to one month's sales in the current year, valued at cost in shadow prices; and
- work in progress based on a production period of 20 days and a working year of 250 days, at the current year's production level, valued in shadow prices.

6.   Basic data has been prepared on annual operating costs at 100 percent capacity utilization (Table 1).

Table 1. Annual Financial and Economic Operating Costs

Components	Financial Cost	Conversion[a] Factor	Economic[a] Cost
Fixed Costs			
Labor - scarce	100.0	1.000	100.0
Nontraded Materials	50.0	1.000	50.0
Total Fixed Cost	150.0		150.0
Variable Costs			
Materials - traded	200.0	1.260	252.0
Utilities - nontraded	60.0	1.000	60.0
Labor - surplus	80.0	0.750	60.0
Total Variable Costs	340.0		372.0
Total Operating Costs	490.0		522.0

[a] Domestic price numeraire (see Appendix 15).

7.   Capacity utilization in this sample processing project builds up over three years at utilization rates of 50, 80, and 100 percent, and then is sustained at maximum capacity. The fixed operating costs include administrative labor and nontradable items for office supplies. The variable operating costs include traded materials with an 11 percent import duty, and negligible handling and transport costs; utility services, which are largely sold at full cost price; and operating labor with an opportunity cost of 75 percent of the annual wage level. A shadow exchange rate factor of 1.4 is applied to the nontax element of traded costs.

8.   Table 2 illustrates the calculation of each component of working capital within a project with a one-year construction period and a ten-year operation period, on the basis of the assumptions above. The annual change in working capital is summarized in the bottom row. It is this annual change in working capital and the corresponding residual value that is entered into the project statement for economic analysis of projects.

Table 2. Calculation of Changes in Working Capital (Economic Costs)

Years	0	1	2	3	4	5	6	7	8	9	10
Capacity Utilization		50%	80%	100%	100%	100%	100%	100%	100%	100%	100%
Operating Costs											
Fixed		150	150	150	150	150	150	150	150	150	150
Variable - materials		126	202	252	252	252	252	252	252	252	252
- utilities		30	48	60	60	60	60	60	60	60	60
- labor		30	48	60	60	60	60	60	60	60	60
Total		336	448	522	522	522	522	522	522	522	522
Working Capital											
Initial Stocks	21	34	42[a]	42	42	42	42	42	42	42	0
Change in Initial Stocks	21	13	8	0	0	0	0	0	0	0	-42
Final Stocks		28	37	44[b]	44	44	44	44	44	44	0
Change in Final Stocks		28	9	6	0	0	0	0	0	0	-44
Work in Progress		12	20	25[c]	25	25	25	25	25	25	0
Change in Work in Progress		12	7	5	0	0	0	0	0	0	-25
Change in Working Capital	21	53	25	11	0	0	0	0	0	0	-110

[a] Two months' worth of materials: $252 \times 2/12 = 42$.

[b] One month's worth of sales at cost: $522 \times 2/12 = 44$.

[c] Value of materials for the production period, plus half the additional value of other variable costs added during processing for the production period:

$$[252 + 0.5 (522-252-150] \times 20/250 = 25.$$

APPENDIX 6
DEPLETION PREMIUM

1.   Many projects involve exploitation of depletable resources, either as an input or an output. The key characteristic of a depletable resource is that it initially exists in a given stock and its use leads to a decline in its stock. Either no process increases the stock in any given deposit, or the rate of use for a given deposit exceeds the rate of replenishment. Normally, mineral and energy deposits are treated as depletable resources. However, environmental goods, such as wilderness, top soil, ozone layers, water aquifers, and endangered species, are also depletable resources. Economic analysis of projects needs to explicitly include the economic cost of depletion.

2.   Depletable resources could be either tradable or nontradable goods. Most energy and minerals goods are tradables, whereas most environmental goods are nontradable. Valuation of depletable resources requires the inclusion of an explicit opportunity cost component for depletion, in addition to the normal market value or marginal extraction costs. This opportunity cost is often referred to as a depletion premium. The depletion premium is an additional amount equivalent to the present value of the opportunity cost of extracting the resource at some time in the future, over and above its economic price today. In the following examples, all values are economic values.

3.   Two cases of depletion premium are encountered:

- with no stock effect, where the cost of extraction is independent of the remaining stock; and
- with stock effect, where the cost of extraction depends on the remaining stock level.

4.   In general, the depletion premium for a particular year can be defined as

$$DP_t \quad = \quad \frac{(PS_T - CS_t)\ (1+r)^t}{(1+r)^T} \tag{1}$$

where DP_t =   depletion premium at time t;
$\quad\quad\ PS_T$ =   price of substitute at the time of complete exhaustion T;
$\quad\quad\ CS_t$ =   extraction cost of present resource, assumed to be constant for all years;
$\quad\quad\ r$ =   discount rate; and
$\quad\quad\ T$ =   time of exhaustion of deposit.

In most projects, the assumption of constant marginal extraction cost is used. However, there are a number of alternative models under different cost conditions.

I.   DEPLETION PREMIUM WITHOUT STOCK EFFECT: NATURAL GAS

5.   Natural gas is a depletable resource and many countries have finite stocks. Consider a project that requires natural gas as an input. The calculation of a depletion premium for natural gas requires the basic data outlined in Table 1. Then using equation (1), assuming the price of the fuel substitute in year 15 to be \$4.5/mmbtu; using 12 percent as a discount rate; and taking 1995 as the base year for calculations ($t=0$), we have

$$\text{Depletion Premium (1995)} = (4.5 - 0.75) \times (1.12)^0 / (1.12)^{15}$$
$$= 0.69$$
$$\text{Depletion Premium (1996)} = 3.75 \times (1.12)^1 / (1.12)^{15}$$
$$= 0.77$$

and so on. The depletion premium increases as the stock diminishes. For the price to reflect depletion, the project economic analysis will include the economic cost of \$0.75 plus the opportunity cost of depletion of \$0.69 in 1995, and \$0.75 plus the depletion premium of \$0.77 in 1996, and so on. The economic value of the natural gas input, therefore, increases over time until the stock is exhausted.

Table 1. Depletion Premium for Natural Gas: Data

Data Required	
Size of deposits	11.0 tcf
Extraction rate	750 bcf
Life of deposit/years to exhaustion	15 years
Present extraction costs (LRMC)	\$0.75/mmbtu
Substitute fuel	fuel oil
Present price of substitute fuel	\$2.25/mmbtu
Price of substitute fuel oil at exhaustion	\$4.5/mmbtu
Discount rate used	12%

tcf = trillion cubic feet   mmbtu = million British thermal unit
bcf = billion cubic feet   LRMC = long-run marginal cost

II.   DEPLETION PREMIUM WITH STOCK EFFECTS: WATER

6.   Some water aquifers also face the phenomenon of depletion when these resources are mined, that is, the natural rate of recharge is less than its consumptive use. This represents a case of depletion with stock effects. In such cases, where significant cost increases take place as the stock depletes, the appropriate valuation of water has to include a depletion premium, irrespective of the time of depletion. The depletion premium here is defined as the present value of future cost increases. The concept is shown very simply in Figure 1. A typical cost function for a constant cost case is a step function:

$$C_t = C_1 \quad \text{for } t < T$$

$$C_t \quad = \quad C_2 \quad \text{for } t \geq T$$

where C_t is cost in time period t, and T is the time when the present cost increases to a much higher level. C_1 reflects the present low cost, whereas after period T, the cost will be significantly higher at the C_2 level, as a result of changing to an alternative water source.

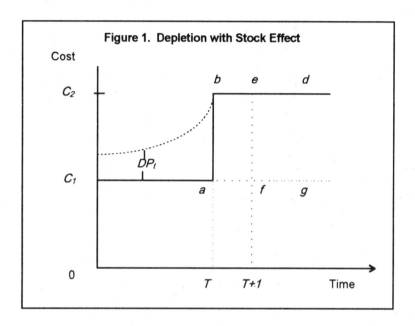

Figure 1. Depletion with Stock Effect

7.   The depletion premium is defined as the present value at time t of the increase in future costs, that is, the open-ended rectangle area *abdg* in Figure 1. While the area *abdg* is infinite, it has a finite present value, that is, if exhaustion can be delayed by one year to $T+1$, the present value of area *abef* will be saved. The depletion premium increases each year as the stock of water diminishes. It can be expressed as

$$DP_t \quad = \quad (C_2 - C_1) \, e^{-r(T-t)}$$

where r is the discount rate.

8.   Table 2 provides estimates for the depletion premium for water. T is assumed to be 20 years. The cost of desalination of water, the alternative source, is $2.00 per 1,000 gallons, compared to the present economic cost of $0.15 per 1,000 gallons from the existing aquifer. The discount rate used is 12 percent per year. Table 2 shows the depletion premium for each year, and the full economic price of water.

Table 2. Depletion Premium and Economic Price of Water

Time (year)	Cost	Depletion Premium	Economic Price
1	0.15	0.21	0.36
2	0.15	0.24	0.39
3	0.15	0.26	0.41
4	0.15	0.30	0.45
5	0.15	0.34	0.49
6	0.15	0.38	0.43
7	0.15	0.42	0.57
8	0.15	0.47	0.62
9	0.15	0.53	0.68
10	0.15	0.60	0.75
11	0.15	0.67	0.82
12	0.15	0.75	0.90
13	0.15	0.84	0.99
14	0.15	0.94	1.09
15	0.15	1.05	1.20
16	0.15	1.18	1.33
17	0.15	1.32	1.47
18	0.15	1.48	1.63
19	0.15	1.65	1.80
20	0.15	1.85	2.00
21	2.00	0.00	2.00

III.   CONCLUSIONS

9.   There are a number of uncertainties inherent in estimating a depletion premium for any resource. The major ones include the present knowledge about the size and life of the deposits, the substitutes to be used, and the level of future prices of both the resource for which the depletion premium is estimated and likely substitutes. It is therefore recommended that analysis of depletion should be carried out in the context of a broader analysis for risk and uncertainty. As far as possible, assumptions about the size or cost of substitutes need to be validated and documented. If there are uncertainties associated with the basic assumptions relating to estimates of a depletion premium, sensitivity analysis should be applied.

APPENDIX 7
THE USE OF CONSTANT PRICES IN THE
ECONOMIC ANALYSIS OF PROJECTS

1.   Project analysis is conducted to determine the economic viability of investing in a project. It entails choosing the project components that are, at the time of approval, expected to provide the highest net economic returns in the future. The stream of future costs and benefits that is compiled is termed the economic project statement. In preparing this statement, prices are used to express the inputs and outputs of a project in value terms to arrive at a common denominator. A consistent set of prices must be used for all future costs and benefits.

2.   There are four different ways to define prices, namely

- financial or shadow prices,
- nominal or real prices,
- current or constant prices, and
- absolute or relative prices.

Financial prices are the actual prices at which inputs are bought and outputs sold and are used in financial analysis. In economic analysis, where prices are distorted due to market or government failure, it is necessary to impute the price that reflects the real economic value of an input or an output—its shadow price.

3.   Nominal price is interchangeably used with current price, and real price with constant price. *Current price* is the term used to define the value of the inputs and outputs, and includes the effects of general price inflation. *Constant price* refers to a value from which the overall effect of a general price inflation has been removed. Where current prices are adjusted for general inflation, it is assumed that inflation will affect the prices of the inputs and outputs in the project statements to the same extent, such that prices retain the same general relationship to each other. Using constant prices ensures that the future costs and benefits of the identified project alternatives are estimated in the same units as the costs and benefits measured at the time the decision to invest in the project is to be made.

4.   Table 1, taken from the World Bank report entitled *Commodity Markets and the Developing Countries*, illustrates the use of constant and current price projections for a set of commodities. For traded items, the appropriate measure of inflation to adopt in adjusting current to constant prices is a measure of international inflation, such as the manufacturing unit value index of the United States. For nontraded items, an appropriate measure of inflation is the projected rate of increase in domestic prices measured through a gross domestic product deflator, a general consumer price index, or a more specific index, such as a construction price index for construction costs.

Table 1. Commodity Price Projections in Current and Constant Prices

Commodity		Year 1	2	3	4	5	6	7
		Price Projections in Current Dollars						
Petroleum	$/bbl	21.2	17.3	17.3	15.3	14.9	15.3	16.0
Coal	$/mt	41.8	44.5	40.6	38.0	36.0	38.0	40.0
Sugar	$/mt	277	198	200	221	261	265	261
Rice	$/mt	287	314	287	270	360	325	315
Wheat	$/mt	156	143	177	193	198	192	184
Palm oil	$/mt	290	339	394	378	497	450	365
Coconut oil	$/mt	337	433	579	450	575	565	545
Jute	$/mt	408	378	320	290	320	323	332
Copper	$/mt	2,662	2,339	2,291	1,913	2,230	2,100	1,980
Urea	$/mt	157	172	140	107	143	147	154
		Price Projections in Constant Year 1 Dollars						
Petroleum	$/bbl	21.2	17.0	16.3	14.6	13.9	14.0	14.4
Coal	$/mt	41.8	40.6	38.1	36.5	33.5	34.9	36.1
Sugar	$/mt	277	193	187	212	243	243	235
Rice	$/mt	287	308	270	259	335	299	284
Wheat	$/mt	156	140	166	185	184	177	166
Palm oil	$/mt	290	332	369	362	463	413	329
Coconut oil	$/mt	337	424	542	432	536	519	492
Jute	$/mt	408	370	300	273	298	301	299
Copper	$/mt	2,662	2,238	2,139	1,836	2,073	1,923	1,736
Urea	$/mt	157	168	132	102	133	135	139

I.   RELATIVE PRICE CHANGES

5.   *Absolute prices* refer to the value attached to an input or output. *Relative prices* refer to the value of an input or output in terms of each other. Even where general price increases are removed through the use of constant prices, it is possible that the relative prices of inputs and outputs would vary because of productivity and technology changes, natural calamity, and even differential inflation. The price of an input may increase either slower or faster than the prices of other inputs and the output, or vice versa. In such cases, the corresponding effects of the relative price change on the project statement should be included. In economic analysis, a change in the relative price of an input is expected to result in a change in the amount that must be foregone by using such an input in the project instead of elsewhere in the economy. Changes in relative prices must be reflected in the economic project statement in the years when such changes are expected.

6.   Suppose an expected 2.5 percent annual increase of nominal wages for unskilled labor over five years is expected, when the annual general price increase for the same period is placed at 12 percent per year. The change in the relative price of unskilled labor will be given by $(1 + 0.025) / (1 + 0.120) - 1 = -0.085$. Therefore, the value of unskilled labor in the economic project statement, drawn up in constant prices, should be reduced by 8.5 percent per

year reflecting this relative price change over the period for which it will continue. Alternatively, suppose there is a scarcity of skilled labor and wages are expected to increase by 15 percent per year for five years. If inflation is assumed at only 12 percent per annum for the same period, then the price of scarce labor in the economic project statement should be increased by 2.7 percent per year for five years calculated from $(1 + 0.15) / (1 + 0.12) - 1 = 0.027$.

II.   REAL INTEREST RATES

7.   An inflation adjustment should also be applied to any interest or discount rate that is used to calculate an annualized value for capital costs or simply a real rate of interest. Where the rate of interest applies to domestic borrowing, a domestic inflation index should be used to deflate the nominal interest rate. Where the rate of interest applies to foreign borrowing, an international inflation rate should be used to deflate the nominal interest rate. For example, a project will borrow at a domestic interest rate of 25 percent when domestic inflation is projected at 21 percent; and at a foreign interest rate of 6.9 percent when international inflation is projected at 2.4 percent. The real interest rates are given by

$$\text{Domestic borrowing} = (1 + 0.25) / (1 + 0.21) - 1 = 0.033 \text{ or } 3.3 \text{ percent}$$

$$\text{Foreign borrowing} = (1 + 0.069) / (1 + 0.024) - 1 = 0.044 \text{ or } 4.4 \text{ percent}$$

Appendix 8
General Methodology for Building Up Project Statements

1.   A summary project statement of economic costs and benefits is required as the basis for project decisions. Both costs and benefits should be valued at constant economic prices. The statement needs to be drawn up for each subproject, for each project alternative, and for a project as a whole. The statement will differ between projects. However, some common conventions are used to represent the different types of cost and benefit over the life of the project.

I.   Investment Costs

2.   Investment costs include initial investments to implement the project, replacement investments during the life of the project, and the residual value of investment assets at the end of the project. Initial investments are generally broken down into subcategories, such as land preparation, buildings and construction, equipment, vehicles, and other costs included in the initial investments, such as environmental mitigation and monitoring. Physical contingencies included in the initial investments for economic analysis should be allocated to these different categories. The initial investments may be concentrated in a single project year, or more generally scheduled over more than one year according to the project phasing and implementation schedule.

3.   Associated with each subcategory of investment is a replacement period in years. On the assumption of normal maintenance activities, this replacement period indicates when the relevant assets will be worn out and will therefore need replacing. Replacement investments are entered in the project statement in the last year of use of the current assets, when commitments to new resources have to be made.

4.   The whole project statement will be drawn up to cover the implementation period of major investments and a certain number of operating years. The number of operating years to include in the statement can be determined by

- the market life of the project—the years over which the project benefits will occur or the output is demanded;
- the technical life of the major investment assets and the number of years of normal operation before the assets are fully worn out;
- the economic life of the same assets—the number of years after which it is worth reinvesting to obtain the benefits of reduced operating and maintenance costs even if the assets are not fully worn out.

For some major economic infrastructure projects with particularly long lives, such as dams or railways, the project period may include 20-25 years of operation with the remaining life of assets represented by a residual value.

5.   Different types of investment asset have different replacement periods. For whatever project period is decided upon, some assets will not be fully worn out at the end of the project period. The remaining value of the assets—their residual value—is entered as a negative investment cost at the end of the project. It is calculated as the proportion of the replacement period still remaining for a particular subcategory, times the value of the assets concerned. If it is envisaged that the remaining assets would be sold when operations cease, this would take some time and the residual value is entered in the year after the last operating year. If it is envisaged that the project will continue in some form at the end of the project period, the residual value is entered in the last operating year, to represent a stream of further benefits discounted to the end of the present project.

6.   Table 1, Part A, illustrates the construction of an investment schedule for a processing project with an implementation period of two years and an operating period of 20 years based on the estimated market life of the output. It includes the initial investments, the replacement investments at intervals, and the residual values of project assets at the end of the project life.

II.   WORKING CAPITAL

7.   The treatment of working capital in project statements has been illustrated in Appendix 5. The processing project holds large initial stocks of raw materials at some times of the year, and no initial stocks at others. The supply is seasonal. An annual average amount for initial stocks and final stocks of output is included in Table 1, Part B, related to the capacity utilization of the assets. A residual value is included at the end of the project life.

III.   ANNUAL COSTS AND BENEFITS

8.   The supply of raw materials for the processing project builds up over two years from the end of implementation. Capacity utilization is 50 percent in the first operating year, and then 100 percent thereafter. Most annual costs (materials, utilities, and labor) are variable and increase with capacity utilization. Overhead costs are fixed. The annual costs include an estimate for the opportunity cost of land; half the land is taken over in the first implementation year, and the other half in the second year of implementation. The annual costs are totaled for each year of the project, as shown in Table 1, Part C.

9.   The processing project will be able to offer a better price for the local raw materials. It may take over some supplies at present going to local small scale processors. However, most of the output will be from additional material supplies. The incremental output is built up with capacity utilization as in Table 1, Part D.

IV.   NET BENEFITS

10.   The investment, working capital, and annual costs are subtracted from the incremental output for each year of the project life, as in Table 1, Part E. The net economic benefits are negative in the two implementation years, and in the later year in which the major equipment is replaced. They are low in the first operating year when the project is at less than full capacity utilization, and are high in the final year where they include the residual value of investment and working capital costs. Such a statement provides the basis on which a decision can be taken as to whether the future net benefits are a sufficient return for the earlier net costs.

Table 1. Processing Project Resource Statement (Economic Prices)

Years / Item	Initial Amount	Replacement Period	0	1	2	3	4	5	6	7	8	9	10	11	12	13	14	15	16	17	18	19	20	21
Capacity Utilization					50%	100%	100%	100%	100%	100%	100%	100%	100%	100%	100%	100%	100%	100%	100%	100%	100%	100%	100%	100%
A. Investment Schedule																								
Land Preparation	80	–	80																					
Construction	1860	30	930	930																				-620
Equipment	900	12		900												900								-300
Vehicles	370	5		370					370					370					370					
Others	60	–	30	30																				
I Total	3270		1040	2230	0	0	0	0	370	0	0	0	0	370	0	900	0	0	370	0	0	0	0	-920
B. Working Capital																								
II Working Capital	230			115	115																			-230
C. Annual Costs	Annual Amount																							
Materials	600				300	600	600	600	600	600	600	600	600	600	600	600	600	600	600	600	600	600	600	600
Utilities	170				85	170	170	170	170	170	170	170	170	170	170	170	170	170	170	170	170	170	170	170
Labor	145				73	145	145	145	145	145	145	145	145	145	145	145	145	145	145	145	145	145	145	145
Overheads	90				90	90	90	90	90	90	90	90	90	90	90	90	90	90	90	90	90	90	90	90
Land Opportunity	35		18	35	35	35	35	35	35	35	35	35	35	35	35	35	35	35	35	35	35	35	35	35
III Total	1040		18	35	583	1040	1040	1040	1040	1040	1040	1040	1040	1040	1040	1040	1040	1040	1040	1040	1040	1040	1040	1040
D. Benefits	Annual Amount																							
IV Incremental Output	1695				848	1695	1695	1695	1695	1695	1695	1695	1695	1695	1695	1695	1695	1695	1695	1695	1695	1695	1695	1695
E. Net Benefits																								
IV-I-II-III			-1058	-2380	150	655	655	655	285	655	655	655	655	285	655	-245	655	655	285	655	655	655	655	1805

Discount rate	12.0%
Net Present Value	329
Internal Rate of Return	13.4%

APPENDIX 9
ECONOMIC VALUATION OF PROJECT OUTPUT AND INPUT

1.   The economic valuation of project output and input is undertaken within a common conceptual framework. This framework distinguishes incremental output from nonincremental output, and incremental input demand from nonincremental input demand. This appendix outlines the conceptual framework and Appendixes 10 and 11 apply the framework to tradable and nontradable goods, respectively.

I.   PROJECT OUTPUT

2.   The economic price (EP) of project output is the gross economic benefit per unit of output. The EP is equal to the gross economic benefit (GEB) of the project divided by project output (Q_P).

3.   The competitive market model provides a framework for valuing project output (see Figure 1). A project is represented by a rightward shift in the supply curve, with output being produced at a lower cost. The market price of project output falls from P_{WO} to P_W and the quantity sold increases from Q_{WO} to Q_W. The project displaces a part of supply that was provided at a higher price. The incremental output of the project is (Q_W-Q_{WO}) and nonincremental output is Q_P less incremental output. The gross economic benefit of the project is therefore made up of two parts: gross benefit from incremental output and gross benefit from nonincremental output.

4.   The GEB from incremental output is represented by the light-shaded area under the demand curve, defined by P_{WO}, P_W, Q_W, Q_{WO}. It comprises incremental revenues (area below the price line) and consumer surplus (area above the price line).

5.   The GEB from nonincremental output is represented by the dark shaded area under the without project supply curve, defined by P_{WO}, Q_{WO}, Q_E, P_W, where Q_E is the supply of output from other sources with the project. It is the cost to the economy of producing nonincremental output without the project.

6.   The GEB of the project is equal to the average market price with and without the project, multiplied by project output, and the EP of project output is equal to the GEB divided by the project output.

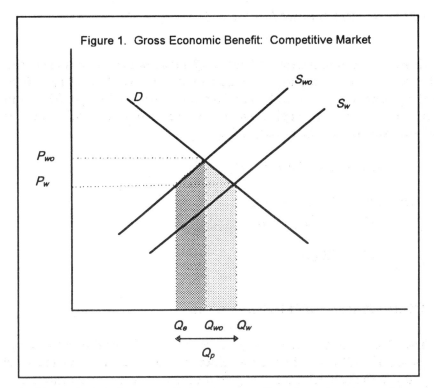

Figure 1. Gross Economic Benefit: Competitive Market

7.   In this illustration, it is assumed there are no distortions in any product or factor markets. However, with government intervention, the market price, demand price, and supply price may differ. Figure 2 shows the result of an ad valorem consumption tax and production subsidy. The consumption tax shifts the demand curve leftward by the amount of the tax, while the production subsidy shifts the supply curve rightward by the amount of the subsidy.

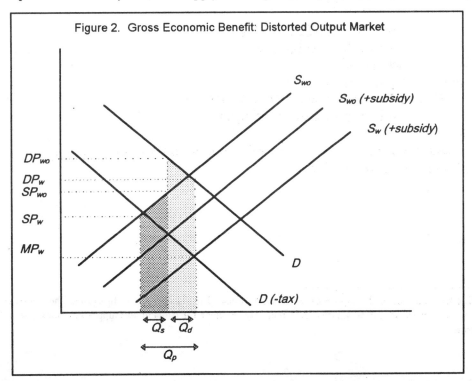

Figure 2. Gross Economic Benefit: Distorted Output Market

8.   Gross benefit from incremental output (Q_D) is shown by the area under the before-tax demand curve, which is equal to the product of the average demand price (DP) with and without the project, and Q_D. Gross benefit from nonincremental output (Q_S) is shown by the area under the before-subsidy supply curve, which is equal to the product of the average supply price (SP) with and without the project, and Q_S.

$$GEB = (DP \cdot Q_D) + (SP \cdot Q_S)$$

where[1] $DP = 0.5\,(DP_{WO} + DP_W)$
$SP = 0.5\,(SP_{WO} + SP_W)$

$$EP = GEB/Q_P$$

II.   DEMAND AND SUPPLY ELASTICITIES

9.   The EP can also be derived using the price elasticities of demand and supply for the project output. The EP is based on the weighted average of the demand and supply price of project output, with the weights depending on the price elasticities of demand and supply.

$$EP = DP \cdot dw + SP \cdot sw$$

where dw is demand weight, and
sw is the supply weight.

$dw = (-D_E \cdot Q_D/Q_S) / [S_E - D_E(Q_D/Q_S)]$
$sw = S_E/[S_E - D_E(Q_D/Q_S)]$
$sw = 1 - dw$

where D_E is the price elasticity of demand, and
S_E is the price elasticity of supply.

Where distortions appear in other commodity or factor markets, the demand price and supply price have to be adjusted for these.

---

[1]   The formulations in this Appendix are based on linear demand and supply functions. The numerical values for the coefficients can be adjusted for circumstances where the demand and supply functions take a different form.

III.   PROJECT INPUT

10.   The EP of a project input is the economic cost per unit of input. The EP is equal to the economic cost (EC) of the project input divided by the quantity demanded (Q_P).

11.   The competitive market model again provides a conceptual framework for valuing a project input (see Figure 3). The input demand by the project is represented by a rightward shift in the total demand curve for the input. The market price of the project input rises from P_{WO} to P_W and the total quantity demanded increases from Q_{WO} to Q_W. At the higher price, the new project bids some supply away from existing projects. The incremental quantity demanded is (Q_W - Q_{WO}) and the nonincremental quantity demanded is $[Q_P - (Q_W - Q_{WO})]$. The economic cost of the project input is therefore made up of two parts: the economic cost of the incremental quantity demanded and the economic cost of the nonincremental quantity demanded.

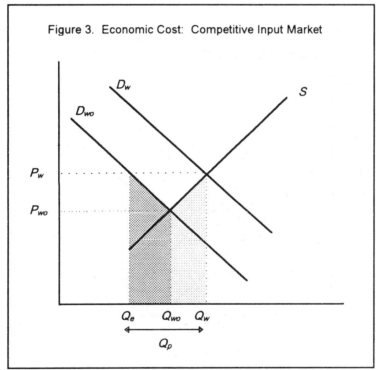

Figure 3. Economic Cost: Competitive Input Market

12.   Without any distortions in commodity or factor markets, the EC of the incremental quantity demanded by the project is represented by the light-shaded area under the supply curve, defined by P_{WO}, P_W, Q_W, and Q_{WO}. It comprises the incremental cost of increasing supply to meet project demand.

13.   The EC of the nonincremental quantity demanded by the project is represented by the dark-shaded area under the without project demand curve, defined by P_{WO}, Q_{WO}, Q_B, and P_W. It comprises the economic benefit foregone by the without project buyers of the project input, as measured by their willingness to pay.

14.   The total EC of the project input is equal to the average market price with and without the project multiplied by the quantity of input demanded by the project. The EP is equal to the EC divided by the quantity of input demanded.

15.   The input market represented in Figure 3 is perfectly competitive. However, with government intervention, the market price, demand price, and supply price may differ. Figure 4 shows the result of an ad valorem consumption tax and production subsidy. The consumption tax shifts the demand curve leftward by the amount of the tax, while the production subsidy shifts the supply curve rightward by the amount of the subsidy.

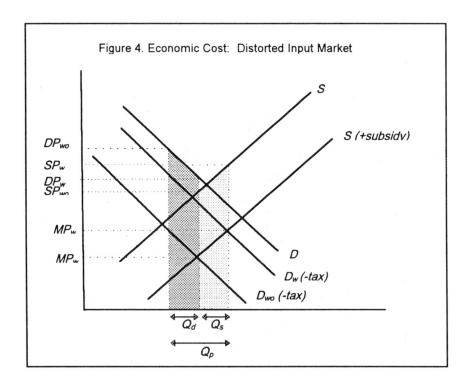

Figure 4. Economic Cost: Distorted Input Market

16.   With no distortions in other markets, the EC of incremental input (Q_S) is shown by the area under the before-subsidy supply curve, which is equal to the product of the average supply price (SP) with and without the project, and Q_S. The EC of nonincremental input (Q_D) is shown by the area under the after-tax demand curve, which is equal to the product of the average demand price (DP) with and without the project, and Q_D.

$$EC = (DP \cdot Q_D) + (SP \cdot Q_S)$$

where $DP = 0.5 (DP_{WO} + DP_W)$; and
$$SP = 0.5 (SP_{WO} + SP_W)$$
$$EP = EC/Q_P$$

IV.   DEMAND AND SUPPLY ELASTICITIES

17.   The EP can also be expressed in terms of the price elasticities of demand and supply for the project output. The EP is based on the weighted average of the demand and supply price of project output, with the weights depending on the price elasticities of demand and supply.

$$EP = DP \cdot dw + SP \cdot sw$$

where dw is demand weight, and
sw is the supply weight

$$dw = (-D_E \cdot Q_D/Q_S)/[S_E - D_E (Q_D/Q_S)]$$
$$sw = S_E/[S_E - D_E (Q_D/Q_S)]$$
$$sw = 1 - dw$$

where D_E is the price elasticity of demand, and
S_E is the price elasticity of supply

Where distortions appear in other commodity or factor markets, the demand price and supply price have to be adjusted for these.

V.   APPLICATION

18.   In principle, the framework provided here can be applied to any project output or input. It is especially relevant on the output side to analyze the effects of a project producing nontraded outputs, where adjustments of both quantities and prices are confined to the domestic economy and are therefore likely to be larger. It can also be applied to all types of project impact, to materials and services, equipment, construction, and labor, as well as to factors of production more broadly defined, such as capital or foreign exchange. In each case, the approach requires the analyst to assess the market structure for a good, and to work out what the incremental and nonincremental project effects will be.

APPENDIX 10
ECONOMIC PRICE OF TRADED GOODS AND SERVICES

1.   The economic price (EP) of traded goods and services is determined within the conceptual framework outlined in Appendix 9. Traded goods and services are those whose production or use by a project has an effect on the country's balance of payments, because either the goods and services themselves are exported or imported, or because they are substitutes for goods that are exported or imported.

2.   Typically, Bank-assisted projects are small relative to the size of world markets. Projects face an infinitely elastic demand for traded output and an infinitely elastic supply for traded input. Consequently, world market prices are not affected by project supply of output or project demand for input. This represents a special case where increases in the supply of output or in the demand for inputs have no effect on their prices.

3.   The valuation of traded goods can be illustrated for the four main cases: exported output, importable output, imported inputs, and exportable inputs. If world demand is elastic, exported output is incremental to world supply and the EP is based on the demand price (DP), which is the free on board (FOB) price. This compares with the financial price (FP) of an export at the border, which can be given by the FOB price less net export taxes (t = export tax less export subsidy) (see Figure 1). If world supply is elastic, importable output is nonincremental to world demand and the EP is based on the supply price (SP), which is the cost insurance freight (CIF) price. This compares with the FP at the border, which is the CIF price plus net import tariff (t = import tariff less import subsidy) (see Figure 2).

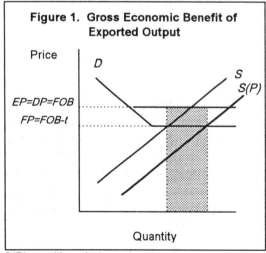

Figure 1. Gross Economic Benefit of Exported Output

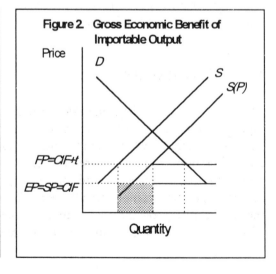

Figure 2. Gross Economic Benefit of Importable Output

S(P) = with project supply.

4.   If the world supply is inelastic, then imported input is incremental to world demand and the EP is based on the SP, which is the CIF price. The FP at the border of an imported input is the CIF price plus import tariff less the import subsidy (see Figure 3).

5.   If world demand is inelastic, an exportable input is nonincremental to world demand and the EP is based on the DP, which is the FOB price. The FP at the border of an exportable input is the FOB price less export tax plus export subsidy (see Figure 4).

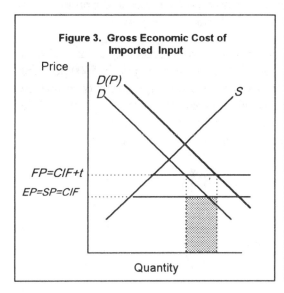

Figure 3. Gross Economic Cost of Imported Input

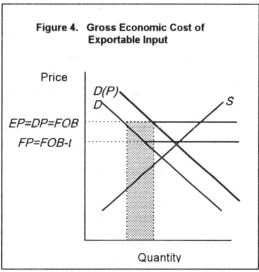

Figure 4. Gross Economic Cost of Exportable Input

6.   The economic price of traded goods need to be adjusted for the location and price level in which the analysis is being conducted. In most cases, the price level is the price level of the project and the location is the project location. The world market price (WMP) needs to be adjusted to the project situation by subtracting or adding handling, distribution, transport, and processing costs between the project location and the port of entry—the result is the border price equivalent value (BPEV). All these nontraded costs need to be expressed in economic prices (see Appendix 11).

7.   When this adjustment has been made, the BPEV can be compared with the FP of the same project output or input at the project location *FP(P)*. This comparison can be expressed in the form of a conversion factor (CF). The CF is given by

$$CF \quad = \quad \frac{BPEV}{FP(P)} \quad or \quad \frac{Border\ Price\ Equivalent\ Value}{Financial\ Price\ at\ Project}$$

Where economic prices are considerably below financial prices, the CF will be significantly less than 1. This will apply for highly protected outputs and inputs. Where economic prices are considerably above financial prices, the CF will be significantly more than 1. This will apply for export products that are heavily taxed.

I.   THE EP OF AN EXPORTABLE OUTPUT

8.   If the output of a project increases the country's supply of an exportable good, and the additional output does not affect the world price of that good, then the economic price of the project's output delivered to the port is measured by the FOB price of the good. The FOB price will in turn be equal to the price received by the producer, plus the financial costs of handling, distribution, transportation, and processing (HDTP) from the project site to the point of export, plus any net export tax on the good. The economic price of an exportable good at the project site is, therefore, the FOB price minus the economic values of HDTP minus net export taxes.

9.   Suppose a country exports timber logs that are used by the wood processing industry abroad. The current level of exports is 40,000 cubic meters per month and the world price is $600 per cubic meter. It has been estimated that if the country decides to increase its logging activity so that the present exports go up by 25 percent, all the output would be incremental to world output, and the FOB price would not be affected. In this case, the various components of the economic benefit or price per cubic meter of logs is described below, with local currency represented in RM:

	Unit	$	RM
FOB price of timber	m^3	600	
Export tax (15% of FOB)	m^3		2,700
Handling charge	m^3		1,500
Transport cost (factory to port)	m^3		900
Official exchange rate	RM/$	30	
Shadow exchange rate	RM/$	36	
SERF (SER/OER)		1.200	
SCF		0.833	

10.   The EP and FP of the timber at the project location can be computed based on the EP of handling and transport items (see Tables 1 and 2).

Table 1. Economic Price of Exportable Output: Timber

	Economic Price[a] (RM per m^3)	Financial Price (RM per m^3)
Timber at port	18,000	18,000
Less: Tax		2,700
Handling charge	1,350	1,500
Transport	684	900
Timber at project	15,966	12,900

[a]   Economic price using world price numeraire.

While the financial price for timber at the project site is RM12,900, the economic price of timber at the project site is RM15,966. The timber is worth more to the national economy than to the timber producers. The conversion factor of 15966/12900 = 1.238 can be used to convert the financial to the economic price of timber at the project (using the world price numeraire).

Table 2. Economic Prices at Border Price Level

	Proportion (%)	Adjustment	Economic Value
EP of Handling Charges			
Traded component	40	1.000	40
Nontraded component	60	0.833	50
	100		90
CF (90/100)		0.900	
Economic Price of Handling Charges (RM)	1,500	0.900	1,350
EP of Transport			
Tax	12.5	0.000	0
Traded component	20.0	1.000	20
Nontraded component	67.5	0.833	56
	100.0		76
CF (76/100)		0.760	
Economic Price of Transport (RM)	900	0.760	684
EP of Timber at Port			
Traded component	100.0	1.000	100
CF (100/100)		1.000	
Economic Price of Timber at Port (RM)	600 x 30	1.000	18,000

II.   THE EP OF AN IMPORT-SUBSTITUTE OUTPUT

11.   If a project produces an import substitute good, its economic price is the foreign exchange saved by the country through reduced imports, adjusted for differences in the economic costs of HDTP. Thus, the benefit of producing such a good is the CIF price of imports, plus the economic costs of HDTP from the port to the domestic market, minus the economic costs of HDTP from the project to the domestic market.

12.   This can be illustrated through the following example where a project will assemble irrigation pumps, which were previously imported, for domestic consumption. It has been estimated that the extra production of pumps will be nonincremental to world output, that is, they will simply substitute for existing imports at prevailing prices. The various components of the economic benefit of the pumps are as follows:

	Unit	$	RM
CIF price of pump	1 pump	35	
Import duties (50% of CIF)	1 pump		525
Port handling	1 pump		30
Transport (port to market)	1 pump		90
Transport (project to market)	1 pump		30

13.   This time, all economic prices will be estimated at the domestic price level. The EP of handling, transport, and the pumps is given in Table 4, using the same values for the official exchange rate of 30 RM/$ and the shadow exchange rate of 36 RM/$. The EP and FP of the pumps at the project site can be compared as follows (Table 3).

Table 3. Economic Price of Import Substitute Output: Pumps

	Economic Price[a] (RM per pump)	Financial Price (RM per pump)
Pumps at port	1,260	1,050
Plus: Tax		525
Port handling charge	32.4	30
Transport (port to market)	82.4	90
Less: Transport (project to market)	(27.5)	(30)
	1,347.3	1,665

[a] Economic price using domestic price numeraire.

While the financial price of pumps at the project site is RM1,665, the economic price at the project site is RM1,347.3. The CF for pumps of 1,347.3/1,665 = 0.804 can be used to convert the financial to the economic price of pumps (using the domestic price numeraire). The pumps are worth less to the national economy than to the project sponsors.

Table 4. Economic Prices at Domestic Price Level

	Proportion (%)	Adjustment	Economic Value
EP of Handling Charges			
Traded component	40	1.200	48
Nontraded component	60	1.000	60
	100		108
CF (108/100)		1.080	
Economic Price of Handling Charges	30	1.080	32.4
EP of Transport			
Tax	12.5	0.000	0.0
Traded component	20.0	1.200	24.0
Nontraded component	67.5	1.000	67.5
	100.0		91.5
CF (91.5/100)		0.915	
Economic Price of Transport:			
Port to market	90	0.915	82.4
Project to market	30	0.915	27.5
EP of Pump at Port			
Traded component	100.0	1.200	1.200
CF (120/100)		1.200	
Economic Price of Pump at Port	1,050	1.200	1,260

III.   THE EP OF AN IMPORTED INPUT

14.   A project's requirement of an imported input will cause an increase in the total imports of the country even if the project does not directly import the item. If the price of the good in the world market does not change with this additional demand, the economic cost of the input at the country's border is the CIF price. The full economic cost of this item at the factory site will include the economic costs of handling and transportation from the port to the project site. This can be computed in a similar manner to the economic price of an import substitute output.

IV.   THE EP OF AN EXPORTED INPUT

15.   A project may use an input that otherwise could have been exported. The relevant cost is the benefit foregone by consuming the good at home instead of exporting it. In this case, the FOB price should be adjusted for the difference in the economic costs of handling and transportation to the port, which is now saved, and to the project site from the source of supply.

V.   IMPORT SUBSTITUTE AND EXPORTABLE OUTPUT

16.   Project outputs and inputs can be incremental and nonincremental. A particular output or input may be both. The project to establish domestic production of irrigation pumps may also produce for export. The EP of exportable pumps is calculated in Table 5 from the FOB price of pumps. The economic value of an exported pump (1124.7) is less than the economic value of an import substitute pump (1347.3).

Table 5. Economic Price of Exportable Output: Pumps

	Economic Price (RM per pump)	Financial Value (RM per pump)
Pumps at port (FOB)	1,212.0	1,010
Less: Tax		0
Port handling charge	32.4	(30)
Transport (factory to port)	54.9	(60)
	1,124.7	

^a Economic price using domestic price numeraire.

17.   Nonincremental (import substitute) output is valued at its supply price based on the CIF cost of a pump. Incremental (exportable) output is valued at its demand price based on the FOB price of a pump. The EP of a pump is the weighted average of its supply and demand price. The weights attached to the supply and demand price in the early project years are 0.8 and 0.2, respectively. Over time, however, it is expected that the project will increase the proportion of output exported. Table 6 shows the weights for the supply and demand price for three phases of the

project and the corresponding economic prices. As the proportion of exports rises, the weighted average EP falls somewhat. Different CFs should therefore be used in different phases of the project to convert the financial price into the corresponding weighted average EP (see Table 6).

Table 6. Weighted Average EP of Pumps

	Years 0-5	Years 6-10	Years 11 +
EP of import substitute	1,347.3	1,347.3	1,347.3
EP of exportable	1,124.7	1,124.7	1,124.7
Weight: Import Substitute	0.8	0.6	0.4
Weight: Exportable	0.2	0.4	0.6
Weighted EP	1,302.8	1,158.3	1,213.7
CF (divided by 1,665)	0.782	0.756	0.729

Economic price using domestic price numeraire.

VI.   LARGE PROJECTS: ELASTICITIES AND PRICE CHANGES

18.   The EP of a good is the weighted average of its demand and supply price. Most projects will have no effect upon the price level of either outputs or inputs. The supply of output will be fully incremental when the demand for project output is price elastic. In this case, the demand weight is 1.0 and the EP is the demand price. Similarly, where the demand for project output is inelastic, the supply of output will be nonincremental, the demand weight is zero, and the EP is the supply price (see Table 7).

Table 7. Combinations of Demand and Supply Price Weights

Item	Market	Demand Weight	Supply Weight	Economic Price
Output	Demand elastic	1	0	Demand price
Output	Supply elastic	0	1	Supply price
Input	Demand inelastic	0	1	Supply price
Input	Supply inelastic	1	0	Demand price

19.   Similar arguments apply to additional project inputs. Where supply of an input is price elastic, the supply weight is one and the EP is the supply price. Where supply of an input is price inelastic, the supply weight is zero and the EP is the demand price.

20.   However, if a project is large or if demand for output or supply of inputs is not perfectly elastic, then the EP of project items needs to be calculated in a way that allows for changes in price between the without and the with project cases. For a large project, the extra supply of output may cause a reduction in price. The with project price can be calculated using elasticity estimates for the elasticity of supply of other producers when the price falls, and the elasticity of demand for other purchasers as the price falls. If the elasticity of supply is large relative to the elasticity of demand,

then the weight on the with project supply price will be large (approaching 1.0 for the import substitute case). If the elasticity of demand is large relative to the elasticity of supply, the weight on the demand price will be large (approaching 1.0 where supply is fixed).

21.   A large project may create additional demand for an input that affects the market for that input in two ways: producers may increase supplies as a response to the increase in price; some consumers may reduce their purchases as a result of the increase in price. The new price of the input will depend on the relative elasticities of supply and demand. If the elasticity of supply is large relative to the elasticity of demand, the EP of the input tends toward its supply price. If the elasticity of demand is high relative to that of supply, the EP tends toward its demand price.

22.   Because large projects may have an impact on the prices of outputs and inputs, the effects on existing suppliers or users also have to be considered. A new project that brings about a reduction in the DP for the output on the world market will cause a loss of earnings to existing producers. This loss should be subtracted from the economic value of the output. A new project that increases the price of a traded input will cause a loss to existing users of the inputs. This loss also must be subtracted from the net economic benefits of the projects.

23.   The following steps summarize the procedure that is followed in valuing tradable outputs and inputs.

    i.   Identify the effects of additional project output. Will the effects be felt in terms of trade?
    ii.   Identify the effects of additional demands for project inputs. Will the effects be felt in terms of trade?
    iii.   Estimate the trade effects of outputs: extra exports, less imports, a combination of the two.
    iv.   Estimate the trade effects of inputs: less exports, more imports, a combination of the two.
    v.   Take account, exceptionally, of price effects in the world market for outputs and inputs.
    vi.   Identify the fob and cif prices for extra exports and extra imports. Identify the equivalent traded good, for substituted imports or exports, and their cif and fob prices. Adjust for quality differences where necessary.
    vii. Estimate the associated costs to/from the market or project site.
    viii. Adjust all values to the chosen numeraire.
    ix.   Summarize the border price equivalent value.
    x.   Compare the economic price with the financial price for the same good.

APPENDIX 11
VALUATION OF NONTRADED OUTPUTS AND INPUTS

I.   NONTRADED OUTPUTS

1.   As with traded goods and services, the economic price of nontraded outputs is derived from a weighted average of the supply and demand price for nonincremental and incremental production. Economic and financial prices differ because of taxes and subsidies on outputs, taxes and subsidies on the inputs being used to produce the nontraded outputs, and the monopoly supply situation of some suppliers. They may also differ because the government regulates prices and does not set prices in relation to costs, and because factors of production are not priced according to their economic value.

2.   The demand and supply of nontraded outputs is affected by their financial price. Because the market for nontraded goods is the market within the domestic economy only, a project may have a significant impact on the supply of output and on the average costs of production. A major project to produce nontraded goods therefore is likely to affect both the supply price and the demand price. In many cases, the with project prices will differ from the without project prices. The extent of nonincremental and incremental production depends on the elasticity of demand and the elasticity of supply in relation to changes in financial prices.

3.   Figure 1 illustrates this situation for a nontraded good produced in a competitive market. As the supply price falls, nonincremental project output will partly substitute for existing production. Existing consumers will benefit as the price falls—a consumer surplus. However, at the same time existing producers will lose income—a loss of producer surplus. The nonincremental output should be valued through the average supply price without and with the project. At the same time, project output will expand overall supply and bring about a fall in the demand price. New users will benefit from the expanded output. The incremental output should be valued through its average demand price without and with the project. Project output as a whole, therefore, should be valued through the weighted average of the supply and demand prices, with the weights depending upon the level of nonincremental and incremental output.

4.   Many nontraded outputs, especially in the public sector, are not produced in a competitive framework. For example, piped water supplies may be produced by a single agency and substitute entirely for nonpiped supplies in the project area. In this case most of the output will be nonincremental, valued through the average of the without and with supply prices. Moreover, the price of piped water supplies may be regulated by government and sold at a fixed price irrespective of the level of costs. In this case, the value of the incremental nontraded output, which may be a small part of total project output, can be valued through its demand price. The basic approach can also be applied to the situation where, along with a project investment, user charges are raised for the nontraded output. The increase in user

charges has to be converted into a projected demand for the output, and the investment scaled accordingly, bearing in mind that demand for nontraded services is affected by factors other than price, for example the growth of the population or the growth in overall production. In this case, there also will be a high level of nonincremental output affected by the increase in price; however, the nonincremental output should still be valued through its average supply price. The incremental output can be valued through its average demand price, taking account of the increase in price.

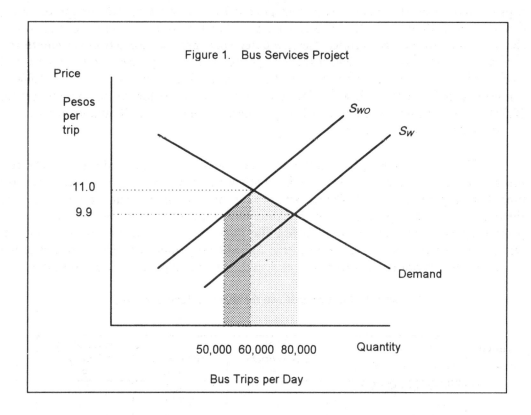

Figure 1.   Bus Services Project

5.   When the quantity and price have been projected without and with the project, the resulting levels of nonincremental and incremental outputs need to be revalued at shadow prices in order to calculate the economic internal rate of return for the project. This involves taking the weighted average of the demand and supply prices and adjusting them for the value of foreign exchange and labor. If the assumptions on price levels and demand and supply responsiveness change, then the projected financial demands, revenues, and costs will change; so too will the average supply and average demand prices, as well as the proportions of nonincremental and incremental project output. In other words, a change in the financial assumptions will also bring about a change in the economic results. Where supply and demand relates to the world markets for traded goods, changes in financial assumptions are unlikely to change economic prices. Where supply and demand relates to the domestic market

for nontraded goods, any change in financial assumptions is likely to alter the balance between economic costs and benefits as well.

The EP of a Competitive Nontraded Output: Bus Services

6.   A public sector company is considering expanding services on a city bus route using newer buses with a larger capacity and lower operating costs. At present there are 60,000 return trips per month on the route. The present price is P11, made up of P10 for the operating company and a 10 percent sales tax. It is not expected that the price or number of trips would change without the new bus project. The new buses would provide 30,000 trips per month at a total price of P9.9, made up of P9 for the bus operator and the 10 percent tax. On the basis of a consumer survey, it has been estimated that the total number of trips would rise to 80,000 at this price level. In other words, a new bus service would substitute for existing bus services for 10,000 trips per month (nonincremental output), and increase the overall number of trips by a further 20,000 (incremental output).

7.   The new bus service, like existing services, would rely on imported vehicles. The cost breakdown for bus services will be similar both without and with the project. This cost breakdown is given in Table 1. The supply price for the driver is approximately 75 percent of the wage that would be paid. The economic price of foreign exchange has been estimated at 20 percent higher than the official rate. Table 1 also shows the cost breakdown of supplying bus services revalued in economic prices using the domestic price numeraire. The extra cost of bus services in shadow prices is 7 percent higher than their financial price to the bus operator.

Table 1. Cost breakdown for Bus Services per Trip

	Cost Breakdown (P)	Conversion Factor	Economic Value (P)
Traded component	6	1.200	7.2
Labor	2	0.750	1.5
Nontraded	2	1.000	2.0
Total Cost	10		10.7
CF ((10.7/10.0)		1.070	

Economic costs using domestic price numeraire.

8.   The gross economic benefits of the bus supply project is given by the nonincremental output times the average adjusted supply price plus the incremental output times the average adjusted demand price. The average adjusted supply price is derived from the without project cost of P10 per trip and the with project cost of P9 per trip. The average supply price of P9.5 is converted to an economic price using the conversion factor from Table 1 of 1.070. This gives an economic supply price of P10.165. The average demand price is the average bus fare per trip

without and with the project. The fare is P11 without and P9.9 with, giving an average demand price of P10.450.

9.   The gross economic benefits for the bus service project can be calculated from the nonincremental and incremental outputs and the economic supply and demand prices (see Table 2). These gross economic benefits can be compared with the revenue to the new bus operator, which will be 30,000 trips at P9 per trip, or P270,000. The resulting conversion factor is 1.151, which can be applied to the revenue accruing to the new bus operator to derive the economic value of the bus services provided.

Table 2. Gross Economic Benefits of the Bus Service Project

Production	Nonincremental	Incremental
Trips	10,000	20,000
Economic supply price	P10.165	
Economic demand price		P10.450
Gross economic benefits	P101,650	P209,000
Total		P 310,650
CF (310,650/270,000)	1.151	

The economic value of the bus services provided by the new project is P310,650, in the domestic price numeraire.

The EP of Piped Water Supplies

10.   The bus services project takes place in a competitive environment. Many public services such as water supply projects take place in an environment that is not fully competitive. In this example a piped water supply project to extend an existing scheme is expected to displace present sources from household wells and private vendors. While the private vendors and households supply and purchase water in a competitive environment, the government subsidizes public supply schemes. The subsidy and the higher quality of the piped supplies ensures that the other water sources will be fully displaced.

11.   Without the project, water demand in the area would be 120,000 cubic meters (m^3) per year. The financial price for these supplies is P40 per m^3 for the 20 percent of water supplies derived from private vendors and P10 per m^3 for the 80 percent of water supplies derived from operating household wells. These financial prices include the costs of home processing of water to a quality close to that of the piped supplies. The price of piped water supplies from the public system is only P5 per m^3, which is lower than its cost of supply. At this level of charge for the new supplies, it is expected that demand will increase to 180,000 m^3 per year.

12.   The nonincremental water should be valued through its without project supply price (SP). This is the cost of water supplies to the customer, that is, after water losses, that will be

saved through the new provision. The financial and economic cost of water without the project is given in Table 3. Fifty percent of the cost of supply from private vendors reflects labor costs, with a supply price 85 percent of its wage. Eighty percent of the supply price of household wells reflects traded components for the pumps, fuel, and treatment process. The economic price of foreign exchange is 30 percent above the official exchange rate, implying a standard conversion factor (SCF) of 1/1.3 or 0.769.

Table 3. Economic Supply Price of Nonincremental Water

Source	Component	Amount	CF	Economic Cost	Proportion
Private vendors	Labor	20	0.85 * 0.769	13.073	
	Nontraded	20	0.769	15.380	
Total		40		28.453	20%
Household wells	Traded	8	1.000	8.000	
	Nontraded	2	0.769	1.538	
Total		10		9.538	80%
FP of nonincremental water					16.000
EP of nonincremental water					13.321

Economic values using world price numeraire.

13.   The incremental water to the customer should be valued through its average demand price (DP). The average cost of water without the project in financial prices is P16 per m^3. With the project this cost will fall to P5 per m^3. The average demand price of P10.5 per m^3. needs to be converted into its world price equivalent using the SCF. The average economic demand price is P8.075 per m^3.

14.   Table 4 calculates the weighted average economic price of water to the customer. The weighted average economic price is applied to the water supply output to give the gross economic value of the water supply output (see Table 4 and Figure 2).

Table 4. Economic Price of Water and Economic Value of Water Supplies

Supply	Economic Price	Weight	Weighted Price
Nonincremental	13.321	0.667	8.885
Incremental	8.075	0.333	2.689
	Weighted average economic price		11.574
	Supplies		180,000
	Economic value		2,083,320

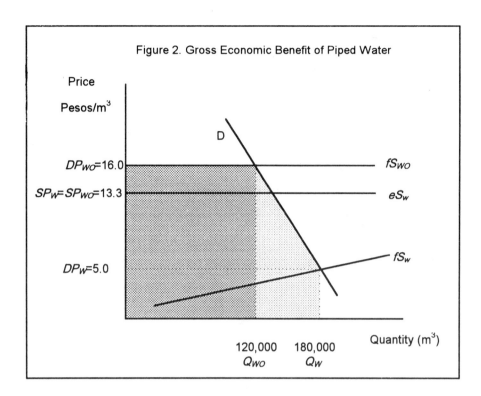

Figure 2. Gross Economic Benefit of Piped Water

15.   The economic value of the water can be compared with the financial revenue from the water supply project, which is 180,000 m^3 at P5 per m^3, or P900,000, to give a conversion factor for water sales of 2,083,320/900,000 = 2.315. This conversion factor is calculated using the world price numeraire. It can be used to convert the supply of water at the level of the customer from its financial to its economic value.

II.   NONTRADED INPUTS

The EP of an Expanding Nontraded Sector: Power

16.   A private sector mineral processing project requires a large amount of power per unit of output. The power sector is being expanded and provision is being made to meet the future demands of the mineral processing project. The power input should be valued at the average of its demand and supply price. In the case of an input, incremental production is valued through its average supply price, while nonincremental production is valued through its average demand price. In this case, the extra demand for power as an input will be met through incremental power output, and so it should be valued through its average supply price (see Figure 3).

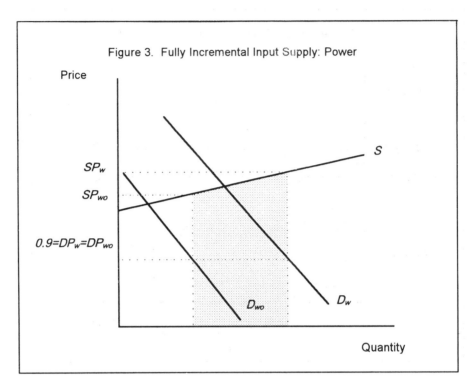

Figure 3. Fully Incremental Input Supply: Power

17.   The power sector is experiencing increasing costs. It is expected that the supply cost of power will increase with the project. The average supply cost in financial prices without and with the project has been calculated; however, this value needs to be converted to economic values, and related to the charge being made for power. Power charges are heavily subsidized, and the cost breakdown for power includes a substantial transfer element. The cost breakdown by proportion without and with the project is assumed to be similar, and is given in Table 5.

Table 5. Economic Supply Price of Power

	Cost Breakdown (P)	Conversion Factor	Economic Value (P)
Fuel - traded	0.90	1.000	0.900
Labor	0.04	0.900	0.036
Capital charges - traded	0.30	1.000	0.300
- nontraded	0.34	0.900	0.306
Nontraded inputs	0.12	0.900	0.108
Total	1.70		1.650
Transfer	-0.80		
Financial	0.90		
CF (1.650/0.900)		1.833	

Economic values using world price numeraire.

18. The present charge for power is P0.90 per kwh. This charge includes a financial subsidy of P0.80 per kwh. The economic supply price of power is calculated as P1.65 per kwh. Where the extra demand for power from the mineral processing project will be met through the expansion of the power sector, that is, entirely from incremental production, the conversion factor of 1.833 should be applied to convert the cost of power to the project into its economic value to the economy as a whole.

The EP of Water Inputs

19. A new industrial project has a high demand for water per unit of output. The water will be drawn from the public supply and treated further in the industrial plant itself. The treatment costs have been included in the project costs. Three-quarters of the extra demand for water by the industrial project will be met from an expansion of supply. This incremental water supply should be valued through its average supply price.

20. The new public water supplies will in part use water that at present is being used for agricultural purposes as there is a strict limit on the amount of water that can be drawn from the common water source. One quarter of the extra demand for water will be drawn away from agricultural uses. This nonincremental water input should be valued through its average demand price. For simplicity, it is assumed that the demand price for agricultural uses is not affected by the project, that is, the without and with demand prices are equal.

21. The cost of extra water supplies to consumers can be converted from financial to economic value (see Table 6). It is assumed that the cost structure for existing water is not different from the new project. Because water is heavily subsidized, its economic value is much greater than its financial value. Also, part of the cost of water includes the cost of power, which itself is subsidized (see the previous example). The SCF for the country is 0.9, and the supply price of labor is 85 percent of its wage.

Table 6. Economic Price of Incremental Water

	Cost Breakdown (P)	Conversion Factor	Economic Value (P)
Tradable inputs	29	1.000	29.0
Power	72	1.833	132.0
Capital charges: construction—nontraded	25	0.900	22.5
equipment—traded	7	1.000	7.0
Labor	74	0.765	56.6
Nontradable inputs	13	0.900	11.7
Total	220		258.8
Transfer	-120		
Financial price	100		
Economic price			258.8
CF (258.8/100)		2.588	

Economic values using world price numeraire.

22.   The value of water in agricultural uses is estimated through the marginal loss of net agricultural output, at shadow prices, per unit of water diverted to the new users. Agricultural prices for the staple crops grown in the area are regulated, and some of the inputs are subsidized. The net effect is expressed in a conversion factor relative to the financial cost of a unit of water. Again, because agricultural water use is also subsidized, this conversion factor, at 1.673, is considerably above one, even using the world price numeraire.

23.   The CF for the water inputs is the weighted average of the CFs for incremental and nonincremental supplies. Seventy-five percent of project supplies is incremental and 25 percent is nonincremental. The weighted average CF is

$$CF = 0.75 * 2.588 + 0.25 * 1.673 = 2.359$$

The financial charge for water supplies should be multiplied by this CF to give the economic value at the world price level of the project supplies (see Figure 4).

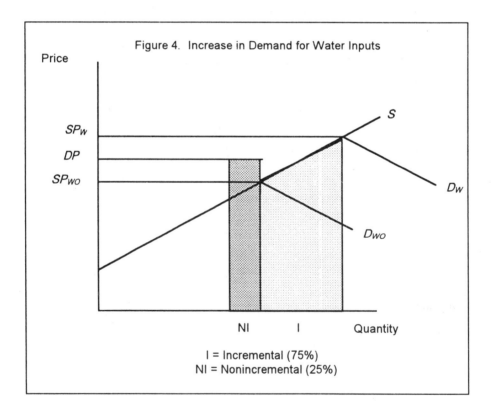

Figure 4. Increase in Demand for Water Inputs

III.   NONTRADED OUTPUTS WITHOUT CHARGES

Estimating Demand for Public Service Projects

24.   In many public projects, no price is charged for the output. Where the marginal costs of an extra person using a public good is close to zero, the efficiency price is also close to zero. In these circumstances, it is expected that 100 percent of those having access would use the public good concerned. To value the output of the public good, it is necessary to construct a surrogate demand curve showing the demand for the service at different levels of hypothetical charges.

25.   As an example, a primary health care project supplying free health care to a poor community is to be established. At present, supply is only available on a private basis in a nearby town. However, this facility is already fully utilized, even though it involves the cost of consultation and treatment as well as the cost of getting there and back. Because the primary health services will therefore be fully incremental to existing supplies, they should be valued at their average demand price.

26.   Figure 5 illustrates this situation, and provides a surrogate demand curve through which the health services can be valued. One extreme point of the demand curve is for the new provision, where all the population demand basic health services at a price of zero. The other extreme of the demand curve is given by the present full cost of access and treatment at the private clinic in the town. At this price, there is no incremental health service provision. The gross economic benefits of the health service project are given by the incremental quantity provided $(Q_W - Q_{WO})$ valued through the average demand price $(P_{WO} - P_W)/2$. Where the without quantity is zero, and where the with project charge is zero, this reduces to $(Q_W * P_{WO})/2$, and the economic value per unit of output can be valued through $P_{WO}/2$. This value can then be converted to economic prices by making adjustments for the value of foreign exchange and labor.

27.   An additional example is a rural water supply project that would provide reliable supplies to a village. At present the water supply is free and all households in the village use it. However, contingent valuation has been applied in the village through a survey to test how many households would be willing to pay different levels of fees to be introduced with the supply improvement. The basic result is that only 60 percent of households would be willing to continue using the supply at a fee level of Rs250 per month for access to the water.

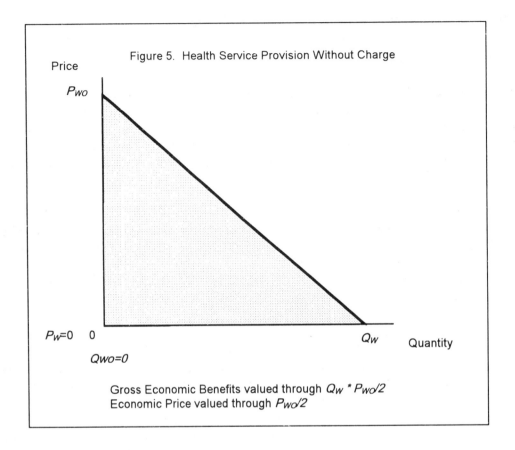

Figure 5. Health Service Provision Without Charge

Gross Economic Benefits valued through $Q_W * P_{wo}/2$
Economic Price valued through $P_{wo}/2$

28.   These two points can be used to derive a surrogate demand curve for the water supply (see Figure 6). One hundred percent of households would use the supply at a zero charge; 60 percent at a charge of 250. The slope of the demand curve is -250/(100 - 60) or -6.25. By extrapolation, all households would give up using the supply at a charge of Rs625 per month. The water supply project can then be valued through its average demand price, 625/2 (using the domestic price numeraire).

29.   There are two basic problems with such a procedure for deriving surrogate demand curves through contingent valuation methods. The first is the difficulty of obtaining reliable answers to how households would react in hypothetical situations. Often households undervalue public services in the expectation that they will be free anyway. The second is the simple assumption about the shape of the demand curve, a straight line, through which the maximum charge of Rs625 is derived. Other shapes can be used over a smaller range when it is felt that the approach here is not realistic.

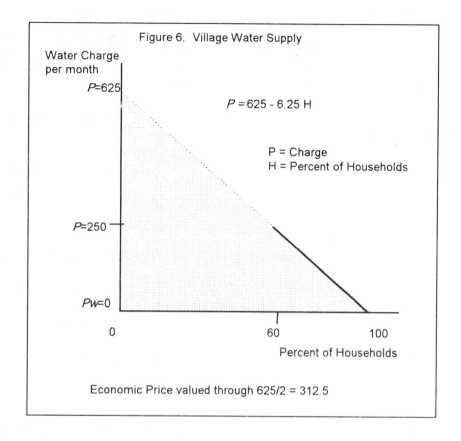

Figure 6. Village Water Supply

Water Charge per month

$P = 625$

$P = 625 - 6.25 H$

P = Charge
H = Percent of Households

$P = 250$

$P_W = 0$

0   60   100

Percent of Households

Economic Price valued through 625/2 = 312.5

30.   Rather than rely on contingent valuation, where hypothetical situations are posed to respondents, as far as possible surrogate values can be derived through related market behavior. Where a nonmarketed good is an intermediate product, for example irrigation water, it can be valued through the market value of the extra crop production to which it contributes. In the same spirit education expenditures for which there is no charge can be valued through the incremental income that accrues to those with better qualifications.

31.   Where the nontraded good or service has a close substitute or a complementary good, either may be used to derive a price through which it can be valued. An example of substitution is that of the public and private health services above. An example of a complementary good would be the demand for television sets through which a television transmission project could be valued. The market value of the transmission project can be taken to be at least equal to the amount people or enterprises are willing to spend to access the transmission. Where different neighborhoods experience different levels of pollution, a project oriented to reducing pollution could be valued through the difference in property prices or rents between neighborhoods.

32.   Where nontraded outputs without charge have no close substitutes or complements, and where resources or circumstances are not conducive to contingent valuation methods, valuations for similar projects in a different location or even a different country could be applied to a new project. Such benefit transfer approaches must be closely scrutinized and argued, with appropriate adjustments for differences in context.

33.   The following steps summarize the procedure for estimating the economic value of nontraded outputs and inputs.

    i.   Identify the effects of project outputs and inputs. Will the effects be limited to the domestic market for the outputs and inputs?

    ii.   *For project outputs:*
What is the market structure?
What will be the effect of the project on quantity and price, of the project output and of any substituted products?
How much of the project output will substitute for the output of other producers (nonincremental) and how much will add to supply (incremental)?
What are the marginal costs of substituted outputs, as a combination of traded and nontraded costs?
What is the willingness to pay per unit for the incremental supplies?

    iii.   *For major project inputs:*
What is the market structure?
What will be the effect of project demands on the quantity and price of the input?
How much of the additional project demand will be met by extra supply (incremental) and how much by reduced supplies to others (nonincremental)?
What are the marginal costs of producing the incremental supplies, as a combination of traded and nontraded goods?
What is the willingness to pay per unit for the nonincremental supplies?

    iv.   Adjust the willingness to pay and the cost estimates to the chosen numeraire.
    v.   Calculate the weighted average economic value of the project output, using the proportions of incremental and nonincremental demands as the weights.
    vi.   Calculate the weighted average economic value of the project input, using the proportions of incremental and nonincremental demands as the weights.
    vii.   Compare the resulting economic prices with the financial prices.

Appendix 12
Shadow Wage Rate and the Shadow Wage Rate Factor

1.   In the financial analysis of a project, money wages (and other benefits) paid to employees are treated as the financial price of labor. The shadow wage rate (SWR) is an estimate of the economic price of labor.

I.   General Principles for Calculating the Shadow Wage Rate

2.   The economic price of labor is measured through its supply price. At very low wages, people may prefer leisure to work. The supply price of labor depends upon several factors, such as the value placed on leisure and other nonwage activities, family income, the cost of migration, and the nature of employment and other benefits accruing from that employment. The reservation wage, below which people in an area will not offer their labor, varies across classes of labor and geographic locations.

3.   There are large variations in the types of labor, depending on skills, regions within countries, and even individual jobs. It is thus often necessary to use a set of shadow wage rates, one for each skill, location, economic sector, and even season, rather than a single rate for the whole country. A simplified approach based on the prevailing wage rates for the various types of skills and locations, and the degree of unemployment relating to those skills can be used to estimate the SWR. For purposes of analysis, workers may be divided into three categories: skilled, semiskilled, and unskilled, corresponding to different degrees of scarcity.

4.   Since skilled workers are generally in short supply in DMCs, prevailing market wages in the project area may be taken as corresponding to their supply price. Other benefits, such as housing and provident fund contributions, also should be included in the supply price estimates.

5.   For semi-skilled workers, wages in the informal or unprotected sector, beyond the effective control of wage regulations and labor unions, adjusted for the degree of unemployment in the project area, can be used in estimating the SWR. In the formal or protected sector, wages can be held above the market-clearing level by minimum wage laws, collective bargaining agreements, or by the hiring policies of companies. Thus, the supply price of semiskilled labor can be estimated as a weighted average of the informal and formal wage sectors, with the weight given by the proportion of labor drawn from each.

6.   For unskilled workers, the SWR should be estimated on the basis of the unprotected wage rate for the number of days and gainful employment during the year. Most DMCs report a high degree of unemployment and underemployment in both rural and urban areas, with most of the unemployed being unskilled. In determining the SWR for such workers, it should be borne in mind that unskilled workers in urban areas engage in many informal activities. In rural areas, the

unemployed may provide help in family farms, do seasonal work in nearby industries or work on construction projects. These alternative activities should also be included when estimating the SWR.

7.   In estimating the SWR, the degree and nature of unemployment and underemployment in the project area and its environs should be carefully assessed. It is preferable that independent surveys made in the project or surrounding areas be used to confirm the estimates obtained from official sources.

8.   Estimation of the SWR is particularly important in projects where the wage component in the total cost or benefit stream is significant, and where technological options exist in formulating projects. For these projects, expected changes in the SWR over the project cycle should be assessed, on the basis of forecasts about the supply and demand for labor. Other projects may involve only a few workers. For projects that have a very small wage component, and that are not sensitive to the valuation of labor, it will not be necessary to estimate a project specific SWR.

9.   If the market works fairly well, minimum wage legislation is absent, and unemployment is low, but there is an income tax imposed on wages, the SWR would be the average of the market wage which represents the value to the employer of the foregone labor, and the net-of-tax wage received by labor. On the other hand, new vacancies created by the project will reduce unemployment compensation payments and this will result in savings of public funds.

10.   It should be noted that the procedure outlined thus far establishes the SWR in terms of the value of output foregone at domestic market prices. In economic analysis, the SWR has to be defined in border price equivalents. This can be done by applying appropriate conversion factors.

II.   ILLUSTRATIVE EXAMPLE: CALCULATING THE SHADOW WAGE RATE FOR UNSKILLED LABOR IN A GOVERNMENT RURAL PROJECT

11.   Consider the case of a government corporation that is undertaking a labor-intensive sugar project in a rural area. The project requires unskilled workers on a temporary basis and pays a gross-of-tax wage that varies by the month. This amount will be subject to a 5 percent income tax. The following schedule shows in column (3), the after tax monthly wage rate for landless labor working in several alternative formal sector activities in the area, and, in column (4), the project's monthly requirements for person-months.

12.   To estimate the economic cost of the unskilled labor to the project, we first need to calculate the monthly share of the annual person-months required by the project. This is obtained in column (5), above, by dividing the number of person-months for a particular month by the total yearly person-months.

Table 1. Shadow Wage Rate for Unskilled Labor

Month	Wage to Employer Before Tax	Wage to Employee After Tax	Person-Months	Monthly Share of Annual Person-months
(1)	(2)	(3)	(4)	(5)
January	126.3	120	1,800	0.2
February	105.3	100	1,800	0.2
March	189.5	180	1,800	0.2
April	189.5	180	900	0.1
May	105.3	100	900	0.1
June	157.9	150	0	0.0
July	189.5	180	0	0.0
August	126.3	120	0	0.0
September	157.9	150	900	0.1
October	115.8	110	0	0.1
November	157.9	150	900	0.1
December	189.5	180	900	0.1
Total			9,000	1.0

13.   The weighted average monthly wage for casual labor is then calculated as

$$= 120 * 0.2 + 100 * 0.2 + \ldots + 150 * 0.1 + 180 * 0.1$$

Average monthly wage after tax   = 141 rupees per month, and
Average monthly wage before tax = 148 rupees per month
Shadow wage rate   = (141 + 148) / 2 = 144.5

III.   THE SHADOW WAGE RATE FACTOR

14.   The shadow wage rate factor (SWRF) for a certain type of labor is the ratio between its shadow wage rate and its price. If project labor is paid a wage of 200 rupees per month, then the SWRF is calculated as: 144.5/200 = 0.723 in domestic prices. Where the world price numeraire is being used, this SWRF has to be revalued again using a standard conversion factor or a specific conversion factor for the output of this type of casual labor.

APPENDIX 13
THE ECONOMIC PRICE OF LAND

1.   Nearly all projects involve an additional use of land. Whether land is purchased or allocated to a project, it has an economic cost. The economic cost of land should be included in the project resource flow for calculating the economic internal rate of return (EIRR). Different values of the economic cost of land will be included in different project alternatives, for example, for different alignments of a road.

2.   The first step in calculating the economic cost of land is to analyze the changes in land use that the project or project alternative will bring about. Some rehabilitation or updating projects may require no additional land and therefore no change in land use. Expansion or new projects will require a land allocation and therefore a change in land use. Where existing activities are displaced and not terminated, there will also be an indirect change in land use at the site to which they are relocated. A survey is therefore required for

- demarcation of the project full land requirement,
- demarcation of land required for relocation,
- identifying those areas where land use will not change, and
- identifying those areas where land use will change.

3.   The change in land use as a result of a project is illustrated in Figure 1.

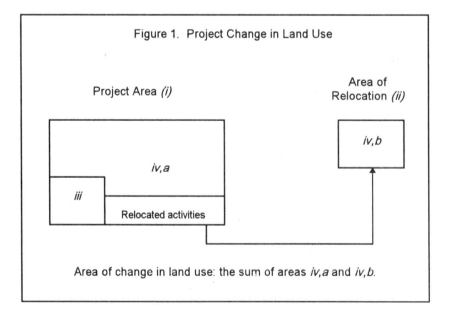

Figure 1. Project Change in Land Use

Project Area *(i)*

Area of Relocation *(ii)*

iv,b

iv,a

iii

Relocated activities

Area of change in land use: the sum of areas *iv,a* and *iv,b*.

Area *iii* includes existing activities that will be incorporated into the project: there is no change in land use. The economic cost of land relates to area *iv,a,* the additional land required for the project from terminated activities, and area *iv,b,* where some activities on this land are to be relocated. Relocated activities may include household dwellings, agricultural activities, factories, and social facilities. There may also be some external effects of the project on land use, for example, consequential changes in land use neighboring the project area because of interrupted rights of way or because of induced economic changes.

4.   The economic price of land is based on those areas where there will be a change in land use. The use of this land without the project provides the basis for its economic price. The without project situation should be based on the next best use of this land area. The basic measure to use as the cost of the land where use is changing is the output, net of all inputs, including labor and equipment, that would be produced on the land without the project. This opportunity cost of the land should be measured at shadow prices. Because of current trends or expected changes in the future, the opportunity cost per unit of land may change in the without project situation. Land productivity may increase where new agricultural methods can be anticipated or where infrastructure investments are planned. Land productivity may decline where, for example, soil erosion or exhaustion is occurring or where rainfall is becoming more scarce. The net output of the land in the without project situation should be estimated for each year of the project.

5.   The opportunity cost of land will differ from place to place. In broad terms a distinction can be made between changing land use in rural areas, where agricultural production will be lost, in city areas, where a range of services and activities may be displaced, and in special development zones, where the production structure is changing rapidly.

6.   In rural areas, changes in land use will result in lost agricultural production. The existing land use should be assessed and a land suitability analysis carried out for the best without project alternative. Commonly, a specific product or small number of products will be selected to represent the lost net output from the land. Estimates can be made on a per hectare basis and then projected onto the total land area. Where it is observed that agricultural techniques or cropping patterns are changing, an annual adjustment to the lost output per hectare can be made to reflect changing productivities. The cropping intensity, or number of harvests per year, will differ from place to place. The net benefits per harvest from the selected products are adjusted by the cropping intensity to give the annual loss of net output for the land area as a whole. A typical calculation can be summarized as

$$EPL_t \;\; = \;\; NB_o \; * \; CI \; * \; (1+g)^t$$

where EPL_t = the economic price of land per hectare in year t,
NB_o = the net output or benefit in shadow prices per hectare per crop in year zero,
CI = the cropping intensity, and
g = the productivity growth factor (positive or negative).

This expression gives the opportunity cost or economic price of the land per hectare for each year of the project.

7.   In city areas, for example, because of the construction of a new ring road, the effects are more complex. There may be several types of service or activity being displaced by the project. It is more likely that the displaced activities will be relocated where there are already existing activities, and so the opportunity cost of land in the project area and in the area of relocation can be equally complex. The economic price of the land is the summation of the several changes in land use measured according to the type of activity being displaced. Table 1 illustrates the possibilities for a road project in an urban area. It specifies the present or without project use of land, the areas of land where land use will change, the area of relocation for displaced activities, and the method of estimating the opportunity cost of the land occupied by different activities without the project.

Table 1. Opportunity Cost of Road Project Involving Mixed Urban Land

Without Project	Area	Area of Change in Use	Relocation Area	Method of Estimation
Factories	40	40	Farmland	As for farmland
Commercial	30	20	Farmland	As for farmland
Roads	40	--	--	--
Housing	30	20	Farmland	As for farmland
Government	10	0	0	Cost difference
Recreation	5	5	0	Willingness to pay
Farmland	20	20	0	Production foregone

8.   These different types of land use can be discussed in turn. Factories will be relocated using the same area of land, displacing agricultural production. There may be efficiency improvements for the factories, but the economic price of the land is the agricultural production foregone. Commercial enterprises and housing will be relocated. However, the newly designed buildings will be more compact than the structures that will be displaced, and so less land is reassigned at the relocation site. The economic price of the land is given through lost agricultural production. Existing roads will be widened as part of the new road, and hence there is no change in land use for the existing road area. Some Government offices will be displaced. They will not be replaced. Existing functions will be fitted into existing Government premises nearby entailing no further loss of land. The cost of the associated land can be estimated through the cost difference in providing Government services. This cost difference may be negative, that is, the cost of providing services may be lower after displacement than before. A small amount of recreational area will be lost. It can be valued through an estimate of willingness to pay, measured through contingent valuation techniques where no revenues are collected for the recreational services that are being lost. Finally, the

farmland, and the associated agricultural production, that is lost directly as a result of the road will not be compensated elsewhere. Those involved will be provided with other jobs. The economic price of land for the different effects of changes in land use should be measured in or converted to shadow prices.

9.   In special development zones or greenfield sites, the purpose of development is to change the land use rapidly. Present land uses will not be a good indication of the future opportunity cost of the land. In principle, the economic price of the land for a new project in this situation can be estimated by considering the next best alternative use of the land after development of the site. However, such uses are likely to be similar to the project under assessment and the difference in their overall returns will become an indicator of project acceptability rather than a measure of the economic price of the land. In these circumstances, the purchase or lease price of the land can be used as an indicator of willingness to pay for use of a site.

10.   The market for land can never be fully competitive because supply cannot be increased. Purchase or lease prices can be set through different means, for example, auctions, competitive bids, or negotiated prices. In general, auction prices will provide the best indication of willingness to pay. Where the economic price of land is estimated through its market price, a conversion factor has to be applied to convert the price to the appropriate price level.

11.   Where the economic price is estimated through the annual lost production in agricultural or other activities, this is usually included in the project resource statement for each year. Occasionally, the stream of annual amounts is converted to a present value using the discount rate (12 percent). Where the economic price is estimated through an adjusted purchase or lease price, this will be included as a single payment in the first project year. It can also be annualized across the project years using the discount rate.

APPENDIX 14
TREATMENT OF RESETTLEMENT COMPONENTS OF PROJECTS

1.   The costs of resettlement should be included in the project financial and economic costs, in addition to the economic price of land. Projects with no change in land use are likely to involve no resettlement. However, most projects involve a change in land use. For many, the resettlement of population and economic activities will be small. For some, it may form a significant proportion of the project costs.

2.   The Bank requires that the involuntary resettlement of populations be treated as an integral part of project design. A resettlement plan is required, and assistance can be provided for its design and implementation. The financial cost of the resettlement component of projects is eligible for Bank financing.

3.   The financial costs of resettlement may include

- compensation for lost income for a specified period,
- compensation for the loss of assets or the reconstruction costs of housing and workshops,
- compensation for temporary production losses during relocation,
- the cost of removal, and
- the cost of managing the resettlement process.

Compensation for lost income for a specified period is a transfer payment and reflects the opportunity cost of lost production from the land and should be excluded from the costs of resettlement where the economic price of land has already been estimated. Other forms of compensation payments need to be substituted by the actual costs of removal and reconstruction. Where compensation schemes are welldeveloped and funded, the financial costs of resettlement may exceed its economic cost. Where compensation schemes are rudimentary, the financial costs may be less than the economic costs.

4.   In estimating the economic costs of resettlement, not only should transfer elements be excluded, but all resource costs should be converted to shadow prices. Table 1 illustrates the calculation of the economic costs of resettlement from their financial costs.

5.   In this case, there is a welldeveloped compensation scheme, and the economic costs of resettlement are less than the financial costs. The economic cost at shadow prices should be included in the project resource flow in addition to the economic price of land.

Table 1. Economic Costs of Resettlement

Item	Financial Cost ($ m)	Resource Cost (RC) or Transfer (T)	Conversion Factor [1]	Economic Cost ($ m)
Land compensation [2]	3.500	T [4]	0.00	0.000
Reconstruction of buildings	10.788	RC	0.90	9.709
Temporary production losses [3]	0.300	RC	0.85	0.285
Removal costs	0.750	RC	0.90	0.675
Management costs	0.782	RC	1.30	1.017
Total Financial Cost	16.120			
Total Economic Cost				11.686

[1]   Using world price numeraire, standard conversion factor = 0.90.
[2]   Seven years lost average production per hectare.
[3]   Net income from one harvest/three months workshop net income.
[4]   Economic cost of land calculated separately.

6.   A minimum requirement in planning resettlement, sufficient in most cases, is that no person should be worse off after resettlement than before. However, resettlement can also be seen as an opportunity to improve the living standards of those being resettled, through resettlement with development. Compensation payments may be used voluntarily to establish a new economic activity with improved prospects. In other cases, changes in economic activity and living standards must be planned along with the project causing the resettlement. Net benefits to those being resettled can be greater with the project than without. Any estimated increase in net benefits as a result of resettlement, measured in shadow prices, should be subtracted from the estimated economic costs of resettlement.

APPENDIX 15
CALCULATING ECONOMIC PRICES AT THE DOMESTIC MARKET PRICE OR WORLD MARKET PRICE LEVELS

1.   The application of economic analysis to projects requires that all incremental outputs and inputs be valued at their opportunity cost. The resource effects of project outputs and inputs can be summarized into their traded good and nontraded goods components. For many items, the opportunity cost will be represented by their border price equivalent value (BPEV). For example, traded goods can be measured directly in terms of their trade effect; the opportunity cost of land and surplus labor may also be expressed in terms of traded goods. For other items, the opportunity cost will be estimated initially in terms of nontraded goods measured in domestic market prices. This breakdown of resource outputs and inputs into their traded and nontraded components must be done for all project capital, operating and working capital costs, and for all project benefits. Project capital costs are usually divided between foreign currency and local currency costs. Foreign currency costs refer to traded good inputs. A substantial proportion of local currency costs may also refer to traded goods, that is, goods produced and used domestically but having a trade effect on the economy in terms of imports or exports foregone. Local currency costs should be broken down between traded and nontraded good components.

2.   In nearly all economies, domestic market price levels are higher than world market price levels. Where some project resource effects are estimated at world market prices and others are estimated at domestic market prices, there is a need to bring all resource effects to a common basis so that they can be aggregated into an estimate of project net benefits. To do this, it is necessary to define a unit of account, that is, to choose a price level—domestic or world market price level—and to choose a currency—national or foreign currency—in which to express all project resource effects.

Table 1. Unit of Account

Price Level	Currency	
	National	Foreign
Domestic prices	Domestic, rupees	Domestic, dollars
World prices	World, rupees	World, dollars

3.   The simplest unit of account to adopt is to express all project effects at the domestic price level in national currency. This means converting all world market price values measured in national currency to the domestic price level using a shadow exchange rate factor (SERF). This procedure is most suitable where a large proportion of the project costs and especially the project benefits are nontraded goods. It also facilitates an analysis of the distribution of project effects. Alternatively, all project effects can be measured at the world price level in national

currency. In the simplest form of analysis, this requires that a standard conversion factor (SCF) be used to revalue nontraded goods at their world market price level. This procedure is most suitable for small open economies where there is a very small proportion of nontraded inputs and outputs. Occasionally all project effects are measured at the world price level but in foreign currency. This option may seem suitable where most project effects are estimated in foreign currency anyway. However, it still requires that an SCF be applied to the value of nontraded goods to bring them to the world market price level.

4.   The differences in the units of account can be illustrated through a simple example. A project will produce extra quantities of rice that will substitute for imported rice. At the official exchange rate of Rs10 to $1, the financial value of the rice output amounting to Rs400 can be broken down as in the first column of Table 2.

Table 2. Different Units of Account

	Financial Value	Domestic (National)	World (National)
Import price/traded component	300	x 1.25 = 375	x 1.00 = 300
Handling & transport/nontraded component	50	x 1.00 = 50	x 0.80 = 40
Import duties & excise taxes	50	x 0.00 = 0	x 0.00 = 0
Financial Value	400		
Economic Value		425	340

A shadow exchange rate of Rs12.5 to $1 has been estimated for the country concerned, implying a SERF of 1.25. When this SERF is applied to the traded goods component of the imported rice that will be substituted, and when all taxes on the imported rice are excluded, the economic value of the rice at the domestic price level in national currency is Rs425. Alternatively, an SCF of 0.8 can be applied to the nontraded component of the imported rice. With all taxes similarly excluded, this gives an economic value of the rice at the world price level in national currency of Rs340.

5.   Both of these values, Rs425 and Rs340, represent the same thing: the economic value to the country of imported rice that will be substituted by the project. They are expressed in different units of account. The value of the rice at the domestic price level is 1.25 times the value of the rice at the world price level; put the other way, the value of rice at the world price level is 0.8 times the value of the rice at the domestic price level.

6.   Where project effects are measured at the domestic price level, all their values will be greater than the same project effects measured at the world price level. They will all be greater by the same fixed ratio. This applies equally to outputs and to inputs. Where all project outputs and inputs are greater by a fixed ratio, the economic internal rate of return will be the same. Valuing project effects at the domestic price level in national currency will give a net present value that in absolute terms is greater than valuing all project effects at the world price

level in national currency. However, the economic internal rates of return will be the same, and so the project decision will be the same whichever unit of account is being used.

7.   The use of different units of account in the economic analysis of a project is illustrated by the following example for a railway project. Table 3 summarizes the economic effects of project inputs and outputs into their traded and nontraded goods components. The civil works element of capital costs involves both traded and nontraded goods components. All machinery and equipment is treated as traded goods wherever it is purchased. The opportunity cost of land is measured in traded goods while resettlement costs are treated as nontraded. For operating costs, the opportunity cost of surplus labor is estimated in terms of traded goods, while administrative expenses are treated as nontraded goods. There are two forms of project output: avoided road transport costs and extra net output achieved through releasing congestion on the system. The latter is estimated directly in traded goods. The opportunity cost of scarce labor and the avoided road transport costs, in principle, represent a mixture of traded and nontraded goods. However, they have not been separated. The opportunity costs have been estimated initially in domestic market prices and so they are treated as nontraded good components.

Table 3. Structure of Railway Project Costs and Benefits

Project Costs	National Currency (Ym)			Foreign Currency ($ m)		
	Traded Goods World Prices	Nontraded Goods Domestic Prices	Total	Traded Goods World Prices	Nontraded Goods Domestic Prices	Total
Capital Costs						
Civil works	720.0	1360.0	2080.0	90.0	170.0	260.0
Machinery & equipment	336.0	0.0	336.0	42.0	0.0	42.0
Land & resettlement	0.0	320.0	320.0	0.0	40.0	40.0
Consultant services	24.0	16.0	40.0	3.0	2.0	5.0
Total Capital Costs	1080.0	1696.0	2776.0	135.0	212.0	347.0
Operating Costs						
Fuel	32.0	0.0	32.0	4.0	0.0	4.0
Labor (surplus)	25.0	0.0	25.0	3.1	0.0	3.1
Labor (scarce)	0.0	28.0	28.0	0.0	3.5	3.5
Other	0.0	56.0	56.0	0.0	7.0	7.0
Total Operating Costs	57.0	84.0	141.0	7.1	10.5	17.6
Project Benefits						
Avoided road transport costs	0.0	280.0	280.0	0.0	35.0	35.0
Additional net output	240.0	0.0	240.0	30.0	0.0	30.0
Total	240.0	280.0	520.0	30.0	35.0	65.0
Official Exchange Rate (Y/$)	8.000					
Shadow Exchange Rate Factor	1.080					
Standard Conversion Factor	0.926					
Discount Rate	0.12					

8.   Table 3 presents the summary of project costs and benefits in two currencies, domestic currency or yuan, and foreign currency or US dollars. The official exchange rate is taken as Y8 to $1. However, a SERF of 1.08 has also been estimated implying that the domestic prices in which the nontraded components are estimated on average are 8 percent higher than the world price equivalents in which the traded good components are estimated. Tables 4a, b, and c illustrates three ways in which the project inputs and outputs can be brought to a common unit of account. Table 4a presents the project economic statement in national currency at the domestic price level, by applying the SERF to the value of all the traded goods components. Table 4b presents the project economic statement in national currency at the world price level, by applying the SCF to the nontraded goods components. Table 4c presents the project economic statement in foreign currency at the world price level, again by applying the SCF to the nontraded goods components.

9.   The absolute value of the discounted net benefits differs between the first and the other two cases (see Table 5). Over a 26 year project period, and ignoring residual values, the net present value (NPV) using a 12 percent discount rate is 201 in national currency in the first case. In the second case, the NPV using the same discount rate is 186 in the same currency, and 23 in foreign currency. These last two cases differ only in the currency in which the project effects have been expressed. The first two cases differ because different price levels have been used to determine the unit of account. However, regardless of the unit of account used, the economic internal rate of return (EIRR) is the same in all three cases. If consistency is maintained in the use of a unit of account, it does not matter which is used for the basic project accept or reject decision.

Table 4a. Project Economic Statement, National Currency, and Domestic Price Level

	Present Values	Years			
		0	1	2	3-25
Capital Costs					
Civil works		2,138			
Machinery & equipment		363			
Land & resettlement		320			
Consultant services		42			
Total Capital Costs	2,556	2,862	0	0	0
Operating Costs					
Fuel			35	35	35
Labor (surplus)			27	27	27
Labor (scarce)			28	28	28
Other			56	56	56
Total Operating Costs	1,019	0	146	146	146
Project Benefits					
Avoided road transport costs			280	280	280
Additional net output			259	259	259
Total	3,776	0	539	539	539
Net Benefits	201	-2,862	394	394	394
Net Present Value	201				
EIRR (%)	13.1				

Table 4b. Project Economic Statement, National Currency, and World Price Level

	Present Values	Years			
		0	1	2	3-25
Capital Costs					
Civil works		1,979			
Machinery & equipment		336			
Land & resettlement		296			
Consultant services		39			
Total Capital Costs	2,366	2,650	0	0	0
Operating Costs					
Fuel			32	32	32
Labor (surplus)			25	25	25
Labor (scarce)			26	26	26
Other			52	52	52
Total Operating Costs	944	0	135	135	135
Project Benefits					
Avoided road transport costs			259	259	259
Additional net output			240	240	240
Total	3,496	0	499	499	499
Net Benefits	186	-2,650	364	364	364
Net Present Value	186				
EIRR (%)	13.1				

Table 4c. Project Economic Statement, Foreign Currency, and World Price Level

	Present Values	Years			
		0	1	2	3-25
Capital Costs					
Civil works		247			
Machinery & equipment		42			
Land & resettlement		37			
Consultant services		5			
Total Capital Costs	296	331	0	0	0
Operating Costs					
Fuel			4	4	4
Labor (surplus)			3	3	3
Labor (scarce)			3	3	3
Other			6	6	6
Total Operating Costs	118	0	17	17	17
Project Benefits					
Avoided road transport costs			32	32	32
Additional net output			30	30	30
Total	437	0	62	62	62
Net Benefits	23	-331	46	46	46
Net Present Value	23				
EIRR (%)	13.1				

Table 5. Economic Analysis Results

Price Level	Currency			
	National		Foreign	
	NPV	EIRR (%)	NPV	EIRR (%)
Domestic	201	13.1		
World	186	13.1	23	13.1

APPENDIX 16
ESTIMATING THE SHADOW EXCHANGE RATE FACTOR
AND THE STANDARD (OR AVERAGE) CONVERSION FACTOR

I.   INTRODUCTION

1.   The shadow exchange rate (SER) is the economic price of foreign currency. There is a common misconception that if the market for foreign exchange is a free float, the shadow exchange rate (SER) is equal to the market exchange rate. That would be the case only if there were no taxes and subsidies on the demand and supply of tradable goods, if all commodities and factors were priced at their economic value, and if the current account deficit was sustainable. In all cases, the SER will diverge from the market or official exchange rate (OER).

2.   Exchange rates are one of the key macroprices affecting project performance. If the OER is taken as the SER, and the OER is overvalued, then projects producing nontradables with tradable inputs are favored relative to projects producing tradables with nontradable inputs. On the other hand, if the OER is undervalued, projects producing tradables with nontradable inputs are favored relative to projects producing nontradables with tradable inputs. In the event that the OER is depreciated to attain external competitiveness, or the OER is appreciated to attain internal competitiveness, project performance suffers. In general, the greater the divergence between the OER and the SER, the more likely will depreciation or appreciation occur and affect project performance.

II.   VALUING PROJECT OUTPUTS AND INPUTS

3.   The purpose of economic analysis is to encourage investment in projects that promote the best use of a country's resources. That is not necessarily the same as investing in projects with the highest financial return. Financial returns are based on financial prices. Economic returns are based on economic prices.

4.   The economic price for any good is based on the weighted average of its demand and supply price, with the weights depending on the market impact of the project. Most projects are small relative to market size, and output produced or input demanded is incremental by adding to that sold or bought without the project. Output and input prices are therefore unaffected by small projects. In such cases, the economic price of a project output is based on its demand price and the economic price of a project input is based on its supply price. The demand price is the price that buyers are willing to pay, that is, the market price plus consumption taxes and less consumption subsidies. The supply price is the price at which suppliers are willing to sell, that is the market price less production taxes and plus production subsidies.

5.   Financial prices are different from economic prices. The financial price of a project output is its supply price and the financial price of a project input is its demand price. The relationship between the market price, the financial price, and the economic price for project output or input differs depending on the type of tax levied and other factors. The market price is the financial price when there is only a production tax on a project input and a consumption tax on a project output, whereas the market price is closer to the economic price when there is only a production tax on a project output and a consumption tax on a project input.

6.   A major difference between economic and financial prices is therefore made up of indirect taxes and subsidies. For project outputs, the economic price exceeds the financial price by the amount of the indirect tax. For project inputs, the financial price exceeds the economic price by the amount of the indirect tax. This applies whether project outputs or inputs are tradables or nontradables.

III.   TRADED AND NONTRADED GOODS

7.   In valuing project outputs and inputs, economic benefits and costs are divided into traded and nontraded components. Whether an output or input component is traded or not depends on whether it can be profitably exported or imported. The demand price for an exported output is its FOB price and the supply price for an imported input is its CIF price. Traded output or input is valued at the border price level, that is at the level of FOB prices for exports and CIF prices for imports. FOB and CIF prices are typically expressed in local currency terms, converted from foreign currency at the official exchange rate. Nontraded output and input sold on the domestic market are also valued at economic prices, but are naturally expressed in national currency at the domestic price level.

IV.   THE SHADOW EXCHANGE RATE FACTOR

8.   Market distortions tend to maintain the domestic price level for both traded and nontraded goods at higher or lower levels than if there was no intervention. The extent to which the exchange rate is overvalued or undervalued is proportional to the effect of market distortions on the domestic price level relative to the border price level. To take account of the effect of market distortions on the market price for foreign exchange, the shadow exchange rate factor is estimated.

9.   The SERF is the ratio of the shadow exchange rate to the official exchange rate, with the shadow exchange rate being defined as the weighted average of the demand price of foreign exchange paid by importers and the supply price of foreign exchange received by exporters. The shadow exchange rate is often estimated as the ratio of the value of traded goods and services at the domestic price level to the value of traded goods and services at the

border price level. Alternatively, it can be measured as the weighted average ratio of domestic prices to border price equivalent levels across all goods in the economy.

10.   Where tariff distortions represent the only distortion to trade and there are no distortions in factor or commodity prices, the shadow exchange rate can be approximated by the demand price given by multiplying the market exchange rate by the shadow exchange rate factor, calculated as one plus the weighted average tariff rate. For example, if the weighted average tariff was 25 percent, the SERF would be 1.25 and the shadow exchange rate would be the market exchange rate multiplied by 1.25. Tradables valued at the border price level are revalued to the domestic price level by multiplying by the SERF of 1.25. Alternatively, if the unit of account for the economic analysis was denominated at the border price level, nontradables would be converted to the border price level by multiplying by the reciprocal of the shadow exchange rate factor or the standard conversion factor (SCF), in this case 0.8 (see Appendix 15).

V.   FREE TRADE EXCHANGE RATE

11.   The SER is not the free trade exchange rate. The free trade exchange rate assumes that the markets for tradables are completely free of distortion. The SER is a second-best shadow price. It is second-best in the sense that the SER assumes that current distortions will continue during the life of the project.

VI.   PARALLEL MARKET EXCHANGE RATE

12.   The SER is not the parallel market exchange rate. The parallel market exchange rate is determined by the informal market. Typically, it is lower than the SER but higher than the free trade exchange rate, which is, in turn, higher than the official exchange rate. The smaller the risks involved, and the greater the proportion of foreign exchange traded on the informal market, the closer the parallel market rate will be to the free trade exchange rate.

VII.   EQUILIBRIUM EXCHANGE RATE

13.   Projects are undertaken within a macroeconomic and sectoral policy environment. In practically all cases, the success or failure of projects depends upon the economic and policy environment in which they are undertaken. One of the most important macroprices affecting project performance is the exchange rate. If the exchange rate is not consistent with long-run fundamentals, it will eventually change and affect project performance. In evaluating project costs and benefits, the SERF should be applied to the equilibrium exchange rate (EER) instead of the market exchange rate as presently practiced (see Figure 1).

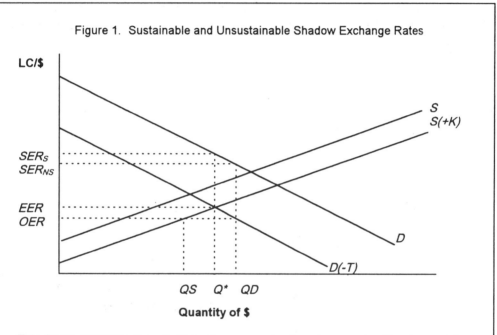

Figure 1. Sustainable and Unsustainable Shadow Exchange Rates

This figure illustrates the situation of an overvalued exchange rate. The demand for foreign exchange (net of the effects of import tariffs) is shown by $D(-T)$ and the supply of foreign exchange (gross of the effects of a sustainable capital inflow) is shown by $S(+K)$. At the official exchange rate, the demand for foreign exchange is Q_D which exceeds supply Q_S. For a small project the shadow exchange rate is indicated by SER_{NS}, which is not sustainable. The sustainable shadow exchange rate is determined by estimating the equilibrium exchange rate for which the demand and supply of foreign exchange are equal, and then determining the demand price of foreign exchange or SER_S.

VIII. Current Account Sustainability

14.   Traditionally, the SERF, or its reciprocal the SCF, has been based on the ratio of the value of traded goods and services at domestic prices to their value at border prices. When tariffs represent the main distortion in the market for foreign exchange, the SERF has been approximated by one plus the weighted average tariff rate. These approaches assume however that the country's current account is sustainable and this is not always the case. An estimate of the SERF can be based upon judgments about the sustainability of any level of current account deficit, as incorporated in the following illustration.

IX.   Shadow Exchange Rate for the Philippines: An Example

16.   The Philippines has long been experiencing trade deficits sustained in the short run by capital inflows (such as, foreign investment and development aid), remittances of overseas contract workers, and drawdowns of foreign exchange reserves. The shadow exchange rate has been estimated for the Philippines under three different cases for illustration purposes, as presented in Table 1. The following paragraphs describe the adjustments and assumptions made.

Data Requirements and Adjustments

17.   *Price-Responsive Imports.* The total import value, converted from $ to P using the average official exchange rate (OER), was obtained from the Foreign Trade Statistics of the Philippines (FTSP). Adjustments in the total import value to arrive at price-responsive imports included special transactions and goods on consignment (heading 931 of Standard Trade Commodity Classification (STCC)), which are eventually reexported. To determine what other sectors are not price responsive to the foreign exchange rate, regression analysis was conducted on ten-year data on foreign exchange and imports by STCC. All sectors showed price-responsiveness to foreign exchange movements.

18.   *Price-Responsive Exports.* The deductions from total exports (obtained from the FTSP) included special transactions and goods on consignment, reexports, and other nonresponsive exports. Reexports are defined as exports of imported goods that do not undergo physical and/or chemical transformation in the Philippines. Using regression analysis on ten-year data on official foreign exchange and exports, two sector classifications are found not to be responsive to foreign exchange. These are: crude materials, excluding fuel (sector 2 of STCC), and animal and vegetable oils and fats (sector 4 of STCC). Other nonresponsive exports included logs, lumber, plywood, and veneer, the exportation of which is regulated.

Table 1. Economic Cost of Foreign Exchange

Items	Variables/Equations	Unit	Value (1994)
Total imports	M	P million	598,028
Special transactions	SM	P million	102,894
Other nonresponsive imports	NM	P million	0
Net Imports	dM=M-SM-NM	P million	495,134
Total exports	X	P million	356,180
Special transactions	SX	P million	124,345
Reexports	RX	P million	4,781
Other nonresponsive goods	NX	P million	24,364
Net exports	dX=X-SX-RX-NX	P million	202,690
Trade deficit	dQ=dM-dX	P million	292,244
Import tariffs	IT	P million	81,405
Net tariff equivalent of QRs	TR	P million	6,873
Import tariff rate	tm=(IT+TR)/dM		0.18
Export taxes	XT	P million	0
Net tax equivalent of QRs	XX	P million	17
Export subsidies	XS	P million	0
Export tax rate	tx=(XT+XX-XS)/dX		0.00008
Elasticity of supply	es		1.89
Elasticity of demand	ed		-2.85
Weight on supply	Ws=es/[es-{ed*(dM/dX}]		0.21
Weight on demand	Wd=-{ed*(dM/dX)} / [es -{ed*(dM/dX)}]		0.79
Official exchange rate	OER	P/US$	26.42
Balanced Trade			
Shadow exchange rate	SER = Ws*OER*(1-tx) + Wd*OER*(1+tm)	P/US$	30.12
Shadow exchange rate factor	SERF = SER/OER		1.14
Standard conversion factor	SCF = OER/SER		0.88
Unbalanced Trade (if 100% sustainable)			
Equilibrium nominal exchange rate	EER = OER*{1+dQ/(es*dX-ed*dM)}	P/US$	30.72
Shadow exchange rate	SER = EER * {Ws*(1-tx)+Wd*(1+tm)}	P/US$	35.03
Shadow exchange rate factor	SERF = SER/OER		1.33
Standard conversion factor	SCF = OER/SER		0.75
Unbalanced Trade (if 60% sustainable)			
Fraction of current BOP deficit sustainable	F		0.60
Equilibrium nominal exchange rate	EER = OER*{1+((1-F)*dQ)/(es*dX-ed*dM)}	P/US$	28.14
Shadow exchange rate	SER = EER * {Ws*(1-tx)+Wd*(1+tm)}	P/US$	32.08
Shadow exchange rate factor	SERF = SER/OER		1.21
Standard conversion factor	SCF = OER/SER		0.82

Notes:
1. Other nonresponsive exports include crude materials excluding fuel, and animal and vegetable oil and fats found insensitive to foreign exchange rate movements, as well as exports of logs, lumber, veneer, and plywood, which are regulated and slapped with a 20 percent export duty.
2. Preliminary data on import tariffs from Department of Finance and on exports of logs, lumber, veneer, and plywood from the Forestry Management Bureau of the Department of Environment and Natural Resources.
3. QRs - quantitative restrictions.

Sources: Asian Development Bank, 1995. *Key Indicators*, and Foreign Trade Statistics of the Philippines.

19.   *Import Tariffs.* Special transactions and goods on consignment are considered dutyfree since the Tariff and Customs Code provides that refund or tax credit shall be allowed for the duties paid on imported articles used in the manufacture of exports, provided that exportation shall be made within one year after the importation of the materials. The import tariffs used include value added tax on imported goods.

20.   *Quantitative Restrictions on Imports.* According to Circular No. 1389 of the Bangko Sentral ng Pilipinas (BSP), the importation of certain commodities is regulated or prohibited for reasons of public safety, national security, international commitments, and development of the local industry. Such importation requires clearances from appropriate government agencies including the BSP. Among the regulated commodities, the importation of petroleum products; coal and coal derivatives; rice and corn; motor vehicles, parts, and components; and used trucks and automobile tires and tubes were examined.

21.   The importation of rice and corn is allowed only if there is a perceived shortage in the domestic market. The last importation of corn was made in 1990, while rice was imported in 1990 and 1993.

22.   Among the wide range of motor vehicles, available data on imports pertain only to used trucks and the Bus Importation Program. Under Phase I of the Bus Importation Program, 1,600 units will be allowed to be imported. However, from 1989 to 1993, only 1,544 units were actually imported compared with 1,728 approved. Under Phase II, 3,500 units were programmed for importation. However, from 1992 to 1994, only 2,160 units were actually imported compared with 5,006 approved. This experience implies that obtaining import permits was not a deterrent to free importation. Considering also that the available data from the Bureau of Import Services does not distinguish between CIF or FOB prices and that domestic prices are difficult to obtain, the impact of quantitative restrictions on motor vehicles and used trucks was not included in the computation of the average tariff.

23.   On refined petroleum products, the 1994 Tariff and Customs Code of the Philippines specifies tariff rates ranging from 10 to 20 percent. Products such as kerosene, aviation gas, gasoline, and liquified petroluem gas (LPG) carry an additional special duty of ₱1.00/liter. The rates of tariff equivalent of quantitative restrictions range from 9.7 percent to 110.7 percent (see Table 2). On coal and coal derivatives, the tariff equivalent does not deviate very much from the prescribed tariff rate because of a policy linking the domestic price of coal to its import price. Thus, the net tariff equivalent used in the SER computation pertains to coal and petroleum products, except fuel oil. Due to the cross-subsidization policy in petroleum product pricing, fuel oil is not subject to a specific tax. Thus, since its tariff equivalent is approximately equal to its tariff rate, the effect of quantitative restrictions on its importation is disregarded.

Table 2.   Tariff Equivalent of Quantitative Restrictions

	1994 Imports			1994 Prices			Tariff Rates			Net
	CIF $'000	Volume	Unit	Domestic	CIF	P/unit	Equiv.	TCC Rate	Spec. Duty	Tariff Equiv.
Coal	41,136	1,113	000 mt	1,200.00	976.37	P/mt	22.9%	20%		1,194.58
Diesel	314,958	14,672	000 bbls	6.46	3.57	P/li	81.0%	20%		192,223.64
Fuel oil	107,709	7,404	000 bbls	2.65	2.42	P/li	9.7%	10%		-306.21
Kerosene	15,241	657	000 bbls	6.47	3.85	P/li	67.9%	20%	+ P/li	3,351.57
Gasoline	38,543	1,431	000 bbls	9.43	4.48	P/li	110.7%	20%	+ P/li	26,355.68
Avgas	925	24	000 bbls	13.39	6.40	P/li	109.1%	20%	+ P/li	680.17
LPG	67,411	4,315	000 bbls	5.26	2.60	P/li	102.5%	10%	+ P/li	36,358.57
Total, $'000	585,924									260,164.20
Total, PM	15,478									6,872.76

Note: Tariff revenue may be overstated since petroluem products used for power generation are allowed a refund or tax credit up to 50 percent.

Source: Energy Regulatory Board, Department of Energy, Philippine Chamber of Coal Mines; and 1994 Tariff and Customs Code (TCC).

24.   *Export Taxes and Subsidies.* Although an export tax of 20 percent is levied on exports of logs, lumber, veneer and plywood, this is not included in the estimation of the average tax rate since the corresponding export value has already been deducted from total exports. Also, export subsidies were disregarded for three reasons. First, the data are not readily available. Second, export incentives are mainly in the form of duty-free importation of capital and intermediate inputs and there are no direct subsidies. Third, although the Board of Investments (BOI) grants income tax holidays to registered firms, previous studies showed that export incentives constitute very low effective output subsidy rates.

25.   *Quantitative Restrictions on Exports.* The calculation of the SER included the effects of restrictions on the exports of petroleum products (see Table 3). Export of petroleum products requires permits from the Department of Energy to ensure that the exportation will not lead to shortages in domestic supply. In the near future, however, this will not be the case in view of moves towards the deregulation of the petroleum industry. The large export tax equivalent is accounted for by the high domestic excise tax rates on petroleum products.

Table 3. Export Tax Equivalent of Quantitative Restrictions

	1994 Exports			1994 Prices			Export Tax Rate (%)		Net
	FOB ($'000)	Volume	Unit	Domestic	FOB	P/unit	Equiv.	TCC	Tax Equiv.
Fuel oil	9,065	925	000 bbls	2.65	1.63	P/li	62.9	0	581.50
Regular gas	914	41	000 bbls	8.95	3.71	P/li	141.5	0	58.00
Total, ($'000)	9,979								639.51
Total, PM	264								16.89

Source: Department of Energy, Energy Regulatory Board.

26.   *Weight on Demand and Supply.* The regression analysis conducted for imports and exports yielded demand and supply elasticities of -2.85 and 1.89 respectively. These elasticity values have been incorporated in the weights applied to demand and supply of foreign exchange.

27.   *Assumption on Sustainability.* In Case 3 below, 60 percent of the trade imbalance is assumed to be sustainable.

Results of SER Calculations

28.   The SER estimates for 1994 under a partly sustainable trade imbalance and under a balanced trade regime are shown in Table 4.

Table 4. SER Estimates for 1994

	Unbalanced Trade	Balanced Trade
Sustainability	60%	100%
Official exchange rate	26.42	26.42
Equilibrium nominal exchange rate	28.14	26.42
Shadow exchange rate	32.08	30.12
SER factor	1.21	1.14
Standard conversion factor	0.82	0.88

It is recommended that a SERF of 1.21 be used for the Philippines, equivalent to an SCF of 0.82.

APPENDIX 17
EXAMPLE OF AN ECONOMIC RATE OF RETURN:
AN IRRIGATION REHABILITATION PROJECT

1.   A project to rehabilitate an irrigation system covering 90,000 hectares of land has been proposed and costed. The main benefits from the rehabilitation would be an increase in the proportion of land that was irrigated, with corresponding increases in cropping intensity and yields. Also, the scheme at present requires a lot of maintenance work; there would be some decline in operation and maintenance costs with the project. The investment would take place over a three-year period and the life of the scheme with normal maintenance has been estimated at 25 years. The total cost of the investment including construction activities and institutional support during the implementation period is about Rs1,800 million. The annual operating and maintenance (O&M) costs will decline from Rs10 million to around Rs7.9 million.

2.   Table 1 shows the expected impact on area, cropping intensity, and yields without and with the project. Irrigated areas are used to grow rice, and these areas will increase with rehabilitation. Unirrigated areas are used to grow vegetables for the local market, and these areas will decrease with rehabilitation. Taking all these factors into account, it is expected that there will be a substantial increase in rice production from the irrigation scheme area, but an overall decline in vegetable production. For both rice and vegetable production, yield increases are expected to build-up uniformly to the with project levels of Table 1 over the first five years after full implementation.

Table 1.   Production Without and With the Project

Item	Unit	Without Project		With Project		Increment	
		Irrigated	Unirrigated	Irrigated	Unirrigated	Irrigated	Unirrigated
Area	ha	55,000	35,000	75,000	15,000	20,000	-20,000
Cropping intensity	%	130	110	180	130		
Yield, rice	mt/ha	2.4		2.9			
Yield, vegetables	mt/ha		5		6.5		
Production	mt	171,600	192,500	391,500	126,750	219,900	-65,750

3.   The project investment and O&M costs, together with the agricultural inputs and outputs, have been estimated at financial prices. They need to be reexpressed in economic prices. A shadow exchange rate factor of 1.33 has been estimated for the country and used in a number of other recent projects. In the project area, a shadow wage rate factor at domestic prices for hired labor of 0.8 has been estimated. Economic project costs and benefits will be estimated in national currency at the domestic price level, in the first instance using just these two general conversion factors.

4.   The farm-gate price of rice in the project area is Rs6,335 per metric ton. However, rice is imported into the country and the incremental rice as a result of the irrigation rehabilitation will substitute for imports. In economic prices, rice is valued at its cost insurance freight (CIF) price to the country, plus the additional costs of getting the rice to the project area where most of it will also be consumed. The cost breakdown of the border price equivalent value (BPEV) of rice is 80 percent foreign currency and 20 percent of other nontraded costs in the country. This cost breakdown is given in Table 2. Table 2 also gives the cost breakdowns of the financial price values of the other project outputs and inputs. The vegetables are grown and sold in the project area; they are not of sufficient quality to be considered for export or to substitute for imports. Other agricultural inputs are basically nontraded, except for fertilizers, which are imported with a small import tax and some handling and transport charges. Extra demand for fertilizer, as well as extra demand for other agricultural inputs, are valued at their supply price converted to economic values. The investment costs are a mixture of imported equipment and materials together with nontraded materials sourced locally, and labor that is surplus in the area. The institutional support costs are dominated by international consultants with a small expenditure on domestic consultants and office services. The O&M costs are predominantly labor costs, with some input of imported parts for equipment and nontraded construction materials.

Table 2. Cost Breakdowns and Conversion Factors

	Cost Breakdowns (%)				Conversion Factors
	Foreign Exchange	Labor	Taxes	Nontraded Goods	
Rice	80			20	1.26
Vegetables				100	1.00
Fertilizers	80		10	10	1.16
Labor		100			0.80
Other				100	1.00
Investment	50	30	5	15	1.06
O&M	10	60		30	0.91
Institutional Support	80	10		10	1.26
National Parameter	1.33	0.80	0.00	1.00	

Conversion factors using domestic price numeraire.

5.   The cost breakdowns of financial price values have been used, together with the SERF and SWRF, to derive a conversion factor for each project item. These are also shown in Table 2. At the domestic price level, several of the conversion factor values are above 1.0 showing mainly that the foreign exchange they use or save is worth more to the national economy than is given by the official exchange rate. On the other hand, the labor component of project items is revalued downward by the SWRF, which represents the opportunity cost of labor at the domestic price level.

6.   These conversion factors can be applied to the estimates of agricultural net output with and without the project. It is anticipated that input costs per ton will rise for irrigated rice

production compared with unirrigated, while inputs into vegetable production per ton will remain the same in quantitative terms without and with the project. Table 3 shows the effect of converting to economic prices for agricultural production in the without and with project cases. Despite lower economic than financial prices, the economic costs of rice production rise because of higher input use with the project. This is partly compensated for by the higher value given to rice output at economic prices. Nevertheless, the economic net output per ton of rice is less with the project than without the project. The project rice benefits come from the increase in area, cropping intensity and yield that the irrigation rehabilitation brings about. At the domestic price level, the nontraded vegetable output is valued the same at economic and financial prices. However, the economic cost of inputs into vegetable production is less than their financial cost and so there is an improvement in economic net output per ton and per hectare.

Table 3. Net Agricultural Output at Economic Prices (Rs per ton)

Inputs	Rice Without		Rice With		Vegetables	
	Financial	Economic	Financial	Economic	Financial	Economic
Fertilizer	100	116	600	698	0	0
Labor	300	240	400	320	600	480
Other	600	600	700	700	300	300
Total Inputs	1,000	956	1,700	1,718	900	780
Output	6,335	8,007	6,335	8,007	3,000	3,000
Net Output	5,335	7,051	4,635	6,289	2,100	2,220

Economic values in national currency at the domestic price level.

7.   These net output estimates at economic prices are used, together with the project investment and O&M costs at economic prices, to derive the project economic statement at shadow prices. Project economic costs and benefits are shown in Table 4. The project costs include the investment and O&M costs. It has also been assumed that one-tenth of irrigated and nonirrigated production will also be lost as a result of implementation activities. The project benefits include the agricultural net output with the project less the agricultural net output without the project, together with the saving in without project O&M costs. There is only one other adjustment that is taken into account. For both the rice output and the fertilizer input there is expected to be a change in relative price in the next few years. The real price of rice is expected to fall by about 26 percent over the next ten years. Over the same period, the real price of fertilizer is expected to rise by about 8 percent. Both estimates are taken from the World Bank Commodity Price projections. Taken together, these imply a decline in the value of net output of rice at economic prices that will in part offset the increases in cropping intensity, rice area and yields. These forecast changes in real prices have been used to adjust the estimate of incremental net output from rice production over the first ten years of the project.

8.   The economic internal rate of return (EIRR) calculated in Table 4 is 19.0 percent. This rehabilitation project is not a marginal project. There is no major nontraded input that needs to be revalued through a specific conversion factor; in other words there is no need for a second iteration of project economic analysis as described in the main text. However, this basic EIRR result should be subject to sensitivity and risk analysis to see how robust it is and where the project risks might lie (see Appendix 21).

Table 4. Project Economic Statement: Irrigation Rehabilitation Project

	Years							
	0	1	2	3	4	5	6	7-28[a]
Rice price forecast factor	1.000	0.879	0.782	0.774	0.763	0.755	0.744	0.741
Fertilizer price forecast factor	1.000	1.017	1.042	1.058	1.075	1.016	1.108	1.083
Costs (Rs m)								
Investment	553.9	553.9	553.9					
Institutional Support	94.8	94.8	94.8					
O&M				7.2	7.2	7.2	7.2	7.2
Total Costs	648.7	648.7	648.7	7.2	7.2	7.2	7.2	7.2
Benefits (Rs m)								
With Project (Net Output)								
Rice				1498.3	1523.2	1572.8	1573.2	1631.7
Vegetables				229.4	242.4	255.4	268.4	281.4
Without Project (Net Output)								
Rice	121.0	104.3	91.0	898.4	882.9	872.8	855.8	848.9
Vegetables	42.7	42.7	42.7	427.4	427.4	427.4	427.4	427.4
Without project O&M				9.1	9.1	9.1	9.1	18.3
Total Benefits	-163.7	-147.0	-133.7	702.7	679.2	679.6	636.6	640.0
Net Benefits	-812.4	-795.7	-782.4	604.0	457.3	530.1	560.4	631.7
Net Present Value @ 12%	1440.2							
EIRR	19.0%							

[a]   Some values change annually up to year 10.
Economic values using domestic price numeraire.

APPENDIX 18
EFFECT ON NET FOREIGN EXCHANGE AND BUDGET FLOWS:
AN EXAMPLE

1.   Some projects are sufficiently large to have a significant impact on the country's foreign exchange flows and on the government's budget. This applies particularly in small countries where a major project can impact on foreign and domestic currency flows. It can also apply in the case of large projects, in relatively large countries, especially where there is a persistent foreign or budgetary deficit. In such cases, it is useful to have a statement of the direct impact of a project on foreign exchange and government revenue and expenditure flows.

I.   NET FOREIGN EXCHANGE FLOWS

2.   The project resource flow at economic prices measures the total foreign exchange effect on the national economy. Some of these effects are indirect, such as the opportunity cost of local labor or the foreign exchange component of nontraded goods, while some of them are direct. A project will have a direct effect on the availability of foreign exchange through foreign exchange earned or saved as a result of incremental output, and as a result of the foreign exchange used in the provision of project inputs.

3.   The irrigation rehabilitation example of Appendix 17 can be used to illustrate a project's direct foreign exchange effect. That project used irrigation and incremental agricultural inputs to produce more rice and less vegetables. The incremental rice production has a direct foreign exchange effect in the form of savings of imported rice. The direct foreign exchange costs of the project are the proportions of project input costs that are foreign exchange expenditures, given in the cost breakdowns at Table 2 of Appendix 17. These include the foreign exchange component of investment costs, institutional support, operations and maintenance (O&M) with the project, and incremental fertilizer imports. The direct foreign exchange generated by the project includes the savings of incremental rice imports and the foreign exchange component of O&M without the project. These direct foreign exchange flows of the project are given in Table 1.

4.   The net direct foreign exchange flows are initially negative while investment is ongoing, and then become very large and positive as the incremental rice production substitutes for imports. The accumulated effect on net foreign exchange shows an accumulated negative effect at first, which turns positive as soon as the fifth year of the project. Overall, this irrigation rehabilitation project has a substantial and positive effect in terms of direct foreign exchange. The only problem consists of the large amounts of foreign exchange needed during the investment phase.

Table 1. Direct Foreign Exchange Flows
('000)

	Year 0	1	2	3	4	5	6	7	8	9	10
A. Before Financing											
OUTFLOWS											
Investment	262,500	262,500	262,500	0	0	0	0	0	0	0	0
O&M	0	0	0	788	788	788	788	788	788	788	788
Institutional support	60,000	60,000	60,000	0	0	0	0	0	0	0	0
Without Project											
Fertilizer cost, rice	1,373	1,396	1,430	14,529	14,758	13,941	15,215	15,101	14,966	14,872	14,872
With Project											
Fertilizer cost, rice	0	0	0	171,454	181,119	177,674	201,097	206,712	205,146	203,580	203,580
Total Net Outflows	321,127	321,104	321,070	147,712	167,149	164,521	186,669	192,399	190,947	189,496	189,496
INFLOWS											
Without Project											
Rice revenue	86,967	76,425	68,040	673,215	663,632	656,444	646,861	646,861	644,465	644,465	642,070
Present O&M	0	0	0	1,000	1,000	1,000	1,000	1,000	1,000	1,000	1,500
With Project											
Rice revenue	0	0	0	1,324,095	1,357,448	1,394,384	1,424,910	1,475,793	1,470,327	1,470,327	1,464,861
Total Net Inflows	-86,967	-76,245	-68,040	651,880	694,817	738,939	779,049	829,932	826,862	826,862	824,292
Direct Foreign Exchange Flows	-408,094	-397,530	-389,110	494,168	527,668	574,418	592,380	637,533	635,915	637,367	634,796
Accumulated Effect	-408,094	-805,624	-1,194,734	-700,566	-172,898	401,520	993,901	1,631,434	2,267,349	2,904,715	3,539,512
B. After Financing											
Net direct flows	-408,094	-397,560	-389,110	494,168	527,668	574,418	592,380	637,533	635,915	637367	634,796
Net loan payments	-309,638	-296,775	-270,610	61,855	61,855	61,855	61,855	61,855	61,855	61855	61,855
Foreign Exchange Flows After Financing	-98,456	-100,754	-118,500	432,313	465,813	512,563	530,525	575,678	574,060	575511	572,941
Accumulated effect	-98,456	-199,211	-317,711	114,601	580,414	1,092,978	1,623,503	2,199,181	2,773,241	3348752	3,921,693

Note: Loan covers direct foreign exchange investment costs only.

5.   The direct foreign exchange flows can be amended to allow for the effects of foreign borrowing. A loan is being provided by the Bank to cover the direct foreign costs of the investment costs and institutional support. It involves the usual ordinary capital resources (OCR) repayment terms consisting of a grace period corresponding to the investment period, a commitment fee of a proportion of undisbursed amounts during the investment period, and loan payments over the life of the project. The inflation adjusted real interest rate is almost 4 percent. The loan can be added as a foreign exchange inflow, the loan payments can be added as foreign exchange outflows.

6.   The loan reduces the initial foreign exchange outflows by meeting the foreign exchange component of initial costs; the initial outflows are reduced just to the annual interest and commitment charges. There is then a very rapid accumulation of foreign exchange from the first year of incremental production. At the end of the project life, after 25 operating years, there is a large accumulation of foreign exchange.

II.   GOVERNMENT BUDGET EFFECTS

7.   The irrigation rehabilitation project has a very positive impact overall on direct foreign exchange flows for the country. However it also involves a very substantial increase in budget expenditures. The project effect on the government budget depends on the project institutional structure. The government will be responsible for meeting initial investment and institutional support costs of the project. It will save the without project O&M costs. In addition, the project is designed so that the with project O&M costs are met by the farmers, both in kind for undertaking some maintenance activities and through an irrigation charge that covers the financial O&M costs. Hence with project O&M will become a financial contribution of the farmers and no longer draw on the government budget. In return for the initial investment expenditures, however, the government will receive very little in the way of tax revenue. Tax revenue will come in the form of the tax component of project costs (indicated in Appendix 17, Table 1), which includes a small tax on investment goods and a relatively small tax on imported fertilizers. (It has been calculated separately that the average farmer, even at the higher cropping intensities and yields with the project, will not be subject to income tax.)

8.   The net effect on the government budget is given in Table 2. There will be substantial budget expenditures for investment. These expenditures should be compared with the total government development budget and scheduled into the government's overall public investment program. They may be a large proportion of investment expenditures for the whole government or for the sector. The small amount of annual tax revenue can also be compared with the total government recurrent budget. It is expected to represent only a small increase in total government revenues. Table 2 also shows the accumulative effect on the government budget. The accumulative effect builds up as a negative amount during the investment period, and remains negative even beyond the end of the project.

Table 2. Effects on Government Budget
('000)

						Year					
	0	1	2	3	4	5	6	7	8	9	10
A. Before Financing											
EXPENDITURES											
Investment costs	525,000	525,000	525,000	0	0	0	0	0	0	0	0
Less without O&M	0	0	0	10,000	10,000	10,000	10,000	10,000	10,000	10,000	15,000
Net Expenditures	525,000	525,000	525,000	-10,000	-10,000	-10,000	-10,000	-10,000	-10,000	-10,000	-15,000
REVENUES											
Investment goods tax	26,250	26,250	26,250	0	0	0	0	0	0	0	0
Net fertilizer import tax	-172	-174	-179	19,866	20,986	20,587	23,301	23,951	23,770	23,589	23,589
Total Revenues	26,078	-26,076	26,071	19,866	20,986	20,587	23,301	23,951	23,770	23,589	23,589
Net Government Budget Effect	-498,922	-498,924	-498,929	29,866	30,986	30,587	33,301	33,951	33,770	33,589	38,589
Accumulated budget effect	-498,922	-997,846	-1,496,775	-1,466,909	-1,435,923	-1,405,336	-1,372,035	-1,338,084	-1,304,314	-1,270,725	-1,232,137
B. After Financing											
Net budget effect	-498,922	-498,924	-498,929	29,866	30,986	30,587	33,301	33,951	33,770	33,589	38,589
Net loan payments	-309,638	-296,775	-270,610	61,855	61,855	61,855	61,855	61,855	61,855	61,855	68,155
Total Budget Effect	-189,284	-202,149	-228,319	-31,989	-30,869	-31,268	-28,554	-27,904	-28,085	-28,267	-23,267
Accumulated effect	-189,284	-391,433	-619,752	-651,741	-682,610	-713,879	-742,433	-770,337	-798,422	-826,689	-849,956

Note: Project life extends to 25 operating years.

9.   The large negative impact on the government budget is ameliorated by the foreign loan in the investment period. However, the loan meets only the foreign exchange component of investment: there are still substantial budget net expenditures at the beginning of the project. When incremental outputs commence so also do loan payments. The loan payments exceed annual incremental tax revenues, and so the negative effect on the budget grows over time. (The accumulated negative budget effect at the end of the project is larger with the loan than without because of the loan charges.)

III.   CONCLUSIONS

10.   Taken together, these two statements of direct foreign exchange flows and net government budget flows provide further light on the project and its funding than is simply given by the EIRR. They demonstrate that the project will generate a substantial amount of net savings of foreign exchange, but, within the planned institutional structure, through substantial budgetary support of irrigation expenditures. The current design allows for meeting only irrigation O&M costs through irrigation charges on farmers; the question arises as to whether a proportion of the irrigation capital costs could also be passed on to the farmers to relieve the negative accumulative impact on the government budget. This question should be addressed in the context of a financial analysis of the incremental net incomes for farming households.

APPENDIX 19
LEAST-COST ANALYSIS AND CHOOSING BETWEEN ALTERNATIVES

1.   Least-cost analysis aims to identify the least-cost project option for supplying output to meet forecast demand. The selection of the least-cost project from mutually exclusive, technically feasible project options promotes productive efficiency. By itself, least-cost analysis does not provide any indication of the economic feasibility of the project since even a least-cost project may have costs that exceed its benefits. Where least-cost analysis ends, benefit-cost analysis begins by comparing the cost stream of the least-cost solution with the benefit stream to determine whether the net present value is positive.

2.   Least-cost analysis enables the ranking of mutually exclusive project options, alternative ways of producing the same output of the same quality. Since benefits are the same, it is necessary only to compare costs and to select the alternative with the lowest present value of cost, discounted by the opportunity cost of capital. Alternative options may consist of different designs, technologies, sizes, and time phasing of what is essentially the same project. A project alternative may also consist of the same project in an alternative location. Being mutually exclusive, the project options must be realistic, such that the selection of one project means the rejection of others. In comparing project options, least-cost analysis must be based on economic prices. In cases where the benefits of mutually exclusive projects are not the same, that is, there are differences in output or service quality, a normalization procedure must be undertaken to ensure equivalence.

3.   For project alternatives that deliver the same benefits, it is possible to estimate the equalizing discount rate between each pair of mutually exclusive options for comparison. The equalizing discount rate (or the cross over discount rate) is the discount rate at which the preference changes. It is also the rate at which the present values of the two cost streams are equal.

I.   LEAST-COST ANALYSIS: EXAMPLE

4.   Consider a geothermal power plant with an aggregate capacity of 880 MW in 16 units of 55 MW each. The most technically feasible project alternative is a 900-MW coal-fired plant in 3 units of 300 MW each. Since the coal-fired plant generates a little more electricity than the geothermal plant, the cost stream of the geothermal plant is normalized by including the foregone benefits from the output differential priced at long run marginal cost. While capital outlays for the geothermal project start earlier than the coal project due to steamfield development, its operating costs are lower. The coal plant's recurrent costs are much higher due to coal inputs. Table 1 presents the present worth of both project options at discount rates of 8 and 13 percent. The ranking of the geothermal and coal alternatives, based on the cost stream with the lowest present worth, may change between lower and higher discount rates. If

the opportunity cost of capital is 8 percent, the geothermal project is selected. On the other hand, if the opportunity cost of capital is 13 percent, the coal-fired project with the delayed investment constitutes the least-cost option. Between 8 and 13 percent, the least-cost option changes from the geothermal plant to the coal-fired plant. The equalizing discount rate at which the switchover occurs is estimated at 10.1 percent. The equalizing discount rate is less than the hurdle rate of 12 percent. The additional costs of the geothermal alternative are not worthwhile. The coal-fired alternative should be chosen.

**Table 1. Choosing Between Power Project Alternatives
Through the Equalizing Discount Rate**

Year	Alternative 1: Geothermal			Alternative 2: Coal-fired			Difference in Cost Streams
	Capital + O&M	Present Worth @		Capital + O&M	Present Worth @		
		8%	13%		8%	13%	
0	200	200	200	150	150	150	50
1	3,000	2,778	2,655	150	139	133	2,850
2	9,000	7,716	7,048	4,500	3,858	3,524	4,500
3	16,000	12,701	11,089	9,800	7,780	6,792	6,200
4	20,000	14,701	12,266	13,000	955	7,973	7,000
5	8,000	5,445	4,342	11,900	8,099	6,459	-3,900
6	8,000	5,041	3,843	7,500	4,726	3,602	500
7	1,370	799	582	4,690	2,737	1,994	-3,320
8	1,370	740	515	4,690	2,534	1,764	-3,320
9	1,370	685	456	4,690	2,346	1,561	-3,320
10	1,370	635	404	4,690	2,172	1,382	-3,320
11	1,370	588	357	4,690	2,011	1,223	-3,320
12	1,370	544	316	4,690	1,862	1,082	-3,320
13	1,370	504	280	4,690	1,725	958	-3,320
14	1,370	466	248	4,690	1,597	847	-3,320
15	1,370	432	219	4,690	1,478	750	-3,320
16	1,370	400	194	4,690	1,369	664	-3,320
17	1,370	370	172	4,690	1,268	587	-3,320
18	1,370	343	152	4,690	1,174	520	-3,320
19	1,370	317	134	4,690	1,087	460	-3,320
20	1,370	294	119	4,690	1,006	407	-3,320
Total		55,699	45,590		58,673	42,831	
Incremental IRR							10.1%

Notes:
1. Investment cost for Geothermal Plant includes steamfield development.
2. Costs streams are expressed in economic terms at constant prices.
3. With different plan factors, station use, and transmission losses, net power generation is the same, project options can be considered mutually exclusive projects with the same benefits.

II.   LEAST-COST ANALYSIS: AVERAGE INCREMENTAL ECONOMIC COSTS

5.   Alternatively, if the effect or outcome of project alternatives is a homogeneous product of the same quantity and quality, the average incremental economic cost (AIEC) can be estimated. Consideration of the AIEC aims to establish the project alternative with the lowest per unit costs. The AIEC is the ratio of the present value of the incremental investment and annual costs to the present value of incremental output.

6.   Selecting the least-cost option through a comparison of the AIECs can be illustrated by the following example. Table 2 presents the cost streams of two alternative water supply projects where the source of water for alternative 1 is surface water while alternative 2 involves drilling for groundwater. At a discount rate of 12 percent, alternative 1 is selected, being the least-cost option as indicated by the lower AIEC. However, the choice changes if the discount rate is reduced below 7 percent, when the AIEC for the groundwater option will be lower than for the surface water.

**Table 2. Choosing Between Water Project Alternatives
Through the Average Incremental Economic Cost**

Year	Alternative 1: Surface Water					Alternative 2: Groundwater					Difference in Total Costs
	Capital + O&M	Other Costs	Total Costs	Water Sales	Adjusted Water Sales*	Capital + O&M	Other Costs	Total Costs	Water Sales	Adjusted Water Sales	
0	3,000	0	3,000	0	0	5,500	0	5,500	0	0	-2,500
1	2,000	0	2,000	0	0	200	0	200	0	0	1,800
2	300	30	330	200	258	200	40	240	200	258	90
3	300	31	331	208	268	200	42	242	208	268	89
4	300	32	332	216	279	200	44	244	216	279	89
5	300	34	334	225	290	200	45	245	225	290	89
6	300	35	335	234	302	200	46	246	234	302	89
7	300	36	336	243	314	200	48	248	243	314	89
8	300	38	338	253	326	200	49	249	253	326	89
9	300	39	339	263	340	200	51	251	263	340	89
10	300	41	341	274	353	200	52	252	274	353	89
11	300	43	343	285	367	200	54	254	285	367	89
12	300	44	344	296	382	200	56	256	296	382	89
13	300	46	346	308	397	200	57	257	308	397	89
14	300	48	348	320	413	200	59	259	320	413	89
15	300	50	350	333	430	200	61	261	333	430	89
16	300	52	352	346	447	200	63	263	346	447	89
17	300	54	354	360	465	200	65	265	360	465	89
18	300	56	356	375	483	200	67	267	375	483	89
19	300	58	358	390	503	200	70	270	390	503	89
20	300	61	361	405	523	200	72	272	405	523	89
Net Present Values @ 12%		7,012		2,175			7,320		2,175		-308
Incremental IRR											7%
AIEC				3.22					3.37		

*   Water supplied by the project is assumed to be distributed as follows: 70% sold and paid for, 10% sold but not paid for (bad debts), 10% consumed but not sold (nontechnical losses), and 10% technical losses. Water sales are therefore adjusted to include bad debts and nontechnical losses, i.e., water sales are adjusted by the ratio of water consumed (90%) to water paid for (70%) or 1.29 times water sales.

Notes:
(1) All costs expressed in economic terms at constant prices.
(2) Other costs include opportunity cost of water, depletion premium, and effluent costs.

III.   COST-EFFECTIVENESS ANALYSIS

7.   Least-cost analysis is applied to projects where the effects or outcomes can be quantified and priced. In other cases, where project effects can be identified but not adequately valued, project selection may be based on the results of cost-effectiveness analysis (CEA). The purpose of cost-effectiveness analysis is to find the means (activity, process, or intervention) that minimizes resource use to achieve the desired results; or in the presence of resource constraints, the means that maximizes results. In CEA, the objective of the process or intervention need not be expressed in monetary terms. It can be applied to any process or intervention, provided the objective is quantifiable.

8.   For example, CEA may be applied in the health sector. However, quantifying the objectives of health sector projects in terms of a common denominator is not always easy, since the ultimate objective of health care is good health and long life. While a health sector project may aim to reduce the incidence of illness, death, or disability, illness and disability tend to vary in duration and severity. A common denominator is therefore necessary to assess the impacts of individual health disorders and the cost-effectiveness of various interventions.

9.   In the health sector, project effects may be expressed in terms of disability-adjusted life years to estimate the burden of disease. In other cases, the concept of quality-adjusted life year or healthy life day is used. Cost-effectiveness may also be measured in terms of births averted as in population control projects. An important limitation of CEA is that a number of other interventions could also affect project outcomes. The project alternative under consideration needs to be separated from these other effects.

10.   The procedure for calculating the health effects of health care programs assumes that the amount of health a society has is measured by the number of healthy life days its population lives as a proportion of the total potential number of healthy life days people could enjoy in the absence of disease. Where a person availing of service from a health care program can extend his or her healthy life by a year, there is a gain of 365 healthy life days. CEA involves the calculation of the ratio of the discounted present value of program costs to net health effects, as in the following illustration.

11.   In improving a certain population's health status, a combination of vaccination programs and village health worker programs are being considered. The results of an epidemiological study reveal that a vaccination program is estimated to save between 50 and 75 healthy life days per vaccination while a village health worker program is estimated to save between 7 and 15 healthy life days per visit. Different program designs are compared, providing different combinations of vaccinations and visits and having different cost implications, as presented in Table 3. Since Program 2 is indicated to have the least cost at $4.71 per healthy life day, it is the most cost-effective solution.

**Table 3. Choosing Between Health Project Alternatives
Through Cost-Effectiveness Analysis**

		Program 1	Program 2	Program 3
1	Annualized cost, $	300,000	200,000	160,000
2	Number of VHW visits per year	2,000	2,500	2,100
3	HLDs saved by VHW visits			
	(number of VHW visits x 10 HLDs per visit)	20,000	25,000	21,000
4	Number of vaccinations	500	350	200
5	HLDs saved by vaccinations			
	(number of vaccination x 50 HLDs per vaccination)	25,000	17,500	10,000
6	Total HLDs saved	45,000	42,500	31,000
7	Cost per HLD saved, $	6.67	4.71	4.16

VHW = village health worker
HLD = healthy life day

12.   The most cost-effective solution is not necessarily the most effective. Program 2 is the most cost-effective solution, but Program 1 will save more healthy life days. The problem is that it will do so at a higher cost. The annualized cost of Program 1 exceeds that of Program 2 by $100,000. It generates an extra saving of 2,500 HLDs. The cost of the extra HLDs generated by Program 1 are therefore $40 each. If Program 2 can be duplicated or expanded, it will generate the most HLDs saved for a given budget. However, if there is a constraint on expanding one of the components of Program 2, for example, a shortage of village health visitors, then a decision should be taken as to whether the extra HLDs of Program 1 are worth the cost of achieving them.

13.   Because of the uncertainty involved in forecasting future demand and the complex interrelationships between the cost of output and the price charged, least-cost analysis should be an iterative process. The analysis should also take into account the value of flexibility, that is, the ability to adapt to changing demand conditions. For example, in the case of uncertain demand in a water supply project, it may be more costly but preferable to consider postponing the start of construction until demand is more certain, employing more flexible technology, or staging construction. Adding capacity in small amounts gives the water enterprise flexibility, but is also more costly. Hence, it is important to be able to value this flexibility. One way to do this is to find out how much lower the capital cost of the smaller plant would have to be to make it the preferred choice. The economies of scale associated with the larger, cheaper option would have to be equal to, or greater than, that amount to make giving up flexibility of the smaller project economical.

APPENDIX 20
ESTIMATING THE ECONOMIC OPPORTUNITY COST OF CAPITAL

1.   The economic opportunity cost of capital (EOCK) is the weighted average of the demand and supply price of capital. The demand price for investible funds can be determined by the marginal productivity of capital and the supply price of savings by the social rate of time preference. The EOCK will therefore equal the opportunity cost of the marginal unit of investible funds to both investors and savers. While Bank practice is to use 12 percent as a hurdle rate, this does not necessarily reflect the cost of capital in a particular DMC. A different discount rate may be used in appraising projects provided that it is based on a country-specific estimation of the EOCK.

2.   To ensure that a proposed project contributes positively to the country's economic output, the project must generate a rate of return at least equal to the economic return foregone from deferred investments, plus the cost of any funds borrowed abroad to finance the project. In a closed economy, the additional demand for funds of a new project will be met either by displacing other projects from the capital market, or by inducing savers to supply additional savings. The financing required for the new project increases the demand for funds and the financial cost of funds. The higher rate of interest forces some of the existing demanders of funds to postpone their projects, thereby reducing the quantity demanded. At the same time, this rate induces some new savers to postpone their consumption and increase the supply of savings. The opportunity cost of funds used by the project is therefore the weighted average of the foregone marginal product of the displaced investment and the value of the foregone consumption. In principle, both of these values should be estimated in shadow prices in the appropriate numeraire.

3.   The estimation of the EOCK is closely linked to the capital market, which allows the injection into, or sourcing of, funds from the rest of the economy. The weight of the impact of savings and investments on the EOCK may be expressed in terms of elasticities of demand and supply of funds with respect to changes in the financial cost or rate of return. Interest rates are basically determined by the willingness of both domestic residents and foreigners to save, as well as by the availability of investment opportunities. However, due to taxes, inflation, and risk premiums, the market interest rate will generally not reflect either saver's time preference for consumption or the economic return generated by investments.

4.   The estimation of the EOCK should allow for the impact of several groups of savers and investors by incorporating their respective elasticities, rates of return, and rates of time preference. Investors may be grouped into categories that generate different rates of return, such as corporations, small scale industries, agriculture, and housing; while savers may be divided into groups of low-income households, middle-income households, and high-income households. With foreign borrowing, the analysis essentially remains the same. The difference is that the interest rate of borrowing has to be adjusted upward because the additional

borrowing from capital markets is usually available at a higher interest rate as compared to the interest charged on previous loans. The marginal cost that is relevant is given by the sum of the cost of borrowing of the additional unit and the extra financial burden on all other borrowings that are responsive to the market interest rate.

5.   For an open economy that is not heavily indebted, the supply curve for investible funds will be elastic. In this case, capital will be a traded good for the country and EOCK will be the world supply price of capital. This will be the interest rate at which the country can borrow on the international capital market, typically LIBOR plus some premium specific to a country. This can be seen in Figure 1 where the relevant supply curve for capital is not the domestic supply curve S_D but the perfectly elastic world supply curve S_W. Although the project demand for capital shifts the after-tax demand curve from D to $D(+P)$, this does not affect the cost of capital, which will remain at the world cost of capital, i_w.

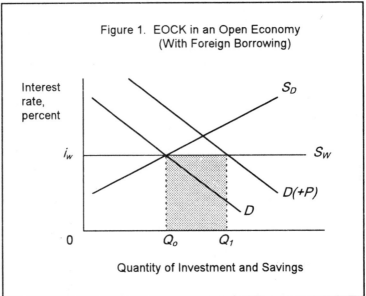

Figure 1. EOCK in an Open Economy
(With Foreign Borrowing)

6.   Table 1 presents an estimate of the EOCK for the Philippines in 1993. The shares of each class of saver (S_i/S_t) and investor (I_i/S_t) in total savings and investments is calculated from the gross savings and gross investments in the 1993 flow of funds summary matrix. Households include noncorporate business, while business includes financial intermediaries. The nominal interest rate (i_m) for domestic savers is the Treasury Bill rate for 1993. The average interest rate from new commitments from private creditors of 6.7 percent is used as the interest on foreign borrowing (i_f), adjusted for a 20 percent withholding tax imposed by the Philippines on all foreign loans. The tax rate for savers (t_i) refers to withholding tax on savings. The foreign inflation rate is represented by the average annual weighted trade price deflator. The proportion of total borrowing (k) responsive to the interest on foreign

Table 1. Economic Opportunity Cost of Capital, Philippines 1993

Reference	Item	Variables	Households	Business	Government	Foreign
1	Savers: Share	S_i/S_t	43.08%	20.81%	30.51%	5.60%
2	Nominal interest rate	i_s	12.45%	12.45%	12.45%	8.04%
3	Tax rate	t_s	20.00%	0.00%	0.00%	20.00%
4	Proportion of total borrowing responsive to foreign interest rate	k				32.21%
5	Return on savings/nominal marginal cost of foreign borrowing	$n_s = i_s*(1-t_s)$	9.96%	12.45%	12.45%	7.81%
6	Inflation rate	p	7.60%	7.60%	7.60%	-0.37%
7	Real return/real marginal cost of foreign borrowing	$r_s = (n_s-p)/(1+p)$	2.19%	4.51%	4.51%	8.08%
8	Elasticity	e_s	0.5000	0.0	0.0	1.5000
	Group weight	e_s*S_i/S_t	0.2154	0.0	0.0	0.0840
	Group weight * real return	$e_s*(S_i/S_t)*r_s$	0.0047	0.0	0.0	0.0068
	Sum of Group Weights	A	0.2994			
	Sum of Group Weights * Real Return	B	0.0115			
1	Investors: Share	I_i/S_t	30.77%	22.50%	26.46%	20.28%
9	Nominal interest/earnings rate	i_r	14.56%	20.00%	14.56%	30.00%
	Real return on investment	$r_r = (i_r-p)/(1+p)$	6.47%	11.52%	6.47%	30.49%
8	Elasticity	e_r	-1.0000	-1.0000	0.0	-1.0000
	Group weight	e_r*I_i/S_t	-0.3077	-0.2250	0.0	-0.2028
	Group weight * real return	$e_r*(I_i/S_t)*r_r$	-0.0199	-0.0259	0.0	-0.0618
	Sum of Group Weights	C	-0.7354			
	Sum of Group Weights * Real Return	D	-0.1076			
10	Economic Opportunity Cost of Capital	EOCK=(B-D)/(A-C)	11.51%			

Reference:
1. Flow of Funds Summary Matrix by Sector from Annual Reports of Bangko Sentral ng Pilipinas. Savers' shares from gross savings. Investors' shares from gross investment.
2. 1994 International Monetary Fund, International Financial Statistics. For households, business, and government, Treasury Bill rate is used. World Trade Tables (1994-1995): External Finance for Developing Countries, vol. 2, World Bank. For the foreign sector, interest rate is the average for new commitments from private creditors of 6.7% which is adjusted for withholding tax imposed on all loans contracted after 1 August 1986, pursuant to Chapter 3, section 25 of the National Internal Revenue Code
3. Tax rate for savers (t_s) refer to withholding tax on savings. t_s for households is the average income rate for individual taxpayers, from a study of the National Tax Research Center from actual income returns filed for 1988.
4. World Debt Tables (1994-95). k=ratio of Philippine debt from private creditors and nonguaranteed private debt to total debt outstanding. k refers to average ratio from 1990-1993.
5. Nominal marginal cost of foreign borrowing = $i_s*(1-t_s)*(1+k*(1/e_s))$.
6. Philippine Statistical Yearbook, 1994 for domestic inflation rate. 1995 ADB Key Indicators of Developing Asian and Pacific Countries for calculating average annual weighted trade price deflator (1981-1991) as foreign inflation rate.
7. Real marginal cost of foreign borrowing = $((n_s*(1+t_s)-p/(1+p))*(1+k*(1/e_s))$.
8. Elasticities are estimates based on information from similar economies.
9. Earnings rate for households and government at lending rates. For business and foreign sectors, return on equity was computed from top 5000 corporations, but 15.7% was considered too low to attract investments. Thus, rates of 20% and 30% were assumed for business and foreign sectors, respectively. If rates of 25% and 35% are used, the EOCK will be 13.15%.
10. This estimate is made at real financial prices.

borrowing is the 1990-1993 average ratio of Philippine debt from private creditors and nonguaranteed private debt to total debt outstanding.

7.   The elasticity of supply of savings (e_i) and the elasticity of demand for investment (n_j) are based on information from similar economies. The EOCK in the Philippines in 1993 is estimated at 11.5 percent. This estimate of the EOCK is in real financial prices. In principle, it should be converted to an equivalent value in real economic prices. In most cases, this conversion does not make much difference to the final numerical value. At the aggregate level, the EOCK of 11.5 percent can be interpreted as the ratio of net output derived from investment. This ratio can be adjusted by the ratio of the appropriate conversion factors.

$$\text{Adjustment} \quad = \quad \frac{\text{Conversion Factor for output}}{\text{Conversion Factor for investment}}$$

Whichever numeraire is used in the economic analysis, the ratio of these two conversion factors (CFs) will be the same. In general, the CF for output in general will be less than the CF for investment, because investment goods are typically less protected.. However, the adjustment is generally close to 1.0, and the difference in the rate at economic and financial prices is small.

APPENDIX 21
THE TREATMENT OF UNCERTAINTY IN THE ECONOMIC ANALYSIS OF PROJECTS: SENSITIVITY AND RISK ANALYSIS

I.   INTRODUCTION

1.   The economic internal rate of return (EIRR) of a project is calculated using the most likely forecast values of economic benefits and costs. However, the stream of benefits and costs is influenced by a wide variety of factors that may vary from the base case. Sensitivity analysis shows the extent to which the project EIRR or net present value (NPV) changes for different values of the major variables. Quantitative risk analysis considers the probability that different values will occur, and summarizes the associated risk attached to the project. These techniques can be used to assess the implications of uncertainty for the choice between project alternatives or for project viability.

2.   Both sensitivity and risk analysis focus on alternative assumptions that have an unfavorable effect on the project result. Where the project outcome depends upon one or two major variables that are uncertain, mitigating actions should be included in the project design. Where a high level of risk is associated with a project that promises substantial returns, then the decision of whether to accept the project or not in its present design will depend on the decisionmakers' attitude to risk.

3.   Sensitivity analysis should be applied to all projects and subprojects with quantified benefits and costs. It should be applied also to project financial analysis and to the environmental components of project analysis where these have been quantified. The purpose in all cases is to identify actions that can mitigate the effects of uncertainty, or to redesign the institutional structure of the project to ensure sustainability. It should also be applied to projects, such as in education, health, and family planning , where benefits may not have been fully quantified. In such cases, sensitivity analysis can be oriented around a summary project measure, such as the unit economic cost of providing a new service.

II.   SENSITIVITY ANALYSIS

4.   Sensitivity analysis is undertaken to help identify the key variables that can influence the project cost and benefit streams. It involves recalculating the project results for different values of major variables where they are varied one at a time. Combinations of changes in values can also be investigated. Sensitivity analysis involves four steps:

- selecting those variables to which the project decision may be sensitive;
- determining the extent to which the value of such variables may differ from the base case;
- calculating the effect of different values on the project results by recalculating the project NPV and EIRR; and
- interpreting the results and designing mitigating actions.

5.   Project statements are made up from underlying project data and assumptions. For example, vehicle operating cost savings are made up from traffic projections for different proportions of vehicle type, their division into without project and generated traffic, data on road quality and maintenance operations, and data on the vehicles and their operating costs. Sensitivity analysis of the project benefits for a road improvement project should be based on changes in such underlying variables rather than the aggregate benefit measure. Focusing on underlying rather than aggregate variables facilitates the design of actions to mitigate against uncertainty.

6.   Some of the variables entering into the project cost and benefit streams will be predictable and small in value compared with total costs and benefits. It is not necessary to investigate the sensitivity of the project to such variables. Other variables may be larger and less predictable. Postevaluation studies and previous project experience may indicate both the type of variable that is uncertain and the likely extent of divergence from the base case value. There are some types of variable in every project that are likely to affect the project result and may be key variables for the project.

7.   The quantities of inputs required to produce the expected quantity of outputs will be given in the corresponding technical feasibility study. However this is often subject to considerable uncertainty. Inadequate supplies or maintenance can change the ratio between inputs and outputs and reduce project outputs. In addition, the quantity of output produced for a given set of input supplies will depend upon the incentives created for producers. Changes in management, improved skills, and financial returns to the producer will all influence the output produced from the available inputs. Consideration should be given to both the technical and institutional characteristics of the project as a guide to sensitivity analysis.

8.   Quantities of outputs and inputs can also be affected by changes in technical or market conditions. Quantities should be broken down into their underlying components—for example, agricultural outputs into areas and yields, or vehicle cost savings by type of vehicle, or construction costs into unit costs and quantities—and the sensitivity of the project to each of the components considered. Output quantities will also depend upon demand forecasts and market analyses. The underlying assumptions of these forecasts and analyses should be subject to sensitivity analysis.

9.   Changes in the major values in the project statements—the main outputs, inputs, and investment costs—may occur because of changes in prices for any of these items. Changes can occur in the market prices or shadow prices used in calculating costs and benefits directly or used in the

estimation of opportunity costs. Commodity prices for major outputs and inputs can fluctuate considerably from year to year. The influence of the average annual forecast prices on the project worth should be tested by varying the forecasts, which should take into account the effect of possible changes in the quality of outputs over time on prices. The prices of labor and nontraded goods can also be subject to change although these might not have the same degree of impact on the project worth.

10.   The timing and coordination of project activities may differ from the basecase. The timing of investment costs that occur early in the project life can affect the measure of project worth considerably. Alternative timings incorporating pessimistic assumptions about construction delays should be assessed. Different investment components need to be coordinated, for example, dam completion and resettlement in irrigation projects. The possible costs of delay in one investment component on the others should be investigated through alternative timing assumptions.

11.   Project results can be seriously affected by the extent to which the investment assets are utilized. Lower utilization rates than in the basecase will be reflected in lower output levels and lower operational costs, but without any decline in investment costs. Utilization is commonly expressed as a percentage of feasible capacity use. The effects of a reduction in the rate of utilization should be investigated through adjustments to both benefit and cost streams, where possible distinguishing between fixed and variable costs.

12.   Economic analyses of projects involve the estimation of opportunity costs for the outputs and inputs. In most calculations economic costs and benefits are calculated by using the ratio of the shadow price of a project item, or the resources that go into it, to its market price. The effect of the estimated ratios on the project worth should be investigated through sensitivity analysis. Except for the most labor intensive projects, it is rare that a project result would be significantly affected by a variation of the shadow wage rate for surplus labor; and for most projects, variation in the shadow wage rate for scarce labor is also unlikely to be significant. More significant will be the value assumed for the shadow exchange rate (SER) and therefore the shadow exchange rate factor (SERF), or the standard conversion factor (SCF), whichever numeraire is being used in the economic analysis. Alternative estimates of the SERF will affect both benefits and costs in the sensitivity analysis. Most simple estimates of the SERF (SCF) take account only of the tax and subsidy system and not of other factors separating financial and economic prices, such as monopoly rents; it is pertinent to include in the sensitivity analysis a higher value for the SERF (lower value for the SCF).

III.   PROCEDURE

13.   The following procedure should be followed when assessing the consequences of changes from base case values of major variables.

- Variables to which the project is likely to be sensitive, such as those referred to above, and for which there is some uncertainty, should be listed. Alternative values should be assumed, based on previous project data where available. The change in the value of the variable should be calculated and expressed as a percentage of the original value. The extent of change should be stated for those variables such as timing of activities where a percentage change is not meaningful.

- The project NPV and EIRR should be recalculated for stated changes in variables one at a time. Unless a different country estimate is available, the NPV should be calculated using an economic discount rate of 12 percent.

- A *sensitivity indicator (SI)* summarizing the effect of change in a variable on the project NPV should be calculated. The SI is calculated as the ratio of the percentage change in the NPV to the percentage change in a variable (see Addendum). A high value for this indicator indicates project sensitivity to the variable. For variables where percentage changes are not meaningful, the percentage change in the NPV should be stated along with the stated change in the variable.

- A *switching value (SV)* should also be calculated. Where the base case shows a positive NPV, the SV shows the percentage increase in a cost item (decline in a benefit item) required for the NPV to become zero (which is the same as the EIRR reducing to the cut-off level of 12 percent). The SV is itself a percentage, the percentage change in a variable for the project decision to change (see Addendum). It can be compared with the variation shown in postevaluation studies or in price forecasts. For many variables, the SV will be high, implying a very substantial change in the variable before the project decision is affected. For a few variables, the SV will be relatively low showing there may be a significant risk for the project outcome.

- In deriving the economic costs and benefits of a project, a SERF (or SCF) will have been used along with other general conversion factors. Sensitivity analysis should include changes in the SERF (SCF) and other general conversion factors to see to what extent the project results are sensitive to the conversion factors used in the analysis.

- The change in the NPV should be calculated for combinations of variables, for example, a lower level of demand and a delay in investment completion, or an increase in cost together with a lower output price. The rationale for any combination of variables should be stated, bearing in mind that changes in more than one variable may have a common cause.

- The results of the sensitivity analysis should be presented in a table showing the base case results, the change in each variable considered, the sensitivity indicator, the switching value, and the changes in project worth for cases where these indicators cannot be calculated, or for combinations of variables. The table should include the consequences of alternative values relating to all technical, economic, environmental, and distributional aspects of the project.

14.   The results of the foregoing sensitivity analysis should be reviewed considering the following questions:

- Which are the variables with high SIs?
- Have the calculations used the likely changes in these variables?
- Do the likely changes come close to, or exceed, the switching values that will change the project decision?
- How likely is it that the combinations of the variables investigated will occur?

These questions will help identify the truly key variables for the project, those that have a substantial effect on the project results, where plausible changes come close to or exceed their switching values. For the key variables identified in this way, a statement should be made of the likelihood of the variation tested actually occurring, the switching values for the key variables that should provide a basis for project monitoring, and the measures that could be taken to mitigate or reduce the likelihood of such variations from the basecase.

15.   Where projects are seen to be sensitive to specific variables, steps should be taken to reduce the extent of uncertainty surrounding those variables. This may require actions at the project, sector, or national level, for example:

At the project level

- the agreement of long-term supply contracts at specified quality and prices to reduce uncertainty over operating costs;
- the formulation of training activities to ensure technical ratios are achieved and maintained;
- the development of information or publicity programs to increase access and use of new goods or services;
- the incorporation of external effects into project costs through regulation or taxation to ensure they are taken into account; and
- where there is considerable uncertainty in a large project or program, the implementation of a pilot project or phase to test technical assumptions and to observe users' reactions.

At the sector level

- tariff and price adjustments to ensure appropriate incentives for producers and the financial liquidity of implementing agencies;
- technical assistance programs to develop project and operational management skills; and
- loan covenants to prompt necessary institutional reforms.

At the national level

- changes in tax and credit policy to influence incentives and simplify procedures;
- implementation of legislative reform and regulation to provide a more certain framework for productive activities; and
- changes in exchange rate and fiscal management to provide greater stability in prices and costs.

IV.   SENSITIVITY ANALYSIS: AN EXAMPLE

16.   The irrigation rehabilitation project example of Appendix 17 is used here to illustrate the application of sensitivity analysis. The project involves a predicted increase in cropped area for irrigated rice, in cropping intensity, and in yield, as a result of rehabilitation, with a compensating decline in vegetable cropped area. The base case result, EIRR of 19.0 percent and economic NPV of Rs1,440 million at 12 percent discount rate, is also based on a long-term relative economic price decline for rice and a long-term relative economic price increase for fertilizer. The main variables to which the base case may be sensitive, together with the possible changes in those variables, are selected as follows.

17.   On the basis of previous rehabilitation projects, there is uncertainty over the farmer response to improved irrigation. Postevaluation studies indicate the possibility of lower values for cropped rice area, cropping intensity and yield by 9, 10 and 6 percent, respectively. There is also uncertainty over the levels of cropping intensity and yield of both vegetables and rice, without the project. Increases in these variables of 10 percent have been included in the sensitivity tests.

18.   The forecast price of rice and fertilizer should be key variables in the project analysis, as the project will increase both the quantity of rice output and the quantity of fertilizer input. In the sensitivity analysis, the forecast price of rice, which declines over the first ten years of the project anyway, is predicted to follow the same pattern but to be at the level of the lower range of the 70 percent distribution given together with the basic World Bank price forecasts. This is equivalent to a price 39 percent lower than in the base case. On a similar basis, the fertilizer price is tested at a price 42 percent higher than in the base case, at the higher range of the 70 percent distribution.

19.   Other variables are also included in the sensitivity analysis. There have been delays in the implementation of previous projects. A two-year delay is considered here. The effect of a 10 percent higher investment cost is tested. The project benefits depend upon continued maintenance activities. Rather than a higher level of maintenance costs, the last five operating years of the project are excluded to allow for the possibility of inadequate maintenance activity. The two principal shadow price factors, the SERF and the SWRF, are subjected to

lower and higher values, respectively, by 10 percent. Finally, some combinations of variables are also tested.

20.   The results of these sensitivity tests on underlying and specific benefit and cost factors are given in Table 1. By observing the SVs in each case, very large changes are required in some variables for the project decision to change. This includes investment costs, the economic price of fertilizer, the cropped area for rice with the project transferred from vegetable production, and the SWRF. For some other variables, cropping intensity and yield for rice without the project, the SERF, and the reduced operating life because of inadequate maintenance, not so large but still unlikely differences from the base case would have to occur for the project decision to change.

Table 1. Results of Sensitivity Analysis: Irrigation Rehabilitation Project

Item	Change (%)	NPV (Rs mn)	IRR (%)	Sensitivity Indicator	Switching Value (%)
Base Case		1,440	19.0		
Costs					
Investment Costs	+10.0	1,291	17.9	1.03	97
Fertilizer, economic price	+42.1	753	15.8	1.13	88
Benefits					
Rice economic price	-38.9	-1,427	1.7	5.12	-20
With:					
Rice area	- 9	1,298	18.3	1.10	-91
Rice cropping intensity	- 10	446	14.3	6.90	-14
Rice yield	- 6	844	16.2	6.90	-14
Without:					
Rice cropping intensity	+ 10	873	16.3	3.94	25
Rice yield	+ 10	873	16.3	3.94	25
Vegetables yield	+ 10	1,162	17.7	1.93	52
Delay in Benefits				NPV declines by	
Two years		636	14.9	75 percent.	
Operating Life				NPV declines by	
Reduced five years		1,250	18.6	13 percent.	
Shadow Price Factors					
SERF	- 10	1,084	17.7	2.47	-40
SWRF	+ 10	1,383	18.6	0.40	253
Discount rate (14%)				NPV declines by	
		889	19.0	38 percent.	
Combinations					
A. Investment Cost	+ 10				
Fertilizer price	+ 10				
Rice, vegetable yield, with	- 10	- 16	11.9	10.10	
B. As A, plus					
Rice economic price	- 10	- 612	8.7	14.25	

IRR = Internal rate of return
NPV = Net present value.

21.   There are four variables to which the project is most sensitive and to which most attention should be paid. These include the economic price of rice, the cropping intensity, and the yield for rice with the project. The forecast values for these variables need only be less favorable by 20 and 14 percent for the project decision to change. The project result is also sensitive to delays in implementation. The first variable is outside the control of the producers and the country. The other three are part of the project design and implementation process, which the executing agency can affect with more or less success. The combination of higher costs and lower yields, which has also been tested, shows considerable sensitivity, together with the further combination also involving a lower economic price of rice.

22.   The following recommendations are made in the light of these results of the sensitivity analysis:

- The monitoring of benefits during and after implementation should particularly include the cropping intensity and yields for rice together with its economic price.
- There is considerable risk because the project returns are so dependent on rice production and there is a great degree of uncertainty about the future economic price of rice. Under institutional development, funds should be provided for research activities at an experimental level into alternative crops for diversification purposes, including higher quality vegetable crops.
- The domestic price for rice and the rice marketing system must be reviewed to ensure there is sufficient financial incentive for farmers to switch from vegetable to rice production in early project years, otherwise the economic benefits of the project will be delayed.

V.   QUANTITATIVE RISK ANALYSIS

23.   Quantitative risk analysis provides a means of estimating the probability that the project NPV will fall below zero, or that the project EIRR will fall below the opportunity cost of capital. This irrigation rehabilitation project is subject to uncertainty particularly with respect to cropping intensity and yields for rice together with its economic price. Risk analysis considers combinations of values for these major variables and the probability that they may occur.

24.   In this case, a quantitative risk analysis can be recommended because of the substantial combined risk associated with the main with project crop. The following information is required for each of these variables to conduct the risk analysis:

- the results of the sensitivity tests;
- a range of values above and below the base case value;
- an upper and lower bound and a value in between; and
- a probability of occurring for each of these values.

In this case, a forecast distribution for the price of rice is available from the commodity price projections of the World Bank and can be used to derive this information. Changes in rice yields with irrigation have also been investigated through a number of postevaluation studies for similar projects, and these studies can be used to define the distribution of values for rice yield. Less information is available about cropping intensities, and assumptions will have to be made for this particular variable.

25.   Quantitative risk analysis involves randomly selecting values for these three variables from the probability distributions that have been determined; combining these values with all other base case values to give an NPV result; and repeating such a calculation a large number of times to provide a large number of NPV estimates. These NPV estimates can be summarized in a distribution. The key feature of this distribution is the proportion of NPV values that fall below zero, and hence the probability that the project result might turn out to be unacceptable. There is no fixed criterion for using such a result. High risk probabilities may be associated with projects that have a high expected NPV. The probability of achieving a less than acceptable result is provided as part of the information on which a project decision is based.

VI.   ADDENDUM

1.   Calculation of Sensitivity Indicator

$$SI = \frac{NPV_b - NPV_1}{NPV_b} \div \frac{V_b - V_1}{V_b}$$

where V_b is the value of the variable in the base case
NPV_b is the value of the NPV in the base case
V_1 is the value of the variable in the sensitivity test
NPV_1 is the value of the NPV with the sensitivity test.

2.   Calculation of a Switching Value

$$SV = 100 * (NPV_b / (NPV_b - NPV_1)) * ((V_b - V_1)/V_b) \%$$

where the variables are defined as before.

3.   Example of SI and SV Calculation

The following results are obtained when the price of a project output is varied downward.

Base Case		**Sensitivity Results**	
NPV_b	900	NPV_1	720
V_b	10	V_1	8.5

Calculations:

$$SI = ((900 - 720) / 900) \div ((10 - 8.5) / 10)$$
$$= 0.2 \div 0.15$$
$$= 1.333$$

The percentage change in the NPV is greater than for the price.

$$SV = 100 * (900 / (900 - 720)) * ((10 - 8.5) / 10) \%$$
$$= 100 * 5 * 0.15 \%$$
$$= 75\%$$

The price of the output would need to be 75 percent lower for the NPV to fall to zero.

APPENDIX 22
USER CHARGES, COST RECOVERY, AND DEMAND MANAGEMENT:
AN EXAMPLE FOR PIPED WATER

1.   Competition for water is growing in many water basins throughout Asia. Urban and rural communities want more water than they can get. As water becomes scarce, polluted, and more costly to supply, investments in water-using projects must be looked at from an economic perspective. Water must be priced to minimize costs and maximize use values. This appendix sets out a method for evaluating pricing policies and demand management options that offset both the economic and financial returns from a project.

2.   In theory, the efficient price of water would be determined by supply and demand, with the marginal willingness to pay for water equaling the marginal cost of supplying water. In practice, nonmarket situations apply with the government setting the price for piped water. Assuming that the increasing cost of supply is minimized and that willingness to pay is not distorted by government policies, the economic price charged for water should be set equal to the average incremental economic cost (AIEC) of supply, or, if the AIEC is below the average incremental financial cost (AIFC) of supply, the financial price should be set equal to the AIFC of supply.[1]   Both the AIEC and AIFC should be based on the long-term, least cost expansion path of the water enterprise.

I.   SUBSIDY AND COST RECOVERY

3.   Piped water is typically supplied as a public service at subsidized prices. The difference between the average financial price of water and the AIFC is referred to as the *average financial subsidy*. The difference between the average economic price of water and the AIEC is referred to as the *average economic subsidy*. The economic subsidy may or may not overlap the financial subsidy, depending on the magnitude of nontechnical losses, and the extent of market distortions and environmental costs and benefits. The ratio of the average financial price to the AIFC shows the extent of financial cost recovery and the ratio of the average economic price to the AIEC shows the extent of economic cost recovery.

---

[1]   The AIEC of water is equal to the present value (at the economic cost of capital) of the stream of future capital and operating costs at real economic prices divided by the present value of the future quantity of water consumed (but not necessarily paid for). The AIFC of water is equal to the present value (at the financial cost of capital) of the stream of future capital and operating costs at real financial prices divided by the present value of the future quantity of water sold (and paid for).

II.   DEMAND MANAGEMENT

4.   The economic cost of subsidies paid to the piped water industry is often large. As a consequence of the high cost of subsidizing water, demand management can yield high economic savings, often much greater than the returns from supply expansion. The following example illustrates an approach to evaluating the economic merit of demand management relative to supply expansion. Depending on the price elasticity of demand, increasing the price of water will decrease the quantity of water demanded, increase sales revenue, cut back consumer surplus and operating costs, and, by postponing future expansion, reduce capital costs.

5.   The example compares the benefits and costs of supply expansion, with and without demand management. Table 1 sets out the costs and benefits of expanding supplies when the price charged for piped water is below cost. Project costs are converted to economic prices using the domestic price numeraire. The net economic benefit is positive, providing a rationale for expanding supplies and paying the financial subsidy. Table 2 sets out the costs and benefits of expanding supplies and managing demand. Increasing the price of water by 27.5 percent results in the water enterprise achieving full cost recovery. At this higher water price the demand is lower and all the costs of water are recovered, including the opportunity cost of capital. However, investment has also been scaled down as a result of the lower projected demand. Allowing also for water that is used but not paid for, the scaling down of investment allows the AIEC to remain constant, at a level somewhat below the AIFC in this case.

Table 1. Supply Expansion (Financial Price below AIFC)

				Financial Costs				
	Financial Price	Quantity Demanded	Financial Benefit	Capital	O&M	Financial Cost	Net Finan-cial Cost	Economic Cost
Year	A	B	C=A*B	D1	D2	D=D1+D2	E+C-D	F
0				2,393		2,393	(2,393)	2,632
1	0.40	1,000	400		87	87	313	96
2	0.40	1,050	420		91	91	329	100
3	0.40	1,103	441		94	94	347	104
4	0.40	1,158	463		98	98	365	108
5	0.40	1,216	486	774	102	875	(389)	963
6	0.40	1,276	511		140	140	370	154
7	0.40	1,340	536		146	146	390	160
8	0.40	1,407	563		152	152	411	167
9	0.40	1,477	591		158	158	433	174
10	0.40	1,551	621		164	164	456	180
Present Value		6,793	2,717	2,832	645	3,477	(760)	3,825
Average per m^3			0.40	0.42	0.09	0.51	(0.11)	0.45
						AIFC		AIEC

O&M = Operation & maintenance

**Table 2. Supply Expansion and Demand Management Option
(Financial Price equal to AIFC)**

Year	Financial Price	Quantity Demanded	Financial Benefit	Financial Costs		Financial Cost	Net Finan-cial Cost	Economic Cost
				Capital	O&M			
	A	B	C=A*B	D1	D2	D=D1+D2	E+C-D	F
0				2,169		2,169	(2,169)	2,386
1	0.51	906	464		79	79	385	87
2	0.51	952	487		82	82	405	91
3	0.51	999	512		85	85	426	94
4	0.51	1049	537		89	89	448	98
5	0.51	1102	564	701	92	794	(230)	873
6	0.51	1157	592		127	127	465	140
7	0.51	1215	622		132	132	490	145
8	0.51	1275	653		137	137	515	151
9	0.51	1339	685		143	143	542	157
10	0.51	1406	720		149	149	571	164
Present Value		6,158	3,152	2,567	585	3,152	0	3,467
Average per m^3			0.51	0.42	0.09	0.51		0.45
						AIFC		AIEC

Notes:
1. Quantities in thousand m^3 and costs in thousand units of local currency.
2. Quantity demanded is assumed to grow at an annual rate of 5%.
3. Capacity in Year 0 is sufficient for demand in Year 6.
4. Extension to the project's final capacity should be ready earlier in Year 5.
5. Cost (in Year 0) of supply expansion per m^3 capacity is $1.50.
6. Cost of supply expansion in the future is assumed to increase by 50 percent.
7. O&M is assumed at 3.5 percent of investment cost and is assumed to grow annually by 4.0 percent.
8. Economic cost is greater than financial cost by 10 percent.
9. As part of water produced, revenue water is assumed to be 80 percent.
10. Economic opportunity cost of capital is assumed at 12 percent.
11. Coefficient of price elasticity of demand (assumed constant over time) is -0.40.
12. Annual quantity demanded as a result of price increase is calculated using arc elasticity formula (see Table 2):

$$Q_t = Q_{t-1} * \frac{(1 + eA/2)}{(1 - eA/2)} \quad \text{where } A = \frac{P_t - P_{t-1}}{(P_2 + P_1)/2} \quad \text{or} \quad 0.25$$

6.   Without demand management the financial subsidy, the difference between the average price and the AIFC, is 0.11 or 21.6 percent of costs. With lower economic costs, but allowing for water that is used but not paid for, the equivalent economic subsidy is 0.05 or 11.1 percent. With demand management, the higher charge for water, lower demand, but also lower investment, reduces the financial subsidy to zero — the full financial costs are being met. At this new charge level, because more water is consumed than paid for, the AIEC is lower than the AIFC and therefore lower than the charge for water. There is now a negative economic subsidy, that is, an implicit tax of 0.06 or 13.3 percent.

APPENDIX 23
FINANCIAL RETURNS TO PROJECT PARTICIPANTS:
AN ILLUSTRATION

1.   The design and sustainability of a project must take into account the level of incentive for undertaking and maintaining a project investment. The financial incentive takes the form of the increased income the investment generates for project participants. This can be calculated as the difference between the level of income in the without project case and the level of income in the with project case. Where the main project participant is a corporation, either public or private, a financial statement in real financial prices can be drawn up showing the net income generated by the project investment after allowing for loan inflows and loan payments, and taxation of profit.

2.   The following illustration relates to a water supply project in India, the Channapatna/Ramanagaran water supply project, that would be implemented through a corporate entity. The illustration presents a financial statement for the project from the point of view of the water authority. The financial and economic analysis for this project has been based on various assumptions about project costs, the level and affordability of user charges for water, projected demand for water, and the use of unaccounted-for-water (UFW). All these factors are interrelated and relate to the basic project economics. The level of demand, the use of UFW, and the economic benefits derived from the project supplies, will depend upon user charges. The project has been scaled to meet the projected demand levels, which also determine the financial and economic returns to the project.

3.   The basic features of the project statement are

-   The initial investment is spread over the four years from 1996 to 1999.
-   The project assets are operated for 31 years, after which they have no residual value, with a small replacement investment in the fifteenth year of operation.
-   The operation and maintenance (O&M) costs increase gradually with supply.
-   The average price of water rises over the whole 35 year project period from Rs1.72 per m^3 to Rs6.18 in real terms.
-   Water sales on the basis of the project supplies increase over the first 12 years of the project, then remain at a constant level.
-   Twenty percent of the UFW is assumed to be used without generating any direct revenue.

4.   The project statement drawn up at financial prices includes

-   project net resource benefits (revenues minus investment and O&M costs);
-   loan inflows;

- loan principal and interest payments; and
- profits tax payments.

These are included in Table 1.

Table 1. Return to Equity
(Rs millions)

Year	Net Benefits	Loan Inflow	Loan Payments	Profit Tax	Owner's Net Benefit
1996	-39.4	31.5	0.0		- 7.9
1997	-89.9	72.0	0.0		-17.9
1998	-72.9	58.5	0.0		-14.4
1999	-21.9	18.0	0.0		- 3.9
2000	9.6		0.0		9.6
2001	20.5		26.1		- 5.6
2002	22.1		26.1		- 3.9
2003	23.0		26.1		- 3.0
2004	23.5		26.1		- 2.6
2005	25.9		26.1		- 0.1
2006	26.9		26.1		0.8
2007	27.7		26.1		1.6
2008	28.7		26.1		2.6
2009	30.7		26.1		4.7
2010	31.5		26.1		5.5
2011	31.8		26.1		5.8
2012	32.2		26.1	6.1	0.0
2013	32.4		26.1	6.8	- 0.4
2014	32.6		26.1	7.5	- 0.9
2015	- 0.9		26.1	8.2	-35.1
2016	32.9		26.1	9.0	- 2.1
2017	33.1		26.1	9.8	- 2.7
2018	33.4		26.1	10.7	- 3.4
2019	33.5		26.1	11.7	- 4.2
2020	33.8		26.1	12.7	- 5.0
2021	33.1			13.4	19.7
2022	33.3			13.6	19.7
2023	33.5			13.7	19.8
2024	33.7			13.8	19.8
2025	33.8			14.0	19.9
2026	34.1			14.1	19.9
2027	34.3			14.3	20.0
2028	34.5			14.4	20.1
2029	34.8			14.6	20.2
2030	34.9			14.7	20.2
Return to Equity					4.4%

5.   The financing arrangements allow for India to take a loan to cover 80 percent of the initial investment costs in each implementation year. However, consistent with Government policy, this is re-lent to the water authority at a nominal interest rate of 12 percent. The loan enjoys a grace period of five years and is then repayable over a 20-year period. Table 2 shows the loan schedule, with the loan payments divided between principal and interest. The water authority makes no payments of interest or principal on the government grant covering 20 percent of the initial investment cost.

Table 2. Loan Schedule
(Rs millions)

Year	Loan	Opening Balance	Interest (8.6%)	Closing Balance	Loan Payment	Interest (8.6%)	Principal
1996	31.5	31.5	2.7	34.2			
1997	72.0	106.2	9.2	115.4			
1998	58.5	173.9	15.0	188.9			
1999	18.0	206.9	17.9	224.8			
2000		224.8	19.4	244.2			
2001				239.2	26.1	21.1	5.0
2002				233.8	26.1	20.6	5.4
2003				227.9	26.1	20.2	5.9
2004				221.5	26.1	19.7	6.4
2005				214.6	26.1	19.1	6.9
2006				207.1	26.1	18.5	7.5
2007				198.9	26.1	17.9	8.2
2008				190.0	26.1	17.2	8.9
2009				180.4	26.1	16.4	9.6
2010				169.9	26.1	15.6	10.5
2011				158.5	26.1	14.7	11.4
2012				146.2	26.1	13.7	12.4
2013				132.7	26.1	12.6	13.4
2014				118.2	26.1	11.5	14.6
2015				102.3	26.1	10.2	15.9
2016				85.1	26.1	8.8	17.2
2017				66.4	26.1	7.3	18.7
2018				46.1	26.1	5.7	20.3
2019				24.0	26.1	4.0	22.1
2020				- 0.0	26.1	2.1	24.0

6.   Allowing for annual O&M costs, depreciation (deflated by anticipated inflation of 3.2 percent per annum), and interest payments, the water authority has an annual loss for most of the first eight years of the project period (see Table 3). Thereafter, the accumulated profit remains negative through the year 2009. The water authority would become liable for profit tax at the rate of 46 percent of gross profit from year 2010 onward. The water authority makes no payments of dividends.

Table 3. Profit Tax
(Rs millions)

	Years	Water Sales	O&M	Depre-ciation	Interest	Taxable Profit	Accumu-lated Profit	Profit Tax
1996	1	0.0	0.0	0.0	0.0			
1997	2	0.1	0.0	1.3	0.0	- 1.1	- 1.1	
1998	3	0.2	0.0	4.1	0.0	- 3.9	- 5.0	
1999	4	0.6	0.0	5.9	0.0	- 5.4	-10.3	
2000	5	11.8	2.2	7.6	0.0	2.0	- 8.3	
2001	6	25.1	4.6	7.4	21.1	-8.0	-16.3	
2002	7	27.2	5.1	7.1	20.6	-5.7	-22.0	
2003	8	28.3	5.3	6.9	20.2	-4.1	-26.0	
2004	9	29.4	5.9	6.7	19.7	-2.9	-28.9	
2005	10	32.2	6.2	6.5	19.1	0.6	-28.6	
2006	11	33.3	6.4	6.3	18.5	2.0	-26.6	
2007	12	34.3	6.6	6.1	17.9	3.7	-22.9	
2008	13	35.5	6.8	5.9	17.2	5.6	-17.3	
2009	14	37.9	7.2	5.7	16.4	8.6	- 8.7	
2010	15	38.9	7.4	5.5	15.6	10.4	1.7	0.8
2011	16	39.8	8.0	5.4	14.7	11.8	13.5	5.4
2012	17	40.2	8.0	5.2	13.7	13.3	26.8	6.1
2013	18	10.4	8.0	5.0	12.6	14.8	41.6	6.8
2014	19	10.6	8.0	4.9	11.5	16.3	57.8	7.5
2015	20	10.8	8.0	4.7	10.2	17.9	75.7	8.2
2016	21	41.0	8.1	4.6	8.8	19.5	95.2	9.0
2017	22	41.2	8.1	4.5	7.3	21.4	116.6	9.8
2018	23	41.5	8.1	4.3	5.7	23.3	139.9	10.7
2019	24	41.6	8.1	4.2	4.0	25.4	165.3	11.7
2020	25	41.9	8.1	4.0	2.1	27.7	193.0	12.7
2021	26	42.1	9.0	3.9		29.2	222.2	13.4
2022	27	42.2	9.0	3.8		29.5	251.7	13.6
2023	28	42.5	9.0	3.7		29.8	281.5	13.7
2024	29	42.7	9.0	3.6		30.1	311.6	13.8
2025	30	42.9	9.0	3.5		30.4	342.0	14.0
2026	31	43.1	9.0	3.4		30.7	372.7	14.1
2027	32	43.3	9.0	3.2		31.1	403.7	14.3
2028	33	43.6	9.0	3.1		31.4	435.1	14.4
2029	34	43.8	9.0	3.0		31.7	466.8	14.6
2030	35	44.0	9.0	3.0		32.0	498.8	14.7

7.   Table 1 shows that the water authority, at projected levels of sales, will earn a return to equity of 4.4 percent. The sales allow recovery of all investment and O&M costs, will meet financing obligations, and will still yield a small return to the authority. It will need no financial subsidy.

8.   How should this return to equity be assessed? The key question is whether it provides sufficient incentive to the owner to undertake and maintain the investment. Without

sufficient incentive, the economic benefits of the project will not be realized. This assessment requires that the return to equity be compared with the cost of investment funds, that is, the return that is required to induce an increase in the availability of savings or foreign investment inflows, or the return that is necessary to induce investment in this project, rather than an alternative project, or a combination of the two.

9.   A return to equity of 4.4 percent is insufficient to induce an inflow of foreign investment funds. Private foreign investors in many countries are looking for returns of 16 to 20 percent in real financial prices. This range includes an allowance for economic and political risks. Nevertheless, it is far higher than is generated by the water supply project. Private domestic investors also are likely to have alternative investment opportunities that yield returns greater than 4.4 percent in real terms. Where interest rates are managed, this may not be in financial assets, but may be in other productive investments or in property. Private investors will be excluded by the level of the return to equity.

10.   Government investment also may be excluded. This depends again upon the cost of investment funds. Recent estimates of the opportunity cost of investment funds for three member countries, combining estimates of returns to savers and investors, and allowing for the elasticity of the demand and supply of investment funds at different real interest rate levels, suggests that the cost of investment in real financial prices is between 10 and 12 percent (see Appendix 20 for an example). This opportunity cost may also be used by government in selecting project investments in financial terms. However, governments will also take into account the economic benefits from the increased supply of treated water. These economic benefits may justify implementing the project even though the financial return is less than could be obtained elsewhere in alternative uses of the investment funds.

11.   Finally, is the return to equity sufficient to justify operating the water supply project on a corporate basis? There is a risk in establishing a corporate authority to operate a project at this level of return to equity. The extent of this risk can be investigated using sensitivity and risk analysis. In this case, the return to equity is very low, and the water authority might require a financial subsidy during implementation and operation if project cost estimates are exceeded or if the projected levels of demand do not materialize. However, it should also be noted that the return to equity is also affected by the terms of relending of external finance. The external finance, borrowed at a nominal rate of 6.9 percent, is re-lent to the water authority at a nominal rate of 12 percent, or a real rate of 8.6 percent. Bearing in mind the effect on the accumulated interest during the grace period as well as the rate itself, if the terms of relending are set equal to the terms of lending, at a nominal 6.9 percent, the return to equity for the water authority improves from 2.9 to 11.9 percent. Therefore, to avoid future reliance on government funds and the consequent risk to water supply operations, the rate of return is sufficient for the water authority to be set up on a corporate basis, but at a lower re-lending rate.

APPENDIX 24
ECONOMIC VALUATION OF ENVIRONMENTAL IMPACTS

I.   BACKGROUND

1.   The methodology of integrating the costs and benefits of environmental changes in economic analysis is still evolving. Therefore, such valuation should be carried out for large or environmentally sensitive projects for which the Bank requires an environmental impact assessment (EIA).[1]

2.   The environment is increasingly being treated as a form of natural capital resource and therefore damaging or using the environment is in a sense similar to the use of any other form of capital. Some parts of this capital, for example, the ozone layer, cannot be replaced or substituted with manufactured capital. Valuation of these resources in the context of projects or programs is thus fundamental to the notion of sustainable development.

3.   Three important conceptual problems need to be addressed at the outset. First, it is necessary to choose a technique for valuing the environmental impact of the project. Second, for all types of project it is necessary to define the boundary of the analysis. Since most environmental impacts include externalities, how far to expand economic analysis is an important issue. For example, in dealing with the impact of waste water, boundaries for downstream effects need to be agreed upon; should it include the area affected immediately or go beyond to account for impacts on irrigation, fishing, and drinking water far away and often beyond the national boundaries. Third, it is also necessary to define an appropriate time horizon. A number of impacts are immediate or within the life of the assets of the project under consideration, whereas there are effects also beyond the project life. For those cases where impacts go beyond the project life, an extended analysis covering the time period for the environmental impact can be attempted, or, alternatively, the concept of capitalized value of net benefits at the end of the project life can be included, a form of salvage value.

4.   The net present value (NPV) of a project is an appropriate criterion to compare the without and with project environmental impacts. Any time, discounting criteria will depend on the choice of the discount rate, which could reflect the opportunity cost of capital or the social rate of time preference. Only one discount rate should be used for any single economic analysis. However, for the Bank discount rate of 10 to 12 percent many long-term environmental impacts tend to become insignificant. Where environmental impacts may extend beyond the life of other project effects, the environmental impact analysis can be combined with a sensitivity analysis for the discount rate, based on a lower rate. If, from the society's point of view, individuals overconsume environmental resources in the present, the

---

[1]   This appendix is based on the *Economic Valuation of Environmental Impacts: A Workbook, 1996*, Office of the Environment and Social Development, Asian Development Bank.

discount rate based on society's time preference would be lower than market-based discount rates. In such circumstances, NPVs for without and with environmental impact values can be examined at alternative discount rates.

II.   INITIAL SCREENING PROCESS

5.   Environmental impact assessments provide the basic information on the physical impacts of different types of stressors as a result of undertaking a project. Using this information, a four-step screening is envisaged as given in Figure 1 to identify major impacts that require quantification. Many potential impacts may not be possible to translate into quantitative terms because of either insufficient data or uncertainty attached to these impacts. A detailed qualitative assessment should be provided in these cases. Following the screening process, it is expected that a list of environmental impacts that require further analysis and quantification, is prepared.

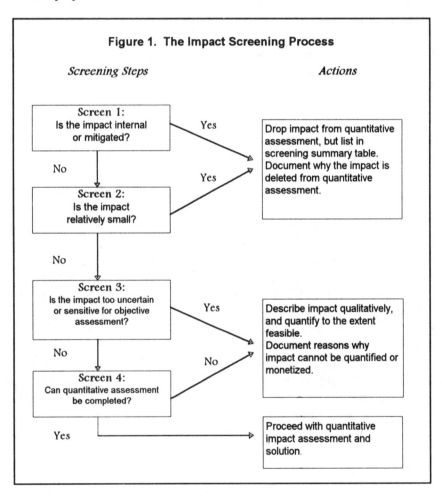

Figure 1. The Impact Screening Process

III.   TYPES OF ENVIRONMENTAL IMPACTS

6.   Different types of environmental stressors impact on different aspects of the environment. Table 1 provides an illustration of major stressors, the potential impact on the air, water, and land, and in three other areas: human health, human welfare, and environmental resources. The human health effects include both mortality and morbidity impacts; for example, environmental changes can be associated with death or increased probability of death, or a higher incidence of illnesses like cancer, malaria, or respiratory disease. Human welfare impacts include damage to property, visual or noise impairment, traffic congestion, changes in soil productivity, changed patterns of recreational uses, loss of homeland, forced relocation, and effects on cultural or religious beliefs. The final category of impacts are on environmental resources, for example, on coastal areas, freshwater ecosystems, biodiversity, and global systems.

IV.   THE GENERAL APPROACH TO VALUATION

7.   Environmental impacts can have both use and nonuse values. Use values can be further divided into direct use value, such as natural parks where individuals are willing to pay for the use; indirect use value where these benefits are derived from ecosystem functions such as mangroves; and option value where individuals are willing to pay for avoiding irreversible change. There are a number of primary valuation methods that are used to value environmental impacts. Table 2 provides a summary of these methods and their underlying basis. Two distinct approaches are used for valuation: objective valuation approaches and subjective valuation approaches. In the first approach, damage functions based on technical relationships between environmental stressors and the degree of physical damage are estimated. In the second approach, assessments are made of possible damage expressed or revealed in market behavior. When these values cannot be assessed from direct behavior, surveys are used, such as in contingent valuation methods to assess willingness to pay from a representative sample of people and organizations.

V.   THE BENEFIT TRANSFER APPROACH

8.   The primary research on project specific conditions is resource intensive and requires a long lead time. Given the data, time, and budget considerations, an alternative method to value environmental impacts in projects is suggested—the benefit transfer approach. The benefit transfer approach essentially uses the primary research data generated elsewhere for valuing impacts after adapting such values to the economic valuation of a given project. If the analysis based on this approach affects the project decision, more site specific information could be gathered, and primary research carried out, wherever feasible, to validate the analysis.

Table 1. Taxonomy for Evaluating Potential Impacts of Environmental Stressors

Effects Category		Human Health		Human Welfare				Environmental Resources					Global Systems
	Stressors	Mortality	Morbidity	Materials	Aesthetics	Resource Use	Social/Cultural	Coastal & Marine Ecosystems	Ground Water	Freshwater Ecosystem	Biodiversity/Endangered Species	Terrestrial Ecosystem	Global Systems
	POTENTIAL EMISSIONS/BURDENS TO AIR												
	Hazardous Chemicals												
1	Inorganics (nonmetals)		✓										
2	Metals	✓	✓									✓	
3	Organics (e.g. VOCs)	✓	✓			✓				✓	✓	✓	✓
4	Pesticides		✓										
	Gases												
5	CO		✓										
6	SO		✓	✓	✓								
7	HO		✓		✓								
8	Oxidants	✓	✓	✓	✓	✓							
9	Greenhouse Gases	✓								✓			✓
10	Aerosols/Particulates		✓	✓	✓						✓		
11	Particulates		✓	✓									
12	Electro Magnetic		✓										
13	Noise				✓		✓						
14	Odor				✓		✓						
	POTENTIAL EMISSIONS/BURDENS TO WATER												
	Hazardous Chemicals												
15	Inorganics (nonmetals)	✓	✓			✓		✓	✓	✓	✓		
16	Metals	✓	✓			✓		✓	✓	✓	✓		
17	Organics	✓	✓			✓		✓	✓	✓	✓		
18	Pesticides	✓	✓			✓		✓	✓	✓	✓		
19	Disease/Pathogens	✓	✓			✓				✓	✓		
20	BOD/COD					✓				✓	✓		
21	Exotics				✓	✓		✓		✓	✓	✓	
22	Acids/Bases		✓		✓	✓		✓	✓	✓	✓		
23	Fertilizers		✓		✓	✓		✓	✓	✓	✓		
24	Waste Products					✓		✓		✓	✓		
25	Acid Deposition					✓		✓		✓	✓	✓	
26	Salinization					✓		✓			✓		
27	Particulates/Sedimentation			✓	✓	✓		✓		✓	✓		
28	Water Diversion/Withdrawal			✓	✓	✓	✓	✓		✓	✓		
29	Channelization/Impoundment		✓			✓	✓	✓			✓		
30	Thermal Alteration					✓		✓		✓	✓		
31	Overharvest				✓	✓	✓	✓		✓	✓		
32	Odor				✓		✓						
	POTENTIAL EMISSIONS/BURDENS TO LAND												
	Hazardous Chemicals												
33	Inorganics (nonmetals)		✓			✓			✓		✓	✓	
34	Metals		✓			✓			✓		✓	✓	
35	Organics		✓			✓			✓		✓	✓	
36	Pesticides		✓			✓			✓		✓	✓	
37	Acids/Bases					✓			✓			✓	
38	Fertilizers					✓			✓			✓	
39	Waste Products		✓		✓	✓					✓	✓	
40	Acid Deposition				✓	✓	✓				✓	✓	
41	Salinization					✓						✓	
42	Erosion					✓						✓	
43	Exotics		✓		✓	✓					✓	✓	
44	Overharvest				✓	✓					✓	✓	
45	Land Use		✓	✓	✓	✓	✓				✓	✓	✓

Table 2. Alternative Valuation Methods

Valuation Methods	Effects Valued	Underlying Basis for Valuation
Change in productivity	Productivity	Technical/Physical
Cost of illness	Health (morbidity)	Technical/Physical
Human capital	Health (mortality)	Technical/Physical
Replacement costs	Capital or natural resources	Technical/Physical
Preventive/mitigation expenditure	Health, productivity of capital or natural resources	Behavior (revealed)
Hedonic approaches	Environmental quality	Behavior (revealed)
Property/land values	Productivity	Behavior (revealed)
Wage differentials	Health	Behavior (revealed)
Travel cost	Natural resources assets	Behavior (revealed)
Contingent valuation	Health, natural resources	Behavior (revealed)
Benefit transfer	All effects	Technical/physical and behavior (revealed)

9.   The approach to valuing environmental impacts using benefit transfer involves three major steps. The first step is to select the appropriate literature given in look-up tables to find reference values and major assumptions regarding the valuation and country conditions. A sample look-up table is presented in Table 3. The evaluator needs to select the most appropriate literature from these tables and a range of values that have been derived from primary research carried out in other country conditions.

10.   The second step is to adjust these values to the location-specific conditions. It is often found that this step involves a lot of subjectivity. It is important to correct for differences between assumptions, such as income, level of human development, wages, cost of time, or price levels, since most primary research studies are carried out in the developed countries. EIAs normally provide information on the baseline conditions. For example, the findings of primary research on the health-related impact of vehicular pollution in urban areas in the United States, when used in the context of other cities like Bangkok, can result in an underestimate if used directly to value environmental impact. It is prudent to document the actual adjustments made from the reference values to project specific conditions and the underlying logic. Finally, using an appropriate range rather than one unique number represents the uncertainties of benefit transfer.

11.   The third and final step is to set these values in the context of the economic analysis framework; values need to be adjusted to economic prices to make these values consistent with other values used for the economic analysis of the project. In particular, environmental costs and benefits need to be expressed using the same numeraire as for the project economic analysis. Where the economic analysis uses the world price numeraire, and environmental effects are valued in domestic market prices, the environmental costs and benefits will have to be revalued using a specific or the standard conversion factor.

**Table 3. Valuing Environmental Impacts: Sample Look-up Tables
Under the Benefit Transfer Methodology**

Resource or Resource Impact	Specific Resource or Impact Being Valued, Country	Monetary Value (1993 US Dollars Unless Noted)	Citation	Comments/Caveats
Forest Preservation of fuelwood	Phewa Tal Watershed Development, a program of sustainability to meet local needs for fuelwood and fodder while arresting the destruction of natural forest areas, Nepal	Annual fuelwood values: - $28 per cubic meter using direct market value - $6 per cubic meter using indirect substitute method - $8 per cubic meter using indirect opportunity cost for other employment	Fleming (1983) as cited in Hufschmidt et.al. (1983) or Dixon, Scura, Carpenter, and Sherman (1994)	The program had a yield five times higher than the production scheme without management. Values calculated using assumptions about wood density and average family gathering, and daily gathering wage of $0.50. The economic rate or return was 9 percent.
Species and Land Habitat preservation	Use and preservation of the undisturbed habitat in the Khao Yai National Park, Thailand	Suggested recreational benefits of approximately $400,000 to $900,000 per year Total existence value, $4.8 million per year	Referenced in Pearce (1993).	Method not explained, but presumed to relate to CVM to obtain estimate of existence values. No details on size or nature of this national park given, but park is near Bangkok and may thus be of value to much of Bangkok area population.
All Water Water pollution	Annual damage in 1986 from all water pollution in the Netherlands	$1.3 to $3.7 billion - magnitudes of pollution not given and reason for range not given	Opschoor as cited in OECD (1989)	OECD study, prepared by Pearce and Markandaya, states that various techniques were used to derive figures and they were, "at best, ball park numbers".
Groundwater	Agricultural groundwater pollution prevention, Dougherty County, Georgia, USA	$747 per household per year (total value)	Sun, et.al. (1992)	CVM used to estimate WTP for groundwater pollution preventing policies for agricultural pesticides and fertilizers in Dougherty County, Georgia
Air Pollution Regional health benefits	Valuation of health benefits from hydrocarbon reductions, U.S.	Range of $131 to $3,400 per ton of avoided pollution for a reduction of ozone of about 30 percent below	Krupnick (1986) as cited in Cannon (1980)	This study estimated that 35.3 million instances of increased coughing would be avoided by the

Resource or Resource Impact	Specific Resource or Impact Being Valued, Country	Monetary Value (1993 US Dollars Unless Noted)	Citation	Comments/Caveats
		1980 levels		northeastern population with this degree of ozone reduction. 124,000 asthma attacks would be avoided.
Health Morbidity effect	Adult chronic bronchitis	$126,000 to $336,000*	Viscussi et.al. (1991), Krupnick and Cropper (1992)	Surveys were conducted to estimate WTP for reducing the risks of developing chronic respiratory diseases. Respondents were presented with trade-off options for the risks versus the cost of living.
	Restricted activity day	$25 to $75	Loehman et.al. (1979)	WTP
	Acute respiratory symptom day	$5 to $15	Loehman et.al. (1979), Tolley et.al. (1986)	WTP

*   = in 1990 US dollar.
WTP   = willingness-to-pay

VI.   CONCLUSIONS

12.   There are a number of important issues that need to be kept in view while valuing environmental impacts. First, most primary research is carried out in developed countries and until data and information based on primary research in developing country conditions are available, recorded values can only provide an approximate range. Second, there is a great deal of uncertainty attached to these values. Therefore, the analysis should be carried out in the context of dealing with uncertainty facing the project. Third, for projects with possible large environmental impacts, additional resources should be devoted for data collection and validation of primary research data. Finally, the evaluator will need to explicitly state omissions and subjective judgments in a transparent manner for an informed decision.

APPENDIX 25
DISTRIBUTION OF PROJECT EFFECTS

1.   The costs and benefits of a project are shared among different groups. There are several ways in which the distribution of project effects can be analyzed. First, the project effects can be allocated among different project participants, usually suppliers, consumers, owners, lenders, workers or producers, and the government representing the rest of the economy. It is usual to expect owners, lenders, workers or producers, and the government all to share in the net project effects. Frequently, consumers and suppliers also do. Second, for projects that involve foreign investors, lenders, management, and labor, the distribution of net project effects between nationals and foreigners can be demonstrated. Third, project effects can be allocated between the public and the private sectors. This may be particularly important for infrastructure developments where public sector expenditures are made in support of private sector operations. Fourth, the net project effects can be allocated not only among different project participants but among participants with different income levels. Fifth, net project effects can be allocated according to whether the project net benefits are likely to be consumed or saved. Finally, costs and benefits can be allocated among different countries participating in subregional projects.

2.   Considerable effort was expended in the past to include the distribution of net benefits between savings and investment into project analysis. The purpose was to identify and give priority to projects that would enhance savings, and therefore investment in the economy, by applying a premium to project effects resulting in extra savings. Considerable effort was also expended to include the distribution of net benefits by income group into project analysis. The purpose here was to identify and give priority to projects that would enhance incomes for lower income groups, by applying a different weight to the incremental incomes of different groups. However, both forms of analysis depend on specifying premia that are essentially subjective and open to disagreement. In addition, enhancing savings can lead to priorities that contradict the enhancement of incomes for lower income groups, and both savings and the distribution of income can be affected more directly by policy changes at the national level rather than through the net effects of new investment projects.

3.   It is recommended that simply a statement of the distribution of project effects be given, without applying any premium to either incomes that are saved or to incomes accruing to particular income groups. There are three reasons for providing such a statement. The first is to assess whether the likely distribution of project effects corresponds with the objectives of the project. The second is to bring the financial and economic analysis of projects together to ensure that the consequences for the economic benefits of projects of changes in financial arrangements are assessed. The third is to assess the likely impact of policy changes on the distribution of project effects.

4.   The following example illustrates the construction of a statement on the distribution of project effects. For simplification, the project excludes the effects of project financing, that is, it does not consider the possible net costs or benefits to lenders. Neither does it include direct tax payments. The illustration concerns a telecommunications project involving 50,000 new lines and associated exchanges that will extend the national network into a rural area through the provision of publicly accessible telephones in villages and rural towns. The analysis of the distribution of project effects is based on the incremental number of calls for the telecommunications corporation and the incremental costs of providing the new telephone facilities. Values for the costs and benefits of the project, at both financial and economic prices, are all given as present values calculated at a discount rate of 12 percent representing the economic price of investment funds in the economy.

5.   The forecast project financial statement at constant domestic market prices is summarized in Table 1. At the projected future charge level, which will apply across the whole telecommunications network and not just in the project area, the telecommunications corporation will not recover the full incremental costs of the project at financial prices inclusive of the opportunity cost of capital. The corporation will have a loss on resources in present value of 100.

Table 1.   Project Net Benefits at Constant Financial Prices

	Present Values (at 12% discount rate)
Benefits Revenue	700
Costs	
Equipment	400
Installation	100
Operating Labor	100
Other Operating Costs	200
Total Costs	800
Net Present Value	-100

6.   The economic analysis of the project introduces three major considerations. First, with project telephone calls will be made at a cost that includes the telephone charge going to the corporation plus the costs of traveling to the telephone. Without the project a high proportion of telephone users would continue to communicate through other means, including traveling to the call destinations. The difference between the cost of communication without the project and the full costs with the project, including the costs of reaching the telephone, represents an economic benefit to telephone users that is not incorporated in the financial charge for the telephone calls. In addition, a further economic benefit will stem from the fact that several small businesses and farmers will benefit from the better access to communication relating to

input and output markets and prices, and transport schedules. Taken together these additional economic benefits can be added on to the financial revenues as a consumer surplus. Second, there is a difference between the economic price of foreign exchange and the official exchange rate. A SERF of 1.3 has been estimated for the country implying that foreign exchange costs have a higher economic than financial cost to the economy. Third, there is a surplus of labor that could easily be trained for telecommunication operations in the area. The opportunity cost at domestic prices for operating labor has been estimated as 90 percent of the wage level, in other words a shadow wage rate factor of 0.9.

7.   The financial project statement has been adjusted by the consumer surplus and the appropriate conversion factors to derive the project economic statement in Table 2. The economic values have been expressed at the domestic price level in national currency. Table 2 also shows the differences between the financial and economic value of resources. These differences give rise to losses and gains among the project participants. As indicated by the consumer surplus, consumers of the new telephone services benefit to the extent to which the economic value of communication cost savings and business efficiency improvements exceed the full cost of making calls. The economic valuation of the equipment for the project exceeds its financial value to the extent of the SERF; the consequent loss because of the overvaluation of the exchange rate is borne by the government representing others in the economy, especially importers. The financial cost of labor exceeds its opportunity cost; the difference accrues as a gain to operating labor. These gains and losses are complemented by the loss to the corporation because not all the full financial costs, including capital costs are recovered. The right-hand-side section of Table 2 summarizes these gains and losses to different project participants.

8.   The overall results for the project are a financial net present value (NPV) of minus 100 and an economic NPV of 40. The economic NPV exceeds the financial NPV by 140. More specifically, as at present structured, two participants lose from the project. The corporation will suffer a loss of 100, and the rest of the economy will suffer a loss of 120 because foreign exchange is available at a price lower than its economic price. On the other hand, two participants will gain. Operating labor will gain by 10 at the project wage level, while consumers will gain from their consumer surplus of 250. These gains and losses in part compensate for each other; the net gain is positive and is equal to the economic NPV of 40.

9.   The differences between the financial and economic values, and the consequent gains and losses for different project participants, provide the basis for considering the impact of policy changes. First, there is a small gain to labor. If there were a completely competitive market for labor this would not occur. However, this is not a major source of difference between financial and economic outcomes. Second, a substantial gain has been identified accruing through the corporation to the consumers as a result of revaluing the foreign exchange element of project inputs. This gain could only be corrected by a general realignment of domestic and world prices, outside the context of project level changes.

Table 2. Distribution of Net Economic Benefits
(Present Values at 12% Discount Rate)

	Financial Present Values	Conversion Factor	Economic Present Values	Difference Economic minus Financial	Distribution of Project Effects			
					Corporation	Government/ Economy	Labor	Consumers
Benefits								
Revenue	700	1.00	700	0				
Consumer Surplus		1.00	250	250				+ 250
Total Benefits	700		950	250				
Costs								
Equipment	400	1.30	520	120		- 120		
Installation	100	1.00	100	0				
Operating Labor	100	0.90	90	- 10			+ 10	
Other Operating Costs	200	1.00	200	0				
Total Costs	800		910	110				
Net Benefits	- 100		40	140	- 100			
Gains and Losses					- 100	- 120	+ 10	+ 250

10.   Finally, the main beneficiary of the project will be the consumers. In part, their benefits could be incorporated into the telephone charges they must pay. If the telephone charge was raised to cover the financial loss of 100, that is, by 100/700 or 14.3 percent on a project basis, most consumers would still be making substantial gains. However, the most marginal consumers may not use the new telephone in these circumstances and so some of the economic benefits would be lost. Moreover, any change in telephone charges in real terms would also impact on existing network users.

11.   The distribution of project effects is of interest for its own sake. It also assists those designing projects by drawing attention to the effects of current policies on the financial and economic results, in this case, exchange rate and pricing policy. Changes in project design within the current policies can be assessed within the same framework. The effects of policy alternatives can be presented in this way to inform policy dialogue with governments and the stipulation of loan covenants.

APPENDIX 26
IMPACT ON POVERTY REDUCTION

1.   Poverty reduction is the most formidable development challenge. To reduce poverty some projects target the poor directly, but most aim at economic growth, benefiting the poor indirectly as well as directly. This appendix shows how to trace the economic impact of growth projects on the poor.

2.   The poverty-reducing impact of a project is traced by evaluating the expected distribution of net economic benefits to different groups. With financial prices determining who controls net economic benefits, the first step is to estimate the present value of net financial benefits by participating group. Next, the difference between net benefits by group at economic and financial prices is added to net financial benefits by group to give the distribution of net economic benefits by group. Finally, the net economic benefits accrue to the poor according to the proportion of each group that is poor. A poverty impact ratio expressing the proportion of net economic benefits accruing to the poor can be calculated by comparing net economic benefits to the poor with net economic benefits to the project as a whole.[1]

3.   This can be illustrated through a publicly funded water utility project selling piped water. The water supply project serves a small rural town. All capital equipment is imported, subject to an import tariff. Labor and electricity account for total operating & maintenance (O&M) costs. Wages are controlled by a minimum wage law, with the economic price of labor being a proportion of the minimum wage. Electricity is subject to a sales tax and a production tax. The water utility is not subject to income tax. All financial and economic values are given in constant year-of-appraisal prices and in present value terms. Tradables are valued at border prices at the domestic price level and nontradables at domestic market prices. Net financial benefits (NFB) and net economic benefits (NEB) are expressed in domestic currency (rupees).

4.   For the purpose of poverty impact analysis, project beneficiaries are divided into three national groups: the poor, the nonpoor, and the government. Net economic benefits by group are distributed between the poor and the nonpoor, according to the extent that they benefit the poor. In the case of net economic benefits to the government, it is assumed that 50 percent potentially benefit the poor.

5.   The present value of project capital costs is $25 million at border prices. Import duties are 30 percent, the official exchange rate (OER) is Rs20/$ and the SERF is 1.20. The market value of electricity is Rs300 million, including a production tax of 20 percent and there is a sales tax of 10 percent. Wages amount to Rs80 million and the supply price of labor is 70

---

[1] The poverty impact ratio is based on the distribution of project net benefits. This differs from the Bank's project classification criterion, that is expressed in terms of the number of beneficiaries.

percent of the average wage rate. Water sales are Rs1,000 million. The quantity of water illegally consumed is 20 percent of revenue water. The economic cost of water consumed and paid for is Rs1,500 million.

6.   The NFB is equal to sales revenue of Rs1,000 million minus capital costs of Rs650 million ($25 million multiplied by the OER of Rs20/$ plus the import tariff of 30 percent), electricity costs of Rs330 million (the market value of electricity plus sales tax), and labor costs of Rs80 million. The NFB of the project shows a loss of Rs60 million in present value (see Table 1).

Table 1. Poverty Impact Ratio for Water Supply Project
(PVs at 12%)

A. Distribution of Project Effects	Financial Returns	Economic Returns	Difference	Consumers	Government/ Economy	Labor
Output	1,000	1,800	800	800		
Capital costs	650	600	50		150-100	
Electricity	330	250	80		80	
Labor	80	56	24			24
Total	- 60	894	954	800	130	24
B. Poverty Impact Ratio	Consumers		Government/ Economy		Labor	Total
Beneficiaries						
NEB-NFB	800		130		24	954
Financial return			- 60			- 60
Benefits	800		70		24	894
Proportion of poor	0.25		0.50		0.333	
Benefits to poor	200		35		8	243
Poverty Impact Ratio: 243 / 894 = 0.271 or 27 percent						

7.   The NEB of the project expressed at the domestic price level is Rs894 million. It is equal to gross benefits of Rs1,800 million (the cost of water increased by the proportion of water consumed but not paid for) minus capital costs of Rs600 million (capital imports converted to local currency at the OER multiplied by the shadow exchange rate factor), electricity costs of Rs250 million (market value of electricity less production tax), and labor costs of Rs56 million (wages valued at the supply price of labor).

8.   The difference between the NEB and the NFB is distributed by group. The difference of Rs954 million is made up of (i) consumer surplus of Rs800 million (the difference between the without project cost of water and the with project expenditure on piped water, plus the value of water consumed but not paid for); (ii) government tax revenues from capital imports of Rs150 million; (iii) government tax revenue from electricity production of Rs80 million (production tax of Rs50 million plus sales tax of Rs30 million); (iv) benefits to labor of Rs24 million (wages of Rs80 million less opportunity cost of Rs56 million); and (v) loss in the economy to government of Rs100 million through overvaluation of the exchange rate.

9.   The NEB-NFB difference is added to the NFB by group to arrive at the distribution of the NEB by group. The government's financial losses from investing in the water supply project amount to Rs60 million. Adding Rs130 million in taxes results in a net economic benefit to the government of Rs70 million. Consumers gain Rs800 million in consumer surplus and laborers earn Rs24 million more than they would have without the project. The NEB by group is Rs894 million.

10.   The final step is to distribute the NEB by group between the poor and the nonpoor. One quarter of consumer surplus and one third of surplus for labor go to those living below the poverty line.   Fifty percent of the return to the government is assumed to benefit the poor. The NEB accruing to the poor is therefore Rs243 million. The PIR of the project is Rs243 million/Rs894 million or 27 percent.

Charges, Benefits, and the Poverty Impact Ratio

11.   The government has decided it can no longer sustain the financial losses of the water supply corporation. The level of water charges is to be raised by 50 percent. It is predicted that, with a price elasticity of demand of -0.4, this will result in a decline in the volume of revenue water of 20 percent. Table 2 depicts the financial and economic returns, and the PIR, in these new circumstances. It is assumed that capital and labor costs are fixed, while electricity costs are fully variable. It is also assumed that nonrevenue water will remain the same proportion of revenue water.

Table 2. Poverty Impact Ratio at Higher Charge Level
(PVs at 12%)

A. Distribution of Project Effects	Financial Returns	Economic Returns	Difference	Consumers	Government/ Economy	Labor
Output	1,200	1,440	240	240		
Capital costs	650	600	50		150-100	
Electricity	264	200	64		64	
Labor	80	56	24			24
Total	206	584	378	240	114	24
B. Poverty Impact Ratio	Consumers		Government/ Economy		Labor	Total
Beneficiaries						
NEB-NFB	240		114		24	378
Financial return			206			206
Benefits	240		320		24	584
Proportion of poor	0.25		0.50		0.333	
Benefits to poor	60		160		8	228
Poverty Impact Ratio: 228 / 584 = 0.390 or 39 percent						

12.   The new level of charges captures some of the consumer surplus. Financial returns become positive and substantial while economic returns, though still positive, are reduced. The distribution of the net benefits between groups changes significantly. The government receives less tax revenue but now receives a surplus from the water supply corporation instead of a loss.

Its share of the benefits increase considerably. The benefits to labor remain the same, while the benefits to consumers decrease substantially, both because of the reduction in consumer surplus per unit of water consumed and because of the decrease in consumption.

13.   The PIR in these new circumstances is 39 percent instead of 27 percent. It has increased significantly but it is not the main parameter to be affected by the increase in charges, which has transferred more benefits to the owner of the water supply corporation, the government. In fact, the absolute amount of benefits going to the poor has decreased with the increase in water charge. This suggests two things. First, the charges may have been raised by too much; given the new financial returns, a lower increase in charges could have ensured the financial sustainability of the corporation. Second, the tariff structure is as important for the PIR as the tariff level. In this case the tariff levels were increased for all types of consumer. An increase in tariff together with a different tariff structure could have captured some of the consumer surplus from the higher income groups while leaving the poor groups unaffected. In other words, the increase in charges could be designed to leave a higher proportion of benefits going to the poor.

14.   By focusing attention on cost recovery mechanisms and tariff structures, PIR analysis can help improve project design by identifying who benefits and who pays, and by how much. Pricing policy can affect the poverty impact of a project; it can also affect the distribution of benefits between the private and public sectors, for example, where the water supply corporation is privately not publicly owned. However, projects designed to have a significant impact on the poor may at the same time have to be provided at a different scale or in a different location, to raise the proportion of benefits going to the poor.

APPENDIX 27
DIFFERENCE BETWEEN ECONOMIC AND FINANCIAL PRICES

1.   Financial returns are based on financial prices. Economic returns are based on economic prices. If the financial and economic boundaries of a project are the same, as in public utility projects for example, differences between financial and economic returns come down to differences between financial and economic prices.[1]

I.   INDIRECT TAXES AND SUBSIDIES

2.   Both financial and economic prices are related to market prices. If governments impose indirect taxes to raise revenues, prices paid by buyers will diverge from prices received by sellers, as taxes drive a wedge between demand and supply prices. For any good the demand price is the price at which buyers are willing to buy, that is, the market price plus consumption taxes and less consumption subsidies, and the supply price is the price at which suppliers are willing to sell, that is the market price less production taxes and plus production subsidies.

3.   Indirect taxes and subsidies, therefore, are important to understanding the difference between economic and financial prices. For project output, the economic price exceeds the financial price by at least the amount of the indirect tax, whereas for project input, the financial price exceeds the economic price by at least the amount of the indirect tax. This result applies whether project output or input is tradable or nontradable.

II.   THE ECONOMIC PRICE OF FOREIGN EXCHANGE

4.   Indirect taxes and subsidies are not the only reason economic and financial prices diverge. Market structures, with monopolized supplies or monopolized stocks, also tend to maintain national price levels at higher levels than world prices. The extent to which the exchange rate is overvalued is proportional to the sum of government and market effects on domestic price levels relative to the level of world prices. To account for these effects on the price for foreign exchange, the economic or shadow exchange rate (SER) is estimated (see Appendix 16).

---

[1]   Depending upon project type and sector, analytical boundaries for financial and economic analyses may not be congruent. Financial analysis may focus on the project's impact on commercial entities whereas economic analysis encompasses the project's impact on the economy. To better understand the impact of government policy on project performance, there are advantages to undertaking analyses at financial and economic prices at both the entity and project level.

5.   The SER is the weighted average of the demand price of foreign exchange paid for by importers and the supply price of foreign exchange received by exporters. Import tariffs and subsidies have the same effect on the foreign exchange rate as would consumption taxes and subsidies on the price of a nontradable. Similarly, export taxes and subsidies have the same effect as production taxes and subsidies. A further major difference between the economic and financial prices therefore stems from the foreign exchange premium. This premium is given by the percentage difference between the SER and the official exchange rate. The foreign exchange premium is in effect a tax paid by exporters to importers.

III.   PRODUCER AND CONSUMER SURPLUS

6.   Economic and financial values can also differ as a result of producer and consumer surpluses. Such surpluses stem from the market impact of projects. For example, if a project is large enough to cause the price of output to fall, the producer surplus of existing producers is reduced and the consumer surplus of both existing and new consumers is increased. Though both producer and consumer surpluses are difficult to quantify, rough estimates can be made, particularly for key project beneficiaries. For example, the difference between the financial price of labor and its economic price is a major source of producer surplus and benefit to the poor.

IV.   EXTERNALITIES

7.   External effects can also cause differences between economic and financial prices. Externalities are in posed by a project on parties outside the project. Positive externalities are known as external benefits and negative externalities as external costs. In cases in which the government imposes a tax to correct for a negative externality, such a tax is incorporated in both financial and economic prices.

V.   DIFFERENCES BETWEEN ECONOMIC AND FINANCIAL VALUES

8.   In sum, the main differences between the economic and financial values of project costs and benefits are made up of government taxes and subsidies, excess operating surpluses from monopolized markets, foreign exchange premia, producer and consumer surplus, and positive and negative externalities. Economic values exceed financial values as a result of output taxes, input subsidies, foreign exchange premia, consumer surplus, and positive externalities. Financial values exceed economic values as a result of output subsidies, input taxes, foreign exchange discounts, producer surplus, and negative externalities.

9.   The difference between economic and financial values is subject, in part, to policy changes. Changes in the level of taxes and subsidy may affect the difference substantially. The difference will also depend on other forms of policy: the extent to which governments ensure external costs are internalized in financial costs, the extent to which governments regulate prices in monopolized markets or open them up for competition, the level of charges for services that will capture some of the consumer surplus. All these forms of government action can be applied at the project level, in the design of projects that are economically viable, that meet all their financial costs and at the same time provide sufficient incentives for project participants.

OCR	-	ordinary capital resources
OER	-	official exchange rate
PAR	-	project assistance ratio
PAC	-	project assistance coefficient
PIR	-	poverty impact ratio
PV	-	present value
PVC	-	present value of cost
ROER	-	real official exchange rate
SCF	-	standard or average conversion factor
SER	-	shadow exchange rate
SERF	-	shadow exchange rate factor
SI	-	sensitivity indicator
SP	-	supply price
SV	-	switching value
SWR	-	shadow wage rate
SWRF	-	shadow wage rate factor
UFW	-	unaccounted for water
WMP	-	world market price
WTA	-	willingness to accept
WTP	-	willingness to pay

APPENDIX 28
USE OF ECONOMIC PRICES IN MEASURING EFFECTIVE PROTECTION

1.   The policy climate affects the productivity of project investments. Just as policies play an important part in shaping project performance, project analysis can help in shaping policy reform. Project economic work contributes to the identification of the best combination of policy, program, and project interventions consistent with government-facilitated, private-sector-led development. The incentives created by domestic policy can affect production and consumption. For sectors where there is a high degree of protection, caution should be exercised in projecting the current policy framework into the future. In this context, the difference between financial and economic prices provides a good understanding of the directions in which adjustment pressures will take prices that will be received and paid by a sector or a project.

I.   FINANCIAL AND ECONOMIC RATES OF RETURN

2.   Comparing financial and economic rates of return for a sector or project can throw light on the effects of policy reform. The ideal policy-investment mix is one that combines a high financial and economic rate of return relative to the cost of capital. If a project is viable at financial prices but not at economic prices, then the project transfers income from the economy to the project investors. However, in such a situation project sustainability may be jeopardized by policy reform aimed at encouraging a more efficient use of resources. If a project is viable at economic but not at financial prices, it would transfer income from investors to others in the economy, including lenders, consumers, and the government. However, such a project would not be sustainable in financial terms, and would require an explicit government subsidy or would go bankrupt.

II.   MEASURING ASSISTANCE

3.   The level of assistance given to a project or sector, explicitly or implicitly, can be defined in terms of the economic net present value (ENPV) and the financial net present value (FNPV). The level of assistance is equal to (FNPV-ENPV), and the ratio FNPV/ENPV is called the project assistance coefficient (PAC). Basically, the PAC indicates the price effects of government policies or market structures on material outputs and inputs. It can also be extended to include the effects of taxes falling on primary factors of production.

4.   The simplest form of assistance measure compares domestic financial prices of outputs with their equivalent economic prices. The ratio of the domestic market to the world market price shows the extent to which domestic policies protect domestic producers from the

direct influence of foreign markets. However, the prices of inputs are affected by government policies as well as outputs. The effective assistance coefficient (EAC) can be calculated at the sector or project level. Like the direct comparison of financial and economic net present values, it takes into account not only assistance on outputs but also assistance on inputs. The EAC is the ratio of value added in domestic financial prices to value added in economic prices.

5.   PACs and EACs can be expressed as percentage rates. When expressed as a rate, the EAC is termed the effective assistance ratio (EAR). The EAR measures the difference in value added measured at financial and economic prices in relation to the value added at economic prices. It is therefore defined as:

$$EAR = ((VA_{dom} - VA_{eco})/VA_{eco}) \times 100 \ percent = (EAC - 1) \times 100 \ percent$$

where VA_{dom} is value added at domestic market prices, and VA_{eco} is value added at economic prices. The EAR gives an indication of the extent to which a particular form of production is favored or discriminated against by government policy. EARs can be calculated for different sectors or projects in a country. In some countries, the coefficients will in general be much higher than in others. However, where domestic prices differ from world prices anyway, it is the dispersion of the EARs around their mean value that is significant. If an EAR is greater than the average for the economy, then the sector or project is relatively protected. If an EAR is less than the average for the economy, then the sector is relatively unprotected.

6.   The cost of assistance is generally passed on to users of a sector's or project's output. For example, where output prices are raised to compensate for tax effects on project inputs, the cost of the taxes will be paid by the consumers through higher financial than economic prices. Higher values for the EAR imply a transfer from users and suppliers to the producers. A higher value for the EAR generally implies a loss to consumers, including the poor. High EAR values across many sectors in an economy are inconsistent with policies to assist the poor.

III.   THE EFFECTIVE ASSISTANCE RATIO: AN ILLUSTRATION

7.   The accompanying Table 1 provides project information in a form suitable for calculating an EAR, and investigating some aspects of the effects of government policy on the level of protection. The table shows the value of project inputs and outputs in domestic market prices and in economic border prices. In general, domestic prices are higher than economic prices because of the effects of the general tax and subsidy system in the country. However, the inputs of pesticide and fertilizer are heavily subsidized. As a result, financial prices for these inputs are considerably below economic prices. In addition, the government has been concerned to provide incentives for expanded exports of cotton. The domestic price for cotton is set at a level higher than its economic price.

**Table 1. Estimating the Effective Assistance Ratio for Cotton Production
at the Farm-gate Level**

	Unit	Total Units	Unit Price	Domestic Price	Conversion Factor	Economic (Border) Price
A. Value of Project Output						
Cotton at farmgate		1	145,325	145,325	0.900	130,793
B. Value of Traded Inputs				7,750		12,128
Pesticides	liters	20	200	4,000	1.838	7,350
Fertilizers	kg	150	5	750	2.451	1,838
Seeds	kg	60	50	3,000	0.980	2,940
C. Value of Traded Components of Nontraded Inputs				27,500		27,301
Tractor fuel	liters	20	250	5,000	0.980	4,900
Tractor lubricants	liters	5	600	3,000	0.817	2,451
Off-farm irrigation costs				7,500	0.980	7,350
Pump costs				12,000	1.050	12,600
Value Added (per ton) (A-B-C)				110,075		91,364
Effective Assistance Ratio	(Value added at domestic prices - Value added at border prices) / Value added at border prices					0.205

This indicates that the domestic value added of the project is raised by 20.5% as a result of the price effects of the Government's policy interventions on the output and inputs of the project, as well as monopolistic market structures.

Assuming the removal of import subsidy on pesticides and fertilizer:

Value added (per ton) (A-B-C)				105,637		91,364
Effective Assistance Ratio	(Value added at domestic prices - Value added at border prices) / Value added at border prices					0.156

This implies that the effective assistance to the project would decline from 20.5% to 15.6%, as a result of the removal of the import subsidy on the pesticides and fertilizer used by the project.

Economic values using world price numeraire.

8.   Comparing value added at domestic and economic prices, the EAR shows a level of protection of 20.5 percent. In other words, the subsidized inputs and the output price incentive more than compensate for the effects of other factors tending to raise the cost of inputs in domestic prices.

9.   This comparison does not allow for the costs of funding the input subsidies and output price incentives. The government has decided that it will eliminate the subsidies on pesticides and fertilizer. If this is done, and if there is no change in the quantity of cotton produced or in the quantity of inputs that are used, the effect will be to reduce the level of protection for cotton growers. The lower part of table 1 shows that, in these circumstances, the EAR falls to a 15.6 percent protection level. In this case, protection is sustained by the output price incentive, as well as by the tax and subsidy regime in general. Protection has been reduced by approximately one quarter by eliminating the input subsidies, but protection has been by no means eliminated.

APPENDIX 29
EXCHANGE RATE ISSUES IN PROJECT ANALYSIS

1.   Several exchange rate concepts may at times be relevant in the economic analysis of projects:

- *Nominal official exchange rate (NOER).* The official exchange rate, in current prices.
- *Real official exchange rate (ROER).* The official exchange rate corrected for changes in purchasing power between domestic and foreign currency units over time.
- *Shadow exchange rate 1 (SER1).* The rate at which nontraded goods and services exchange for traded goods and services. Where tariff distortions represent the only distortions to trade, SER1 is sometimes approximated by a weighted average tariff (WATR) adjustment to the official exchange rate.
- *Shadow exchange rate 2 (SER2).* The exchange rate that would balance trade. This is a theoretical, equilibrium exchange rate.
- *Shadow exchange rate 3 (SER3).* The exchange rate that would balance the current account, which includes invisibles. This, too, is a theoretical, equilibrium exchange rate.
- *Informal or parallel market exchange rate.* The exchange rate in the informal market, which is frequently an illegal market.

I.   FORECASTING EXCHANGE RATE CHANGES

2.   Exchange rates may change over time in response to a number of different forces. Prominent among these forces are: (i) domestic compared to foreign inflation rates, (ii) commercial polices of the Government, including tariff and nontariff barriers to trade, and (iii) international movements of capital and incomes. Anticipating movements in each of the above exchange rates will require analysis of changes in these three critical sets of variables, which often will be causally related to each other.

II.   DIFFERENTIAL INFLATION RATES AND THE NOMINAL AND REAL OFFICIAL EXCHANGE RATE

3.   Analyzing differences between domestic inflation and that of major trading partners will usually be a key factor in anticipating exchange rate adjustments. If, in the face of a high domestic and low foreign inflation rate, the NOER is held constant, then the ROER will appreciate. Similarly, if the NOER adjusts according to purchasing power parity, then the ROER will remain constant. These two cases are illustrated in Tables 1 and 2, respectively.

Table 1. Comparison of Real and Nominal Exchange Rates With Differential Domestic and Foreign Inflation: Nominal Rate Held Constant

Year	Inflation Rate		Exchange Rate (Rs/$)	
	(Domestic %)	(Foreign %)	Nominal	Real[a]
1990			10.00	10.00
1991	15.00	5.00	10.00	9.13
1992	10.00	5.00	10.00	8.72
1993	10.00	5.00	10.00	8.32
1994	10.00	5.00	10.00	7.94
1995	10.00	5.00	10.00	7.58
1996	10.00	5.00	10.00	7.24

[a] At end of respective year, the real official exchange rate adjusts through

$$ROER_n = ROER_{n-1} \times \frac{(1+f/100) \times (1+e/100)}{(1+d/100)}$$

where e% = is the rate of change in NOER, in this case, zero,
f% = is the annual increase in international prices, and
d% = is the annual increase in domestic prices.

Table 2. Comparison of Real and Nominal Exchange Rates With Differential Domestic and Foreign Inflation: Nominal Rate Adjusts to Purchasing Power Parity

Year	Inflation Rate		Nominal[a]	Real
	(Domestic %)	(Foreign %)	Rs/$	
1990			10.00	10.00
1991	15.00	5.00	10.95	10.00
1992	10.00	5.00	11.47	10.00
1993	10.00	5.00	12.02	10.00
1994	10.00	5.00	12.59	10.00
1995	10.00	5.00	13.19	10.00
1996	10.00	5.00	13.82	10.00

[a] Nominal OER adjusts by $\frac{(1+d/100)}{(1+f/100)}$ to maintain real OER constant.

III.   TRADE POLICIES AND THE OER RELATIVE TO SER1

4.   The difference between SER1 and NOER is caused by two sets of factors: (i) border distortions, including tariffs, subsidies, and nontariff barriers to trade, and (ii) domestic distortions, including both policy distortions implicit in, for example, local taxes, and structural distortions implicit in local monopoly power. Most calculations of SER1 focus primarily upon government-induced border distortions. However, methods with a broader focus on the demand and supply of foreign currency for trade purposes can also be used (see Appendix 16), as well as methods which directly compare the economic and domestic prices for a range of traded and nontraded goods.

5.   Trade policy can be used to manipulate the difference between SER1 and NOER. Differential inflation will affect domestic prices in local currency relative to border prices in foreign currency. The combination of the NOER and the border distortions will then affect the domestic prices in local currency relative to border prices in local currency. These relationships are demonstrated in Table 3. The differential inflation rates will affect the exchange rate, SER1. If border distortions stay unchanged, and if the NOER is market determined as opposed to fixed, then NOER will also change in the same proportions as SER1. In spite of the differential inflation rates, the Government can isolate the exchange rate to some extent by increasing the tariff rate on imports and increasing the subsidy rate on exports, that is, by increasing the relative border distortion. Increasing the rate of border distortion has the mathematical effect of decreasing NOER relative to SER1.

6.   The same sequence can be reexpressed in terms of the standard conversion factor (SCF). The SCF may be defined as NOER/SER1. It is another way of measuring the distortions between domestic and border prices implicit in the economy.

Table 3. The Effect of SERF on NOER & ROER via SER1

| Year | Inflation Rate (%) | | SERF | SER1[a] | Nominal OER[a] | Real OER[a] |
	Domestic	Foreign			Rs/\$	
1990			1.000	10.00	10.00	10.00
1991	15.00	5.00	1.095	10.95	10.00	9.13
1992	10.00	5.00	1.095	11.47	10.48	10.00
1993	10.00	5.00	1.202	12.02	10.00	9.55
1994	10.00	5.00	1.150	12.59	10.95	10.45
1995	10.00	5.00	1.200	13.19	10.99	10.49
1996	10.00	5.00	1.200	13.82	11.52	10.99

[a]   At end of the respective year, SER1 adjusts to maintain purchasing power parity. The nominal official exchange rate adjusts to the combined effect of purchasing power parity and changes in border distortions (measured by SERF). SERF is assumed to be adjusted independently, and is an issue of Government policy.

IV.   CAPITAL MOVEMENTS AND CHANGES IN THE EXCHANGE RATE

7.   Deficits or surpluses in capital accounts have had major impacts on movements in the NOER in the past 15 years. This is true for both developed and developing countries. In the case of the developing countries, aid flows and direct foreign investment represent elements on one side of the capital account, while capital income repatriation and capital flight represent factors on the other side. Aid flows and foreign investment inflows tend to cause the NOER to appreciate, while movements of capital the other way tend to cause it to depreciate.

8.   Anticipating major capital movements is difficult, especially in the case of developing countries. In addition, there is a general fear that open prediction of capital movements and exchange rate changes may be destabilizing to international financial markets and may precipitate the changes that are being predicted. However, failure to plan for exchange rate changes can have significant effects on projects.

V.   Project Effects of NOER Charges

9.   Observation of the various exchange rate concepts outlined above can help in anticipating changes in the NOER. Border distortions will be reflected in the SER1 and SERF calculations. As border distortions increase, pressures on the NOER tend also to increase. While border distortion rates of 15 percent to 25 percent may be considered normal in developing countries, average distortion rates greater than 25 percent and rising often will be indicative of mounting problems. This is particularly true where the distortions are nontariff distortions, for example, quotas, bans, import licensing, and foreign exchange allocation systems that may not be fully reflected in some estimates of the SER1 and SERF.

10.   Changes in the NOER during the life of a project may have major positive or negative effects upon profitability. Sensitivity of projects to changes in exchange rates should be tested during project appraisal and steps taken to minimize possible adverse impacts. To facilitate sensitivity analysis of the exchange rate, analysts should maintain separation of traded and nontraded items in the basic project accounts, that is, in the investment budget, the operating budget, the working capital budget, and the revenue budget.

VI.   Switching Value for the Exchange Rate

11.   A major advantage of maintaining such accounts is that the analyst will be able to calculate a switching value for the exchange rate. The switching value for the exchange rate can be calculated from a project account by relating the net present value of the nontraded goods, discounted at the cutoff rate, to the net present value of the traded goods. This ratio can be referred to as the domestic resource cost (DRC) of earning foreign exchange. The ratio may be used to indicate the exchange rate that would make the project rate of return change to the cutoff rate.

12.   In the example in Table 4, the OER at which the project costs and benefits have been calculated is Rs10 to $1, while the DRC for the project turns out to be Rs8.39 per $1. This value gives the switching value for the exchange rate. The project would be viable unless the real exchange rate appreciates to a level of Rs8.39 per $. In most environments, such a strengthening of the exchange rate normally would be considered an unlikely development. Indeed, in most countries the expected change would take the exchange rate in the opposite direction that is, to depreciate. Thus, a project such as this, which uses both imported and local

inputs to produce primarily for the export market, would benefit from devaluation of the exchange rate.

13.	Where the accounts are set up in constant prices, any expected change in the exchange rate would be a change in the real OER. Since the switching value calculation is a variant of the breakeven price calculation, the price that is used in the accounts must be invariate over the range of the period covered in the accounts.

Table 4. Economic Benefits and Costs
(constant prices at border price level)

Year	Traded Benefits ($)	Traded Costs ($)	Traded Net Benefits ($)	Nontraded Benefits (Rs)	Nontraded Costs (Rs)	Nontraded Net Benefits (Rs)
0		500	-500		4,333	-4,333
1	200	30	170	583	500	83
2	200	30	170	583	500	83
3	200	30	170	583	500	83
4	200	30	170	583	500	83
5	200	30	170	583	500	83
6	200	30	170	583	500	83
7	200	30	170	583	500	83
8	200	30	170	583	500	83
9	200	30	170	583	500	83
10	200	30	170	583	500	83
NPV at 12%			461			-3,862
Project NPV ($)			75			
Domestic Resource Cost	8.38					

GLOSSARY OF TERMS

Average incremental economic cost (AIEC). The present value of investment and operation costs at economic prices, divided by the present value of the quantity of output. Costs and output are calculated from the difference between the without project and with project situations, and are discounted at the economic opportunity cost of capital.

Average incremental financial cost (AIFC). The present value of investment and operation costs at financial prices divided by the present value of the quantity of output. Costs and output are calculated from the difference between the without project and with project situations, and are discounted at the opportunity cost of capital or at the weighted average cost of capital.

Benefit-cost ratio (BCR). The ratio of the present value of the economic benefits stream to the present value of the economic costs stream, each discounted at the economic opportunity cost of capital. The ratio should be greater than 1.0 for a project to be acceptable.

Benefit transfer technique. The use of primary research results from other countries, adapted to a particular project, for valuation of project effects. Used especially in the valuation of environmental benefits and costs where national studies of environmental stressors are lacking.

Border price. The unit price of a traded good at a country's border, that is, the free-on-board (FOB) price for exports and the cost, insurance, freight (CIF) price for imports. The border price is measured at the point of entry to a country, or, for landlocked countries, at the railhead or trucking point.

Border price equivalent value (BPEV). The border price for a traded good for the country concerned, adjusted to the project location.

Constant prices. Future price values from which any expected change in the general price level is removed. When applied to all project costs and benefits over the life of the project, the resulting project statement is in constant prices. Expected significant changes in relative prices, that is, in expected price changes for an item compared with the expected change in the general price level, should also be incorporated in the valuation of costs and benefits at constant prices.

Consumer surplus. Savings to existing consumers arising from the difference between what they are willing to pay for an output and what they will be charged with the project. Consumer surplus can arise when expanded supply is associated with a fall in price. It can also arise when the output price is regulated by government and set below the demand price.

Consumption tax. Taxes levied on the consumption of goods and services. Indirect taxes on consumption include excise duties, wholesale or retail sales taxes, value-added taxes, or other taxes on intermediate transactions. Consumption taxes form a wedge between the price paid by the purchaser and the price received by the supplier. For any good or service, the demand price is the market price plus consumption taxes and less consumption subsidies.

Contingency allowance. An allowance included in the project cost estimates to allow for adverse conditions that will add to base costs. Physical contingencies representing the monetary value of additional resources that may be required beyond the base cost to complete the project are included in the economic cost of a project. Price contingencies allow, for financing purposes, for general inflation during the implementation period but are not included in a constant price project statement.

Contingent valuation. A direct means of estimating willingness to pay based on stated preferences of consumers in the situation with the project. Contingent valuation estimates can be used to provide an estimate of the economic value of incremental nontraded outputs and inputs, especially those, such as environmental effects, for which there is no direct market information.

Conversion factor (CF). Ratio between the economic price value and the financial price value for a project output or input, which can be used to convert the constant price financial values of project benefits and costs to economic values. Conversion factors can also be applied for groups of typical items, such as, petrochemicals or grains; and for the economy as a whole, as in the standard conversion factor or shadow exchange rate factor.

Cost-effectiveness analysis (CEA). An analysis that seeks to find the best alternative activity, process, or intervention that minimizes resource use to achieve a desired result. Alternatively, where resources are constrained, analysis that seeks to identify the best alternative that maximizes results for a given application of resources. CEA is applied when project effects can be identified and quantified but not adequately valued.

Cost-effectiveness ratio. The ratio of the present value of project costs to the present value of project effects or outcomes, where costs and effects are discounted at the opportunity cost of capital. Choice of the means with the lowest cost-effectiveness ratio will maximize results for a given input of resources. It also provides the baseline for assessing how much it would cost in terms of extra resources to achieve greater results, through the use of more effective but more costly alternatives.

Cost recovery. The extent to which user charges for goods and services recover the full costs of providing such services, including a return on capital employed. Can be defined in terms of financial cost recovery using financial costs or economic cost recovery using economic costs. See also Subsidy.

Current prices. Future price values that include the effects of expected general price inflation. When applied to all project inputs and outputs, they provide a project statement in current prices.

Demand price. The price at which purchasers are willing to buy a given amount of project output, or the price at which a project is willing to buy a given amount of a project input.

Depletion premium. A premium imposed on the economic cost of depletable resources representing the loss to the national economy in the future of using up the resource today. The premium is frequently estimated as the additional cost of an alternative supply of the resource, or a substitute, when the least cost source of supply has been depleted.

Discount rate. A percentage rate representing the rate at which the value of equivalent benefits and costs decrease in the future compared to the present. The rate can be based on the alternative economic return in other uses given up by committing resources to a particular project, or on the preference for consumption benefits today rather than later. The discount rate is used to determine the present value of future benefit and cost streams.

Distribution effects. An analysis of the net income effects of project costs and benefits on different project participants, including the difference between financial and economic values for project outputs and inputs. Distribution effects can refer to the net income effects between, at least, producers, users, and government, and sometimes workers and lenders, as well, for utility projects; to the particular net income effect for the poor; and to the net income effect for foreign and domestic participants.

Economic efficiency. A criterion for assessing an investment or intervention in an economy. An investment or intervention is said to be economically efficient when it maximizes the value of output from the resources available.

Economic internal rate of return (EIRR). The rate of return that would be achieved on all project resource costs, where all benefits and costs are measured in economic prices. The EIRR is calculated as the rate of discount for which the present value of the net benefit stream becomes zero, or at which the present value of the benefit stream is equal to the present value of the cost stream. For a project to be acceptable the EIRR should be greater than the economic opportunity cost of capital.

Economic opportunity cost of capital (EOCK). The real rate of return in economic prices on the marginal unit of investment in its best alternative use. This rate of return is estimated as the weighted average of the economic demand and supply price of capital, and therefore will be equal to the value of the marginal unit of investible funds to both investors and savers.

Economic price of land. The economic effect of the change in land use as a result of a project. Changes in land use can be the direct result of a project, or indirect, through the consequent displacement and relocation of households or economic activities. The economic price of land is estimated through its economic value in the best alternative use. In practice this is generally taken as the net economic value of production lost when land use changes. This valuation should include anticipated future changes in the productivity of the land. It can also be estimated through the willingness to pay to retain a without project land use.

Economic viability. The assessment that increases in output produced by a project using the least cost method will recover costs, provide an additional required rate of return, and sustain effective production in the face of uncertainty and risk.

Effective assistance ratio (EAR). The ratio of value added generated by an activity measured at financial prices to value added for the same activity measured at economic prices. The EAR provides a summary measure of the protective effect of government policy measures, such as taxes and subsidies, and market structure. Also referred to as the effective protection ratio.

Elasticity. The ratio of the proportionate change in one variable caused by a proportionate change in another variable, all other conditions remaining constant. For example, it is used to refer to the price elasticity of demand, that is, the relative response of demand to price changes; or the income elasticity of demand, that is, the relative response of demand to income changes.

Environmental sustainability. The assessment that a project's outputs can be produced without permanent and unacceptable change in the natural environment on which it and other economic activities depend, over the life of the project.

Environmental valuation. The estimation of the use and nonuse values of the environmental effects of a project. These valuations can be based on underlying damage functions for environmental stressors, identifying the extra physical costs of projects or the physical benefits of mitigatory actions. They can also be based on market behavior, which may reveal the value placed by different groups on avoiding environmental costs or enjoying environmental benefits.

Equalizing discount rate (EDR). The discount rate at which the present values of two project alternatives are equal. It is the same as the internal rate of return on the incremental effects of undertaking an alternative with larger net costs earlier in the net benefit stream rather than an alternative with lower early net costs. The EDR is compared with the economic opportunity cost of capital to determine whether the alternative with larger net costs is worthwhile. Also referred to as the crossover discount rate, the discount rate above or below which the preferred alternative changes from one to another.

Excludability. The ability of suppliers to restrict the availability of outputs to those who can pay for it, or by other criteria. See also Private goods and Public goods.

Externality. Effects of an economic activity not included in the project statement from the point of view of the main project participants, and therefore not included in the financial costs and revenues that accrue to them. Externalities represent part of the difference between private costs and benefits, and social costs and benefits. Externalities should be quantified and valued, and included in the project statement for economic analysis.

Financial internal rate of return (FIRR). The rate of return that would be achieved on all project costs, where all costs are measured in financial prices and when benefits represent the financial revenues that would accrue to the main project participant. The FIRR is the rate of discount for which the present value of the net revenue stream becomes zero, or at which the present value of the revenue stream is equal to the present value of the cost stream. It should be compared with the opportunity cost of capital, or the weighted average cost of capital, to assess the financial sustainability of a project.

Financial sustainability. The assessment that a project will have sufficient funds to meet all its resource and financing obligations, whether these funds come from user charges or budget sources; will provide sufficient incentive to maintain the participation of all project participants; and will be able to respond to adverse changes in financial conditions.

Gross economic benefit. The total economic value of project output, measured as the sum of the economic value of nonincremental output that displaces other supplies and the economic value of incremental output that increases supplies.

Gross economic cost. The total economic value of a project input, calculated as the sum of the economic value of incremental demands that are met by greater supplies of the input and the economic value of nonincremental demands that are met by drawing supplies away from other uses.

Incremental outputs and inputs. Incremental output is additional output produced by a project over and above what would be available and demanded in the without project situation. Incremental inputs are inputs that are supplied from an increase in production of the input over and above what would be produced and supplied in the without project situation.

Least-cost analysis. Analysis that compares the costs of technically feasible but mutually exclusive alternatives for supplying output to meet a given forecast demand. The analysis should be carried out using discounted values over the life of a project, where possible, using the opportunity cost of capital as the discount rate. Such analysis is used to identify the least cost option for meeting project demand.

Market failure. The inability of a system of market production to provide certain goods either at all or at the optimal level because of imperfections in the market mechanism; or the inability of a system of markets to fully account for all costs of supplying outputs. Market failure results in the overproduction of goods and services having negative external effects and the underproduction of goods and services having positive external effects. Market failure occurs for different reasons, for example, inadequate information, inadequate capacity, regulation of the movement of labor and capital, or rent-seeking behavior by producers. The existence of market failure provides a case for collective or government action directed at improving efficiency.

Mutually exclusive project alternatives. Alternative technologies, locations, scales, or timing of project costs such that the selection of one option leads to the rejection of others. Mutually exclusive project alternatives can be compared to arrive at the best project design.

Net present value (NPV). The difference between the present value of the benefit stream and the present value of the cost stream for a project. The net present value calculated at the Bank's discount rate should be greater than zero for a project to be acceptable.

Nominal prices. An alternative expression for current prices. See Current prices.

Nonincremental outputs and inputs. Nonincremental output is output produced by a project that substitutes for supplies that would be available in the without project situation. Nonincremental inputs are inputs that are supplied to a project that, in the without project situation, would be produced and supplied to another project.

Nonmarket failure. Inefficiencies in the implementation and operation of economic activities. These may result from inadequate incentives to those involved in the provision of goods and services, inadequate information about methods and techniques, inadequate resources for maintenance and operation, or lack of accountability for outputs produced. Nonmarket failures can lead to insufficient and costly supplies, especially of public goods produced in uncompetitive circumstances.

Nontraded outputs and inputs. Goods and services that are not imported or exported by the country in which the project is located, because by their nature they must be produced and sold within the domestic economy, for example, domestic transport and construction, or because of government policy that prohibits international trade, or because there is no international market for the product given its quality or cost. Nontraded outputs that are incremental should be valued at their demand price, that is, at the average of their value to new and existing consumers without and with the project. Nontraded outputs that are nonincremental should be valued at their supply price, that is, taking into account the cost of supply of the alternative output being displaced. Nontraded inputs that are incremental should be valued at their supply price, that is, at the marginal economic costs of extra supply. Nontraded inputs that are nonincremental should be valued at their demand price, that is, at the average of the price that existing consumers would be willing to pay to retain supplies, and the price that new consumers would be willing to pay to acquire supplies.

Numeraire. The common yardstick that measures the objective being maximized. In project financial analysis this yardstick is the real income change for the project participants valued in domestic market prices. In project economic analysis, because the scope of the analysis differs, and because domestic market prices do not always reflect the scarcity value of project outputs and inputs, this yardstick is the real change in net national income for the project as a whole valued in economic prices. Generally, the real change in net national income can be measured at two different price levels. These are the domestic price level, where all economic prices are expressed in their equivalent domestic market price level values (the domestic price numeraire), and the world price level, where all economic prices are expressed at their equivalent world market price level values (the world price numeraire). As long as consistency is maintained in a particular calculation across all project effects, project decisions will not be affected by whether the domestic price level or the world price level is used to express the numeraire.

Opportunity cost. The benefit foregone from not using a good or resource in its best alternative use. Opportunity cost measured at economic prices is the appropriate value to use in project economic analysis for valuing nonincremental outputs and incremental inputs.

Poverty impact ratio. The ratio, generally expressed as a percentage, of the net economic benefits accruing to the poor to the total net economic benefits of a project.

Private goods. Goods characterized by very high levels of subtractability and excludability. Subtractability means that one person's consumption of the good reduces the quantity available to others. Excludability means that the producer can restrict use of the product to those consumers who are willing to pay for it, while excluding those who do not meet this or other criteria. Private goods can be produced under private ownership or under public ownership. Except under special circumstances, for example, production in conditions of natural monopoly and where the government lacks the capacity to regulate, production of private goods increasingly is undertaken under private ownership.

Producer surplus. The excess of the revenue received by a producer of a commodity over the minimum amount they would be willing to accept to maintain the same level of supply.

Productive efficiency. Achievement of a specific level of output or objective using the most cost-effective means. Productive efficiency is a precondition for achieving the best allocation of resources among different uses.

Project alternatives. Technically feasible ways of achieving a project's objectives. Project alternatives can be defined in terms of different possible locations, technologies, scales, and timings. It can also refer to alternatives between physical investments, policy changes, and capacity building activities. Consideration of project alternatives, and selection of the best alternative, should precede the assessment of economic viability.

Project assistance coefficient (PAC).   The ratio, generally expressed as a percentage, of the net benefits of a project or activity measured in financial prices to the net benefits of the project or activity measured in economic prices. See also Effective assistance ratio.

Public goods. Goods characterized by very low levels of subtractibility and excludability, by contrast with Private goods above. Low subtractability implies that a good is available to all consumers at the same time, and consumption by one consumer does not use up or reduce the supply available for another consumer. Low excludability implies that if a good is provided to a consumer in a defined region then other consumers in that region cannot be easily excluded from consuming the same good. An example of a pure public good is national security, which is available to all citizens of a country simultaneously. Several other goods are quasi-public, having low levels of subtractibility and excludability. Public goods are generally provided under public ownership, although several can be provided, through contract and regulation, under private ownership.

Real exchange rate. The price of foreign currency in terms of domestic currency where the rate of exchange is adjusted for the relative value of actual or expected domestic and international inflation.

Real prices. An alternative expression for constant prices. See Constant prices.

Relative prices. The future price value of an output or input relative to the price of another input or output, or to the prices of all goods and services in general. If all prices increase at the same rate, all prices will rise but relative prices will remain unchanged. If the price of an output or input increases either more slowly or faster than the prices of other goods in general, then there will be a relative price change.

Return to equity.   The return on capital that will accrue to the owners of a project after all financial obligations to lenders, government, workers, and suppliers are met. It provides an indicator for assessing the incentive to investors to invest in a project compared with other uses of their funds.

Risk analysis. The analysis of project risks associated with the value of key project variables, and therefore the risk associated with the overall project result. Quantitative risk analysis considers the range of possible values for key variables, and the probability with which they may occur. Simultaneous and random variation within these ranges leads to a combined probability that the project will be unacceptable. When deciding on a particular project or a portfolio of projects, decision makers may take into account not only the expected scale of project net benefits but the risk that they will not be achieved.

Sensitivity analysis. The analysis of the possible effects of adverse changes on a project. Values of key variables are changed one at a time, or in combinations, to assess the extent to which the overall project result, measured by the economic net present value, would be affected. Where the project is shown to be sensitive to the value of a variable that is uncertain, that is, where relatively small and likely changes in a variable affect the overall project result, mitigating actions at the project, sector, or national level should be considered, or a pilot project implemented.

Sensitivity indicator. The ratio of the percentage change in NPV to the percentage change in a selected variable. A high value for the indicator indicates project sensitivity to the variable.

Shadow exchange rate. The economic price of foreign currency used in the economic valuation of goods and services. The shadow exchange rate can be calculated as the weighted average of the demand price and the supply price for foreign exchange. Alternatively, it can be estimated as the ratio of the value of all goods in an economy at domestic market prices to the value of all goods in an economy at their border price equivalent values. Generally the shadow exchange rate is greater than the official exchange rate, indicating that domestic purchasers place a higher value on foreign currency resources than is given by the official exchange rate.

Shadow exchange rate factor (SERF). The ratio of the economic price of foreign currency to its market price. Alternatively, the ratio of the shadow to the official exchange rate. This factor will generally be greater than 1. For economic analysis using the domestic price numeraire, the SERF is applied to all outputs and inputs, including labor and land, that have been valued at border price equivalent values, with project effects measured at domestic market price values left unadjusted. The inverse of the Standard conversion factor.

Shadow wage rate (SWR). The economic price of labor measured in the appropriate numeraire as the weighted average of its demand and supply price. For labor that is scarce, the SWR is likely to be equal to or greater than the project wage. For labor that is not scarce, the SWR is likely to be less than the project wage. Where labor markets for labor that is not scarce are competitive, the SWR can be approximated by a market wage rate for casual unskilled labor in the relevant location, and adjusted to the appropriate numeraire.

Shadow wage rate factor (SWRF). The ratio of the shadow wage rate of a unit of a certain type of labor, measured in the appropriate numeraire, and the project wage for the same category of labor. Alternatively, the ratio of the economic and financial cost of labor. The SWRF can be used to convert the financial cost of labor into its economic cost.

Standard conversion factor (SCF). The ratio of the economic price value of all goods in an economy at their border price equivalent values to their domestic market price value. It represents the extent to which border price equivalent values, in general, are lower than domestic market price values. The SCF will generally be less than one. For economic analysis using the world price numeraire, it is applied to all project items valued at their domestic market price values to convert them to a border price equivalent value, while items valued at their border price equivalent value are left unadjusted. The SCF and SERF are the inverse of each other.

Subsidy. In the provision of utility services, the difference between average user charges and the average incremental cost of supply. A subsidy can be estimated in economic terms, using economic costs of supply, or in financial terms using financial costs of supply. The economic effects of a subsidy include the consequences of meeting them through generating funds elsewhere in the economy. Subsidies need explicit justification on efficiency grounds, or to ensure access to a selected number of basic goods.

Subtractability. The extent to which one user's consumption of a good or service reduces the ability of others to consume the good or service without an increase in production cost. See also Private goods and Public goods.

Supply price. The price at which project inputs are available, or the price at which an alternative to the project output is available.

Switching value. In Sensitivity analysis, the percentage change in a variable for the project decision to change, that is, for the ENPV to become zero or the EIRR to fall to the cut-off rate.

Traded inputs and outputs. Goods and services where production or consumption affect a country's level of imports or exports. Project effects estimated in terms of traded goods and services can be measured directly through their Border price equivalent value—the world price for the traded product for the country concerned, adjusted to the project location. Border prices for exported outputs can be adjusted to the project location by subtracting the economic cost of transport, distribution, handling, and processing for export measured at economic prices. Border prices for imported inputs can be adjusted by adding such costs to the project site. Outputs that substitute for imports can be adjusted by the difference in economic transport, distribution, and handling costs between the existing point of sale and the project site. Project inputs that reduce exports can be adjusted by the difference in economic domestic costs between the point of production and the project location.

Transactions costs. The costs, other than price, incurred in the process of exchanging goods and services. These costs include the costs of negotiating and enforcing contracts, and the costs of collecting charges for goods and services provided. The scale of economic and financial transactions costs can affect the market structure for a good.

Transfer payment. A payment made without receiving any good or service in return. Transfer payments transfer command over resources from one party to another without reducing or increasing the amount of resources available as a whole. Taxes, duties, and subsidies are examples of items that, in some circumstances, may be considered to be transfer payments.

Unit of Account. The currency used to express the economic value of project inputs and outputs. Generally the currency of the country in which the project is located will be used as the unit of account. Occasionally an international currency may be used as the unit of account. Economic values using the domestic price numeraire can be expressed in either a domestic or international currency. Similarly, economic values using the world price numeraire can be expressed in either a domestic or international currency.

User charge. A charge levied upon users for the services rendered or goods supplied by a project.

Willingness to accept (WTA). The minimum amount of compensation consumers would be willing to accept for foregoing units of consumption.

Willingness to pay (WTP). The maximum amount consumers are prepared to pay for a good or service. WTP can be estimated as the total area under a demand curve. Changes in WTP can occur when the demand curve itself shifts because of changes in income or in the prices of substitute goods.

Without and with project. The future situation without a proposed project and the future situation with the proposed project. The difference between these two situations constitutes the impact of the investment, policy change, or capacity building activities. To be distinguished from the situations before and after a project that do not allow for expected changes without the project.

World price. The price at which goods and services are available on the international market. The world price for a country is the border price, the price in foreign exchange at which imports are available at the port, railhead, or trucking point, or the price in foreign exchange received for exports at the port, railhead, or trucking point. Significant changes in relative world prices should be incorporated into the economic prices used in the analysis of projects.